Ritual and Its Consequences

Ritual and Its Consequences

An Essay on the Limits of Sincerity

ADAM B. SELIGMAN

ROBERT P. WELLER

MICHAEL J. PUETT

BENNETT SIMON

OXFORD

UNIVERSITY PRESS

2008

OXFORD
UNIVERSITY PRESS

Oxford University Press, Inc., publishes works that further
Oxford University's objective of excellence
in research, scholarship, and education.

Oxford   New York
Auckland   Cape Town   Dar es Salaam   Hong Kong   Karachi
Kuala Lumpur   Madrid   Melbourne   Mexico City   Nairobi
New Delhi   Shanghai   Taipei   Toronto

With offices in
Argentina   Austria   Brazil   Chile   Czech Republic   France   Greece
Guatemala   Hungary   Italy   Japan   Poland   Portugal   Singapore
South Korea   Switzerland   Thailand   Turkey   Ukraine   Vietnam

Published by Oxford University Press, Inc.
198 Madison Avenue, New York, New York 10016

www.oup.com

Oxford is a registered trademark of Oxford University Press

Library of Congress Cataloging-in-Publication Data
Ritual and its consequences : an essay on the limits of sincerity / Adam B. Seligman ... [et al.].
   p. cm.
Includes bibliographical references.
ISBN 978-0-19-533600-9; 978-0-19-533601-6 (pbk.)
1. Ritual.   2. Ritualism.   3. Sincerity.   I. Seligman, A.
BL600.R5775 2008
203'.8—dc22   2007026538

9 8 7 6 5 4 3 2 1

Printed in the United States of America
on acid-free paper

The desires of the heart are as crooked as corkscrews,
    Not to be born is the best for man;
The second-best is a formal order,
    The dance's pattern; dance while you can.

Dance, dance, for the figure is easy,
    The tune is catching and will not stop;
Dance till the stars come down from the rafters;
    Dance, dance, dance till you drop.

—W. H. Auden, "Death's Echo"

Now this is what you shall offer upon the altar: two yearling lambs, day by day, continually.

—Exodus 29:38

For it was fitting that we should have a high priest, holy, blameless, undefiled, separated from sinners, and exalted above the heavens. Unlike the other high priests, he has no need to offer sacrifices day after day, first for his own sins, and then for those of the people; this he did once for all when he offered himself. For the law appoints as high priests those who are subject to weakness, but the word of the oath, which came later than the law, appoints a Son who has been made perfect forever.

—Hebrews 7:26–28

Preface

Like all good ritual—and good science, for that matter—this book is the product of a collective effort. The four of us wrote it together, over the course of time and as part of quite a few ongoing conversations, shared research, a good deal of frustration, and many laughs. "Science," as Werner Heisenberg remarked in his *Physics and Beyond: Encounters and Conversations*, "is rooted in conversations."[1] If shared speech (of a certain kind) makes up the stuff of science, so shared practice (of a certain kind) makes up the stuff of ritual. A book on ritual hovers somewhere between the two: a bit more of a joint social world than shared speech and perhaps a bit less than shared practice.

This book originated in an increasingly expanding conversation with authors and interlocutors, both dead and living. It began with an exercise that Rob and Adam shared in a comparison of Confucian and Jewish funeral manuals. These were texts intended for popular audiences. In the Jewish context, we read the *Kitzur Shulchan Aruch*, a nineteenth-century handbook available to every householder, explaining how to live a ritually correct life. In fact, we used Adam's grandmother's copy, published on Duane Street in New York, in 1900. For the comparable Confucian text we made use of Patricia Ebrey's translation of the eminent neo-Confucian philosopher Zhu Xi's *Family Rituals*, which was first published in the twelfth century, but versions of which remain widely available in the Chinese world.

This exercise was so fascinating that the two immediately realized the need to broaden the conversation. Clearly what was going on in these prescriptive rulings of how to prepare the dead (and the living) for the burial and what followed was quite beyond what we had been prepared for by decades of anthropological theories of ritual. Neither the classic texts nor even their more recent challengers seemed sufficient to encompass the phenomena we were studying. Here we found not only function and meaning, not only practice and performance, but a very particular approach to performance that frames our actions and orientations in a unique manner not always noted in the broader literature on ritual. In trying to make sense of all this, we found ourselves drawn to texts rather beyond some of the recent literature on rituals and began reading and rereading Bateson (*Steps to an Ecology of Mind*) and Huizinga (*Homo Ludens*), Caillois (*Man, Play and Games*) and Gadamer (*Truth and Method*), rather than the works that a study of ritual would more commonly call to mind. We should note at the outset that in these readings, and indeed in this whole project, we were profoundly influenced by Rappaport's *Ritual and Religion in the Making of Humanity*.

We became increasingly convinced that ritual was not some discrete realm of human action and interaction, set apart and distinct from other forms of human action. Instead, we began to see it as a modality of human engagement with the world, one that receives much too short shrift in the contemporary world (of both popular and academic culture). We realized we had to broaden our own conversation. The first step was to invite a group of people who practice and think about ritual to discuss these issues for a few days. We set up a small workshop, inviting rabbis, imams, anthropologists, psychoanalysts, legal scholars, acupuncturists, Confucian scholars, students of the classics, and others to discuss some texts and some practices. The result of this meeting was so positive that we then began a yearlong series of seminars on ritual where many of the original discussants participated, gave papers, and exchanged views. We are grateful to the Humanities Foundation of Boston University for making this possible.

Our group discussion in turn resulted in the decision to write the book you find before you. It was, in every sense of the term, written by all the authors together. Every part of the process was developed consensually. Together we wrote an outline of the book, each author bringing his version to the group for criticism and correction until all had a hand in shaping the form of each chapter. The same was true for the actual parsing out of the agreed-upon themes in each chapter. One of us drafted every chapter and brought it to the whole group, often four or five times, to subject it to collective criticism and recommendations. When the chapters were deemed ready, they then made the rounds of all the authors, each adding, editing, deleting, and shaping the text he found before it was passed on to the next author.

Writing together in this manner is no small matter. It is not simply a curious side effect of an unusual production process. It is, to a great extent, integral to what we are arguing throughout this work. The practice of ritual is not unlike the practice of conversation (at least as the ancients and medievals saw conversation). Both require coordination, shared fellowship, trust, the circumscription of the will, and the ability to abide in silence and sometimes to admit that clarity of one's own expression is not the only "good" to be pursued in the course of the shared enterprise. Both necessitate an opening toward the other, both affirm that truth is not held in one's hand (or even in one's heart) but must be produced in tandem, together with others, through a joint effort. This effort, moreover, shares something with dancing—it requires coordination, circumspection, precision in practice, and a well-tempered attention to what one is about. These are all skills that seem somewhat low on our priorities these days, but this is part of our great misfortune.

Clearly, we have no intention in this work to reproduce or introduce the vast library of work on ritual. Two recent books by Catherine Bell have served a mightily important purpose in recalling and building on the crucial insights of so many studies of ritual into this aspect of the human experience. Bell's work is a landmark of where the study of ritual had arrived by the close of the twentieth century. In this book our aim is somewhat different. We hope to open a conversation on ritual as a particular way of human engagement with the world, an engagement that goes well beyond what we generally think of as ritual activities. We see ritual here as a unique way of accommodating the broken and often ambivalent nature of our world. It is thus a resource that we may dismiss only at our peril, as we hope to clarify in the text that follows.

Before proceeding, however, we would like to thank a number of people who contributed to these conversations, both in the initial workshops and seminars and beyond. These include Paula Fredrikson, Bruce Kapferer, Ted Kaptchuk, Barry Mesch, Arnold Modell, Khaleel Muhammad, Steve Scully, Suzanne Last Stone, Brackette Williams, Rahel Wasserfall, Shlomo Fischer, and Nehemia Polen, to whom we owe special thanks for the juxtaposed quotes from Exodus and Hebrews in our epigraph. We are also very grateful to Nelia Ponte, David Montgomery, and Christal Whelan for their help. Acknowledgments of this sort typically thank people and then absolve them of responsibility. We grant no absolutions, however. This book is the result of a long group effort that goes well beyond the four authors. As with any group, not everyone agrees about everything, but we find ways to live together anyway.

Contents

About the Authors

Adam B. Seligman is Professor of Religion and Research Associate at the Institute for Culture, Religion and World Affairs at Boston University. His books include *The Idea of Civil Society*; *Inner-worldly Individualism*; *The Problem of Trust*; *Modernity's Wager: Authority, the Self and Transcendence*; with Mark Lichbach, *Market and Community*; and *Modest Claims: Dialogues and Essays on Tolerance and Tradition*. He is Director of the International Summer School on Religion and Public Life, which leads seminars every year on contested aspects of religion and the public square in different parts of the world. He lives in Newton, Massachusetts, with his wife and two daughters.

Robert P. Weller is Professor and Chair of Anthropology at Boston University and Research Associate at the Institute on Culture, Religion and World Affairs there. He earned his Ph.D. from the Johns Hopkins University in 1980 and has since written numerous books and articles on Chinese political, social, and cultural change, often with a focus on the relations between religion and civic life. His most recent books include *Discovering Nature: Globalization and Environmental Culture in China and Taiwan*, an edited volume called *Civil Life, Globalization, and Political Change in Asia: Organizing between Family and State*, and *Alternate Civilities: Chinese Culture and the Prospects for Democracy*.

Michael Puett is Professor of Chinese History and Chair of the Department of East Asian Languages and Civilizations at Harvard

University. He received his Ph.D. in 1994 from the Department of Anthropology at the University of Chicago. His interests are focused primarily on the inter-relations between religion, anthropology, history, and philosophy. He is the author of *The Ambivalence of Creation: Debates Concerning Innovation and Artifice in Early China* and *To Become a God: Cosmology, Sacrifice, and Self-Divinization in Early China*.

Bennett Simon is a psychiatrist and psychoanalyst at Harvard Medical School (Cambridge Health Alliance) and the Boston Psychoanalytic Society and Institute. He has long been involved in inter-disciplinary work with the humanities and social sciences in his teaching, research, and writing. He is the author of *Mind and Madness in Ancient Greece, Tragic Drama and the Family* and co-author with Roberta Apfel of *Minefields in Their Hearts: The Mental Health of Children in War and Communal Violence,* and with Elizabeth Lunbeck of *Family Romance, Family Secrets: Case Notes of an American Psychoanalysis.*

Ritual and Its Consequences

Introduction

One of the interesting, if somewhat counterintuitive, developments of the turn of the twenty-first century has been the reemergence of ritual among many sectors of society, including religious society, that had previously distanced themselves from ritual acts. For example, we see the reversal of the leaders of Reform Judaism, who have readmitted ritual to their religious practice in response to congregant demands.[1] We also see the spread of orthodoxies defined in part through ritual action—orthopraxies might in fact be a better term—including the growth of Islamic identities in many regions, the worldwide increase of Jewish orthodox practice, and even the attraction in the United States of neo-paganism and Wicca, or the exponential growth of Yoga centers in cities across the country.[2] The growing concern with a practical theology among mainline Protestant churches is another indicator of this trend.[3] Similarly, the emergence of various forms of neo-Confucianism among Chinese intellectuals also focuses in part on the concept of *li*—ritual in the broad sense that includes both acts of worship and interpersonal rituals of courtesy and diplomacy.[4]

It is not surprising that the worldwide renewal of identities defined in part through ritual has progressed in step with a renewed interest in ritual within certain sectors of the social scientific community. Ritual has been a research focus at various times over the last century, beginning with Durkheim's first theoretical endeavors in *Elementary Forms of Religious Life*.[5] As with any stream of ideas, the flow of work on ritual offers currents and countercurrents in which this book moves. We will not attempt an overview here, but simply place ourselves in relation to the main flow.[6] The dominant current in both anthropology and religious studies has been a search to clarify the meanings of rituals, to show the ways in which their symbols encode and evoke systems of cultural discourse.

It is our contention, however, that such an approach risks being blinded by our own assumptions, all strongly influenced by what can perhaps be termed a post-Protestant or post-Enlightenment vision of ritual action as a referent for meaning whose true essence resides only beyond the ritual itself. The famous Augustinian understanding of the Eucharist as the "visible sign of an invisible grace," although it long predates the Reformation, has become the mode through which much of ritual has been understood. In such a view, the "thing itself" always resides beyond the ritual, and the ritual act is only its instrument. To be sure, this understanding has led to important exegesis of ritual's symbolism, but it also led to an emphasis on inner states like sincerity or belief that may not always be relevant to the social and cognitive contexts of ritual action.

Among other preconceptions, this orientation suffers from an overly subjectivist and individualist emphasis on meaning and interaction. Such a view sees the "essential" or constitutive arena of action (often read as intention) as something within the social actor or actors, with the external, formal ritual seen as but the marker of these internal processes.[7] We will refer to this attitude toward self and world as "sincerity."

In many ways, that is the current against which we are swimming. People certainly can fill ritual with meanings, in some cases providing us with elaborate explanations. Yet ritual can also take place with no concern for meaning (at least in its standard discursive sense), and in many cases informants refuse to spin out meanings, but simply say that they perform rituals in certain ways because that is the tradition. Most of the meanings we can read into ritual, after all, come into play outside the frame of the ritual itself. Ritual, we will argue, is about *doing* more than about saying something.

We are not alone in this view, but jostle together in the countercurrent with a number of earlier authors. Catherine Bell, for instance, sees one of the fundamental characteristics of ritualization as "the simple imperative to *do* something in such a way that the doing itself gives the acts a special or privileged status."[8] Such "doing" appears naturalized and externally defined, she argues, because of the performative and traditionalizing features of ritual. Caroline Humphrey and James Laidlaw, in their study of Jain ritual, argue similarly that "ritualization, by presenting action to experience as already-constituted and hence apprehensible elements, allows a wide variety of actual conduct to be counted unambiguously as successful performance, and that this is independent of the attribution of particular propositional meanings to the acts."[9] Like us, these authors see ritual as a particular form of orientation to action, a frame that tells us how to understand actions like lighting a candle or sitting quietly in a chair.[10] One implication of this approach is that ritual acts cannot be circumscribed within the realm usually termed "religious." Ritual, we will claim, provides an orientation to action and hence a framing of action that is relevant in understanding human activities beyond what may be done in temples, churches, mosques—or the houses of Parliament for matter.[11]

There is, to be sure, a rather grand debate on precisely this subject. Jack Goody and John Skorupski are only two who have weighed in on the debate over using the same terms to refer to such diverse activities as "taking a dog for a walk, watching television, going to the cinema, listening to records, visiting relatives, routines at work, singing at work, children's street games, hunting and so on."[12] If a category is all-inclusive, it is, as many rightly claim, useless. Our own position, however, is that many diverse forms of behavior and action can usefully be understood as ritualistic precisely because the term "ritual" frames actions in certain, very specific ways. It is the framing of the actions, not the actions themselves, that makes them rituals. Thus both partaking of the Eucharist and shaking hands can be understood as actions that are framed ritualistically. They can also be understood nonritualistically, at least on their margins.

Debates over the priestly hand movements and bodily stance when administering the Eucharist focus precisely on the extent of ritual in the administering of the sacred rite.[13] Thus the Protestant Reformation of the sixteenth century replaced the Eucharist as a ritual administrated before an altar, marked off by railings, performed by a priest robed in vestments and surplice to the whole congregation. Instead, in colonial New England, say, the "Eucharist" was enacted as the Lord's Supper, administered at a rough, folding table, by a minister in plain dress, known for his plain preaching, only to those members of the congregation who had given evidence of saving grace.[14] This was precisely about the deritualization of the Eucharist and its framing by a different set of categories and desiderata. Similarly, we can shake hands with a number of strangers we meet following the concert in Symphony Hall in a purely "ritualistic" manner. But we can also shake hands with a former dear friend, where time and age and the different decisions each of us has taken in the decades since we met preclude a warmer embrace, though the sentiments of mutual warmth and care are still there. The handshake is still the same act, physically. The framing of the act, however, is very different. The difference turns, as we shall argue, on the highly ritualized nature of the pre-Reformation Eucharist or the usual handshake, as opposed to the relatively nonritualized orientation of the second. These frames around the early Protestant Eucharist or the heartfelt handshake, to which we shall devote no small amount of attention in our study, we see as the orientation of sincerity.

This is one of the most important ways we see this book building on and moving beyond the insights of others who contribute to the countercurrent that sees ritual as one possible orientation to action, rather than as a set of meanings. Identifying sincerity as an alternative and crucially important orientation allows us to focus on the interaction between the two modes, which has become so important to the social dynamics of the modern world. It has also pushed us to examine the way both orientations relate to problems of social and psychological ambiguity. As we will see, ritual and sincerity shape group and individual boundaries to create very different modes of empathy and interaction. We do not claim that these are the only possible orientations to action, but they are at least two terribly important ones that reveal a lot about our world.

This is, of course, a broad view of ritual, but it is not indiscriminate, compromising its usefulness by including everything and thus explaining nothing. Understood as one mode of framing action juxtaposed to other modes, this concept of ritual may offer a new way to understand diverse social phenomena and develop new insights into hitherto unexplored aspects of our shared social world. By opening up the concept in a way that will lead us to discuss architecture, music, and play as much as liturgy, we do not wish to downplay its importance to how men and women approach the sacred. Ritual can be, of course, an orientation to the sacred, but it is not the only possible such orientation—sincerity is another, of equal importance, and of vastly different import.

We should clarify that by taking ritual beyond the walls of religion, we are not particularly referring to what Moore and Myerhoff called "secular ritual."[15] Most of the studies in their collection were less concerned with the phenomenon of ritual as a frame of action than with secular events that are ceremonial in nature. In these studies, ritual essentially keeps its religious connotations, and activities in other realms of life are seen as functional equivalents of these in one form or another.

We argue instead that ritual is not a particularly or solely religious phenomenon. In fact the only reason that most of us tend to see ritual in this light is because of the Protestant, but more broadly Christian, separation of religious from secular realms that we are all so accustomed to. Rather, we see ritual as one crucial mode of framing activities. As such, it is one among many. We shall claim that the individual and social choices between the ritual or sincere orientations (which primarily concern us here) have considerable social consequences.

Ritualized actions have—at least since the work of Durkheim—been identified by most authors with what society holds sacred, that is, with what we can reasonably call religious. If, as Jonathan Z. Smith proclaims, "ritual is, above all, the assertion of difference," then the sacred in its classic Durkheimian formulation remains the most different of all, totally set apart and separate from the profane.[16] We are not questioning this understanding of the sacred or of the role of ritual therein. What we are cautioning against is the tendency to see this working of ritual—that is, the marking off of difference— as something that exists apart from everyday affairs. This tendency prevents us from understanding the pervasiveness of the way we do, or could do, or sometimes did, frame actions in a ritualistic mode. It is ultimately our own prejudices, our own inability to see the ever presence of differences in life— difference that ritual continually mediates—that leads us to reduce ritual to a representation of the sacred (more on this in chapter 1). It is, we will ultimately claim, our own sincerity—as a form of framing experience and action—that leads us to frame ritual actions in sincere terms, in terms separate from and no longer in continual mediating presence with everyday life.

We thus analyze ritual and sincerity as two "ideal typical" forms of framing experience, action, and understanding that exist in all societies, in tension with one another. We will further claim that our own default position of sincerity makes it difficult for us to understand ritualistic modes of existence beyond the sacred. "Ritual," as Smith noted, "precises ambiguities, it neither overcomes them nor relaxes them."[17] This is a function of its peculiar way of mediating difference and parsing boundaries, rather than seeking to overcome and absolutize them (which, we shall claim, is a common trait of sincere modes of framing action and understanding). Much of the following work focuses on delineating some of these individual and social ambiguities. It explicates how the work of ritual teaches us how to live within and between different boundaries rather than seeking to absolutize them—which is, sadly, often the result of deritualized frames of understanding and action.

We develop four central points in the following chapters. First, we claim that ritual creates a subjunctive, an "as if" or "could be," universe. It is this very creative act that makes our shared social world possible. Creating a shared subjunctive, we will argue, recognizes the inherent ambiguity built into social life and its relationships—including our relations with the natural world. The formality, reiteration, and constraint of ritual are, we argue, all necessary aspects of this shared creation. Ritual, moreover, offers its own capacities for human realization and fulfillment, which are all too often slighted in more contemporary, liberal autonomous versions of a self-created universe of individual choice and of an ideal of autonomy freed from any traditional referents. What we are terming here the subjunctive has cognates within the literature on ritual. As we shall see in chapter 1, Jonathan Z. Smith refers to something similar when talking of the "imaginary" nature of ritual.[18]

Second, we claim that these aspects of a shared "as if" created through ritual pervade many realms of human endeavor. Ritual is not restricted to the realm we moderns define as "religious," or even to "secular ritual." Ritual and ritualistic behavior are not so much events as ways of negotiating our very existence in the world. To be sure, we can find such ritual behaviors in churches, mosques, synagogues, and so on. But we can also find them in public performances, at concerts, in the theater, and, crucially, in more quotidian enactments of civility and politeness among strangers and even intimates. Whenever the expressions "please" and "thank you" are used, when we ask a casual acquaintance, "How are you?" both knowing in advance that we do not really expect an honest answer (which could be disastrous), we are enacting a crucial ritual for the maintenance of our shared social world. This type of ritual behavior (studied in some forms by Goffman) is, we claim here, of the same type and follows the same strictures as behaviors more commonly thought of as "ritualistic"—both create subjunctive universes, both permit the very existence of a shared social world, both hold us in a universe that, without such performatives, would simply not exist.[19] Ritual behavior, then, is to be found in public realms as well as private ones. It occurs in myriad forms of normal everyday behavior, as well as in various forms of social and psychological pathologies. It is to be found in art as in architecture, in music and in poetry, in children's games and in professional tennis. To more fully understand ritual, to accustom ourselves to its presence, we must understand that we are not so much witnessing an event (High Mass in church, animal sacrifice, raising the flag at a military base, etc.) as participating in a concert, whose cadences and rhythms point to ways of living in the world that for us moderns tend to be drowned out by a discourse and narrative of what we have just termed "sincerity."[20]

Our third substantive point, to reiterate our brief discussion from earlier in this chapter, is that ritual modes of behavior can be usefully contrasted to what we term sincere forms of approaching the world. Sincere views are focused not on the creation of an "as if" or a shared subjunctive universe of human being in the world. Instead, they project an "as is" vision of what often becomes a totalistic, unambiguous vision of reality "as it *really* is." The tropes of sincerity are pervasively with us, in both our personal and our shared social world. They appear in the arrogance of what are termed fundamentalist religious beliefs. They are present in our overwhelming concern with "authenticity," with individual choice, with the belief that if we can only get at the core, the fount, the unalterable and inimitable heart of what we "really" feel, or "really" think, then all will be well—if not with the world, then at least with ourselves. This is the attitude that Christian Smith, a sociologist at the University of Notre Dame, attributes to young evangelical Christians in the United States: "If you don't choose it, it's not authentic for you."[21] The further implication of course, the one that need not even be explicated, is that if it is not "authentic" it lacks meaning. This is the same attitude that has informed the publication of niche-market Bibles since the mid-1960s. As Phyllis Tickle, an author of popular prayer books, said, "Instead of demanding that the believer, the reader, the seeker step out from the culture and become more Christian, more enclosed within ecclesiastical definition, we're saying 'You stay in the culture and we'll come to you.'"[22] These examples illustrate the core of the phenomenon that we term sincere and that we contrast with the formalism, reiteration, and externally dictated obligations of ritual.

The tension between ritual and sincerity is not new, but pervasive in human cultures. Different cultures deal with the tensions differently, find different accommodations, and differentially value the one or the other orientation. These differences can be found in politics and in art, in music and architecture, as well as in people's understanding of their own sacred traditions. With these differences in mind, we nevertheless claim that our contemporary period is marked by an overwhelming concern with sincerity at the expense of ritual. This pervasiveness is, to a significant degree, a result of the strong role of Protestant Christianity in the making of our modern world and of contemporary culture (even as this world is shared by Jews, Confucians, Hindus, Muslims, Sikhs, and so on). The importance of sincerity within Protestantism is in many ways a commonplace, familiar through the writings of Lionel Trilling, William Haller, and others. It is, to be sure, not unique to Protestantism. It can be found to be equally salient among Hasidic Jews, Zen Buddhists, or Chinese Mohists of two millennia ago. Henri Peyre has traced its role from the Renaissance through twentieth-century French literature.[23] But it is in and through its Protestant articulation that it has had such a pervasive and formative role in contemporary culture.

This is significant, we claim, to any attempt to understand what are so often termed fundamentalist movements in today's world. If we analyze the phenomena in question (and do not simply use the term "fundamentalist" for anyone whose religious beliefs and commitments we find offensive), it becomes clear that there is a very strong "sincere" component to these contemporary manifestations of religious radicalism—be they Christian, Islamic, Hindu, or Jewish. To no small extent, this sincerity occurs in the romantic expressivism of these movements, almost Herderian in nature.[24] This view understands the religious act—and, all too often, the religious act as politics—as the vehicle for self-expression and self-fulfillment. It is less God's work that is being realized in the world than one's own projection of selfhood. Too often this is the unfortunate result of a privileging of authenticity and choice as touchstones of religious action in today's world. We will therefore be arguing that many acts that are often uncritically assigned to a ritualistic religious impulse instead carry with them strong elements of an all too sincere orientation to self and world that in itself has no necessary correlation to the religious impulse or to sacred traditions.

Ritual has had something of a poor reputation in the contemporary world, relegated to a form of deviance in the structural-functionalism of midcentury American sociology, or extirpated as an empty, external husk, lacking in ultimate spiritual significance, or again, condemned as a form of authoritarian control and dominance. We are often too concerned with exploring the different forms of self-expression and of individual authenticity to appreciate the rhythmic structure of the shared subjunctive that is the deepest work of ritual. Our social vision of a world of market utilizers and contracting agents engaged, in the best of times, in the mutually advantageous pursuit of private goods has deafened us somewhat to the cadences of ritual, to its work, to the spaces of its presence, and to the price of its absence.

Finally, then, our fourth point is that the normative connotations in the subtitle of this book are not coincidental. Only through a reengagement with ritual as a constitutive aspect of the human project will it be possible to negotiate the emergent realities of our present century. The reaction to the cultural and economic forces of globalization, the reemergence of religious commitments and ethnic identities throughout the world, and the currently posited opposition of the "West and the rest" all suggest the failure of our existing cultural resources to deal with ambiguity, ambivalences, and the gentle play of boundaries that require both their existence and their transcendence. All too often the modern world has absolutized boundaries. This occurs, on the one hand, through the construction of unassailable identities (such as racial, ethnic, or what are termed "religious" identities, or even the idea of citizenship in the nation-state), and, on the other, through the destruction of all particularism and denial of all constitutive difference between peoples and communities. Such a disavowal of boundaries lies at the heart of most liberal political agendas, such as the universalization of human rights. The genocidal implications of the former approach to boundaries were made only too clear over the course of the twentieth century, which both began and ended in Sarajevo and the ethnonational wars it witnessed. The insufficiency of the latter approach is all too obvious in the continuing challenge of particularisms that do not wish to assimilate to a global culture—and the particularisms of Western Europe and of the United States are no exception.

Neither of these attitudes toward boundaries addresses the deep human need for boundaries, but also for their existence as negotiable entities, more akin to the walls of a living cell than to those of an impregnable fortress. We are constituted on our boundaries, that is to say, constituted on a plane we do not totally control, one that is always also open to the other, to the stranger, to what is different and unknown and beyond the controlling power of the center. This is what makes boundaries dangerous. Rather than trying to eliminate boundaries or to make them into unbreachable walls—the two approaches that so typified the twentieth century—ritual continually renegotiates boundaries, living with their instability and labile nature. Only by paying closer attention to the play of ritual—to its formal elements, even when those formal rhythms may overwhelm claims of content—can we find the way to negotiate the emergent demands of our contemporary world.

Our first chapter begins by taking up some of the formal properties of ritual, with an emphasis on what it does rather than the more usual social scientific stress on what it means. We have found Roy Rappaport's definition particularly useful for this work. Ritual for him is "the performance of more or less invariant sequences of formal acts and utterances not entirely encoded by the performers."[25] One implication of this is that ritual creates and re-creates a world of social convention and authority beyond the inner will of any individual. We will explore this notion through a serious consideration of the understandings of ritual in traditions that take it as central, especially Judaism and Confucianism. We argue that such traditions understand the world as fundamentally fractured and discontinuous, with ritual allowing us to live in it by creating temporary order through the construction of a performative, subjunctive world. Each ritual rebuilds the world "as if" it were so, as one of many possible worlds.

While we explore secular ritual only in a secondary way, we can see a minor example of such things in U.S. presidential elections in our home state of Massachusetts. Many decades have gone by since a vote for president in this state changed anything. The results are such a foregone conclusion that candidates do not even campaign here. More broadly, a recent column by an economist puzzled about why anyone votes, since more utility is lost than gained: the odds of actually determining the result are tiny, and the loss in time and energy is real.[26] Nevertheless, we and millions of our neighbors in the state vote anyway. Voting in such cases is a ritual with no practical value, but one of great significance because it allows us to re-create a social imaginary, a world where the people control the government. In such cases we vote less to choose a president than to re-create our democracy every four years. In such circumstances, at least part of the reason we vote for a president is akin to the same reason we follows the rules and codes of etiquette and civility in our daily lives—these are the rituals without which our social subjunctives would collapse back into a world of coercion and self-interest alone.

We argue, in addition, that the performative aspect of ritual is critical because ritual addresses the relational aspects of role, and of self and other. Ritual both posits boundaries and allows the move between boundaries. By recognizing limits, ritual provides as well the vehicle for transcending them. In the beginning of the Jewish daily prayers, for example, the devotee proclaims: "What are we? What is our life? What is our goodness? What our righteousness? What our helpfulness? What our strength? What our might? . . . Indeed all the heroes are as nothing before thee, the men of renown as though they never existed."[27] But then, immediately declares as well: "However, we are thy people, thy people of the covenant, the children of Abraham thy friend to whom thou didst make a promise on Mount Moriah."[28] The first set of sentences circumscribes existence and its meaning, the last opens it up.

In a somewhat different register and toward the end of the daily prayers, during the Aleynu prayer, the devoted Jew thanks the Lord "who has not made us like nations of the world and has not placed us like the families of the earth; who has not designed our destiny to be like theirs."[29] But, then, the last sentence of the prayer looks to the overcoming of these distinctions "on that day [when] the Lord shall be One and his name One."[30] Both segments present examples of the way ritual notes both the recognition of limits as well as their overcoming or transcendence. These are of course but liturgical examples of the unique ways different rituals are often used to both instantiate boundaries and overcome them. Chapters 2 and 3 address this important characteristic of ritual in greater detail and from broader perspectives.

Unlike most work on rituals, chapter 2 approaches these issues by linking individual psychology to ritual's broader social work. We look at the development of subjunctive worlds and ritual-like behaviors in children, from things like repeated bedtime rituals to the capacity for fantasy and for invention and deceit. Another stream of the analysis examines more unusual and exotic behaviors like fetishism or extreme examples of lying. These two lines of discussion converge around the ways they allow us to deal with ambiguity, building on the psychoanalytic idea of the split ego. Indeed, a central theme of this chapter is the capacity of human beings not only to tolerate ambiguity but even to generate it creatively as a tool for coping with the contradictory demands of existence in the world. Ambiguity and ambivalence are not just passive experiences. For all of us, at some time in our lives, they are instead something actively generated as a mechanism of adaptation to the contradictory demands and impulses of our lives—as both individuals and social actors. We argue that these capacities rest in no small measure on ritualistic modes of behavior, both psychological and sociological. Together these contribute to the creation of subjunctive "as if" universes that not only posit boundaries between discreet entities but also often blur these very boundaries and sometimes even overcome them.

Following on these insights into our capacity to hold together different, even contradictory, versions or visions of reality, chapter 3 takes up the "as if" worlds of play. The first half discusses how the literature on play helps reveal important variations in the world of ritual by clarifying how ritual relates to notions of self and role. It also helps focus the idea of "ritual" more clearly by asking how it differs from play. The second half of the chapter continues the discussion of boundaries by turning to issues of framing in play and ritual, both of which invariably have boundaries around them but also have mechanisms for crossing those boundaries. We point to exactly this ability to play with boundaries as a crucial feature of the ritual worldview that is missing in a world of pure sincerity.

In its ability to play with boundaries—to see the dual role of boundaries as both separating and uniting—ritual action stands in opposition to modern forms of social organization, which most often tend to absolutize boundaries, either by doing away with them totally or by apotheosizing them into unquestionable and inviolable entities. We take up this issue directly in chapter 4. There we open the discussion of how liberal modes of social organization—and of organizing the self, we might add—maintain interaction and solidarity by doing away with boundaries rather than by teaching how to negotiate them. The only boundaries maintained in such liberal visions are those predicated on instrumental distinctions, that is, on the vagaries of the division of labor.

In many ways this is the heart of the project of modernity as registered in Article I of the Declaration of the Rights of Man and of the Citizen (August 26, 1789) of the French National Assembly: "All men are born and remain free and equal in rights: *social distinctions can not be found but on common utility.*" Social distinctions between men and women are, henceforth, not to be based on anything other than their place in the division of labor, in essence on their utility functions for the working of the social whole. In this modernist vision—repeated in both its socialist and liberal forms—divisions and distinctions between individuals and groups are henceforth to be instrumental rather than constitutive. Denying constitutive boundaries, however, does not seem to work. Not then and not now. One consequence of recent globalization (surely the most radical experiment in boundary deconstruction) has been the reemergence of boundaries and bounded identities often of a markedly xenophobic nature. These have spawned religious struggles in Africa, anti-immigrant sentiment in Western Europe, religious and national conflict on the Indian subcontinent, and much more. Ritual, then, seems a useful area to explore because its very recognition of boundaries may also provide a way of negotiating them with a minimum of violence.

We may add parenthetically that the denial of boundaries and constitutive identities was, in the nineteenth century and following the French Revolution, the key to the integration (and assimilation) of the Jews within the western European political order. Its classic expression was given by Count Stanislav de Clermont-Tonnerre in 1789: "We must refuse everything to the Jew as a nation and accord everything to the Jew as an individual."[31] This became a paradigmatic statement of attitudes toward the other. As we all know, the vision of this form of integration ended in tragic failure and in the mass murder of European Jewry in World War II. Given current attitudes toward Muslims in Europe, whether in France or in Bosnia, or in the continued popular opposition to the incorporation of Turkey into the European Union, it seems timely to propose a serious questioning of this paradigm and an attempt to articulate or at least to open a possible space for an alternative model.

The modern and postmodern worlds have not attended closely to ritual forms of social life and behavior. When the daughters of secularizing elites in Turkey voluntarily take up veiling and when the children of liberal Jews in New York subject themselves to the most stringent dietary proscriptions, we begin to realize that role, ritual, and self-identity are bound up in ways that social scientists have yet to fully fathom. The indicative force of ritual rather than its propositional potential may express fundamental aspects of human relationships, indeed of human existence, that—however inimical to modernist assumptions—cannot be lightly dismissed.

Chapter 4 turns directly to the tension between sincerity and ritual that is always present. Sincerity often appears as a reaction against the perceived hypocrisy of the ritually created subjunctive. Yet those reactions in turn tend to ritualize over time. Sincerity imagines a world "as is" instead of ritual's multiple worlds of "as if." It looks to discursive meanings and unique selves instead of repeated acts and fragmented realities. One crucial implication of the turn toward sincerity over the last few centuries has been a general dissolution of social boundaries in principle, even as people constantly reassert them in fact. Ultimately, we argue, ritual has an important place in this (or any) world, which has not been recognized by most political or social scientific theory.

Chapter 5 extends this discussion by looking at the interplay of ritual and sincerity over time, including reforms demanding more ritual, as well as those demanding more sincerity. Unlike the earlier chapters, this one introduces less new theoretical material and turns instead to various arenas (often beyond religion) where the tension plays out. First, we discuss the interplay of law and love, Judaism and Christianity, ritual and sincerity in Shakespeare's *Merchant of Venice*. Second, we look at the history of architectural ornament, which is ritual-like in its repetitions and rhythms and in its concern with boundaries and framing. Here the ritual/sincerity tension plays out typically as conflict between ornament and pedagogy through either representational art or the banning of images in favor of text. Iconoclasm is a core theme of this section. Finally, we turn to music, which shares many formal features of ritual and often accompanies it. Like ritual, music is a way of establishing and crossing boundaries, and of making order out of a messy world. We can see this in issues like intonation, rhythm, and ornament. The tension between ritual and sincerity shows up in long arguments against complex harmonies or ornaments as distractions from the sung text, and culminates in twentieth-century attempts to move beyond the conventions of tonality completely.

Ritual, as we shall be arguing here, is best approached through what it does rather than through what it may mean, although a focus on meaning has characterized much of the social scientific literature on ritual in the past. While that literature's findings are many and significant, they do tend to blind us to certain core aspects of ritual that gain much from shifting the focus of study from meaning to *doing*.

Ritual acknowledges authority relations and their consequences for human existence in the world by positing existing relationships between bounded entities, rather than by serving as an instrumental information code that conveys descriptive messages. Ritual both relies on and supports shared social convention. To be sure, these conventions include distinctions of role and power, but also the very idea of a constitutive self. While these properties of ritual may make it irreducible to modernist assumptions about the autonomy of individuals, it is nevertheless worthy of fresh study precisely because of the importance of boundaries to the continued existence of both social selves and their shared social world.

We are not arguing that the interplay of ritual and sincere modes of understanding the world provides a full theory of religious or even just ritual experience. Our claim is more modest: that by examining this particular dynamic we can achieve a new and richer understanding of how ritual works, and how it will continue to be important. This is true even in a modern world whose vision has so far focused almost entirely on sincerity—perhaps especially in such a world, whose limits now seem all too clear.

I

Ritual and the Subjunctive

The idea that ritual creates a shared and conventional world of human sociality goes back at least two millennia, as do insights about the resulting problems of self and society, individuality and convention. Such a world is always subjunctive, just one possible alternative. Let us begin our inquiry with a quotation from Xunzi, an early Confucian thinker from the third century BCE: "Heaven and Earth are the beginning of life; ritual and propriety are the beginning of order; the gentleman is the beginning of ritual and propriety."[1] Heaven and Earth generate life, but it is humanity who brings order to the world through the creation of rituals. As Xunzi elaborates:

> Therefore, Heaven and Earth gave birth to the gentleman. The gentleman gives patterns to Heaven and Earth. The gentleman forms a triad with Heaven and Earth, is the summation of the myriad things, and is the father and mother of the people. Without the gentleman, Heaven and Earth have no pattern, ritual and righteousness have no unity; above there is no ruler or leader, below there is no father or son. This is called the utmost chaos. Ruler and minister, father and son, older and younger brother, husband and wife begin and then end, end and then begin. They share with Heaven and Earth the same pattern, and last for ten thousand generations. This is called the great foundation.[2]

Heaven and Earth give life, but they are also fundamentally chaotic, without pattern. And so, therefore, is humanity. Only humans can give pattern and order to the world. In short, order is an artifice of humanity:

> Someone asks: "If man's nature is evil, from where are rituals and propriety generated?" I respond: "All rituals and propriety were generated from the artifice of the sages. They were not originally generated from the inner nature of man. Thus, a potter works clay and makes vessels; as such, the vessels are generated from the artifice of the craftsman, and were not originally generated from the inner nature of man. Thus, a craftsman carves wood and completes implements; as such, the implements are generated from the artifice of the craftsman, and were not originally generated from the inner nature of man. The sages accumulated their considerations and thoughts and practiced artifice and precedents; they thereby generated rituals and propriety, and made laws and standards arise. As such, rituals, propriety, laws, and standards were generated from the artifice of the sages, and were not originally generated from the inner nature of man."[3]

Comparable views occur repeatedly in early Confucian writings. As we are told in the *Book of Rites*: "The Master said, 'As for the sacrificial victims, ritual, and music being properly arranged and flourishing, this is the means by which there is no harm from the demons and spirits and no resentment from the hundred families.'"[4] This chaotic and fragmented world, controlled by capricious and potentially antagonistic demons and spirits, can only be ordered through human rituals.

Let us now turn to a selection from the rabbinic literature. From *The Fathers According to Rabbi Nathan*:

> With ten utterances the world was created. What need do inhabitants of the world have of this? It is to teach you that, for anyone who practices one commandment, and anyone who observes one Sabbath, and anyone who preserves one life, Scripture accounts it to him as if he preserved the entire world that was created with ten utterances.[5]

A clearly well-intentioned deity created this world, and even the most minute ritual action on the part of a human supports that creation.

At first glance, these appear to be two radically distinct visions of ritual. In the one tradition, ritual is a human construct, aimed at bringing order to an otherwise fragmented and chaotic world. In the other, ritual is a divine construct, sent to allow humans to live properly in and even help support a divinely created order.

An earlier anthropology would have dissolved the difference between such visions by simply ignoring the content of the cosmological claims. Ritual, according to figures such as Radcliffe-Brown, simply functions to create social cohesion. It would have served the same function in both the early Chinese and Judaic traditions. The only difference between the two is that China produced some theorists like Xunzi who understood what ritual was really about:

> There is no doubt that in China, as elsewhere, it was thought that many or all of the religious rites were efficacious in the sense of averting evils and bringing blessings. It was believed that the seasons would not follow one another in due order unless the Emperor, the Son of Heaven, performed the established rites at the appropriate times. Even under the Republic a reluctant magistrate of a *hsien* may be compelled by public opinion to take the leading part in a ceremony to bring rain. But there developed among the scholars an attitude which might perhaps be called rationalistic or agnostic. For the most part the question of the efficacy of rites was not considered. What was thought important was the social function of the rites, i.e. their effects in producing and maintaining an orderly human society.[6]

Radcliffe-Brown continues:

> The view taken by this school of ancient philosophers [the Confucians] was that religious rites have important social functions which are independent of any beliefs that may be held as to the efficacy of the rites. The rites gave regulated expression to certain human feelings and sentiments and so kept these sentiments alive and active. In turn it was these sentiments which, by their control of or influence on the conduct of individuals, made possible the existence and continuance of an orderly social life.[7]

In this classic formulation, Xunzi, like modern social scientists but unlike the practitioners themselves, understood that ritual is a human construct to maintain social cohesion. In contrast, practitioners, who would include Rabbi Nathan, mistakenly read ritual as a divine construct.

Much subsequent theory has rightly opposed such a devaluing of indigenous beliefs. Most famously, and certainly most influentially, Clifford Geertz shifted our focus toward the meaning-making subject.[8] Ritual, under such an approach, is to be understood according to the total system of signs that make a given action meaningful to the participants. In the case at hand, this would entail a thick description of early Chinese and Judaic material, focusing on their respective—and thus radically different—systems of meanings.

One of our concerns with such an approach, however, is that Geertz tames ritual practice by interpreting it according to a coherent worldview, instead of looking at its actual workings. As Talal Asad has argued, Geertz's approach to religious practice owes a strong debt to what may be termed a post-Protestant emphasis on the coherence of belief.[9] Such an approach is of dubious universality. Indeed, as we will argue in chapter 4, this reading of religious practice emphasizes a very different pole of activity than ritual. In the cases at hand, such an approach may be particularly dangerous: as we will discuss later, the Chinese and Judaic traditions actually have an enormous amount in common, despite their radically different theological underpinnings.

Finally, Geertz, somewhat ironically, repeats one of the fundamental errors of Radcliffe-Brown, namely, an a priori emphasis on ritual as an encompassing concord. By emphasizing ritual as concord and unity (whether in the realm of social function or in the realm of the totalizing system of cultural meanings), both theorists fail to emphasize some of the key features of ritual—features that our examples will hopefully help to underscore.

We have emphasized the potential inadequacies of both Radcliffe-Brown and Geertz for a particular reason. These two figures represent the two basic poles around which much of twentieth-century and now twenty-first-century theory on ritual has revolved. On the one hand is an emphasis on the social function of ritual, with an overt rejection of the importance of culture. On the other is an emphasis on the worldview that is perceived to underlie the actions of the ritual participants. Such views, we will argue, came to prominence in a particular historical moment. As such, they are of great interest—but not as theories of ritual.

The model we propose instead understands ritual as a subjunctive—the creation of an order *as if* it were truly the case. Or, putting it in different words, the subjunctive creates an order that is self-consciously distinct from other possible social worlds. Unlike Radcliffe-Brown, then, we take cultural meanings very seriously, but unlike Geertz we do not read such meanings as an overriding set of assumptions concerning the world. On the contrary, we emphasize the incongruity between the world of enacted ritual and the participants' experience of lived reality, and we thus focus on the work that ritual accomplishes.

With this point in mind, it is worth returning to our two examples thus far. For Xunzi, the goal of ritual is to bring order, hierarchy, principle, and ethics to a world that is otherwise chaotic, amoral, and indifferent—to live *as if* the world were actually a moral, coherent universe. For Rabbi Nathan, the goal is to enact divinely ordained commandments—to live *as if* enacting them actually preserved the divinely created world. In the Chinese case, rituals are explicitly presented as a human artifice; in the Jewish one, the rituals are presented as a product of a great deity. Both cases, however, imply that ritual action creates a new world, in self-conscious tension with an unritualized world. A rabbinic dictum explicitly recognizes the subjunctive aspect of the human ordering of the world: "He who rules justly is as if he participates with the Holy One, Blessed Be He, in the creation of the world."[10] It is thus not surprising that, as we shall see, the work involved in enacting ritual in these two traditions is remarkably similar.

So what does it mean to analyze ritual as a subjunctive, and how, then, does ritual work? We will tackle the questions first from a theoretical perspective and then in terms of specific examples from the early Chinese and Judaic traditions, as well as elsewhere.

Ritual and the Subjunctive

Ritual activity—and, with it, the construction of a subjunctive universe—occurs throughout many different modes of human interaction, not just religion. The courtesy and politeness of daily life are also modes of ritual action. The truth value of such ritual invocations (like saying "please" and "thank you") is not very important. We are inviting our interlocutor to join us in imagining a particular symbolic universe within which to construe our actions. When I frame my requests with please and thank you, I am not giving a command (to pass the salt), but I am very much recognizing your agency (your ability to decline my request). Hence, saying please and thank you communicates in a formal and invariant manner—to both of us—that we understand our interaction as the voluntary actions of free and equal individuals. "Please" creates the illusion of equality by recognizing the other's power to decline.

Other forms of politeness, of course, construct quite different social illusions. Chinese courtesies have long marked hierarchies instead of imagining equalities. Endless modernizing campaigns by both republican and communist governments over the twentieth century—to say please and thank you or to call everyone comrade—have attempted to substitute other visions of the social world. None, however, has so far succeeded over the long term, because they posit a very different kind of social self underlying the convention.

Note that even in the imagined equalities of American courtesy, the power to decline may not be real. When we ask our children to please clear their plates or our students to please open their books, declining is not a normal option. Nevertheless, we ask *as if* the behavior were voluntary, because that ritual creates the social world that allows our interactions to continue in peace. Rituals such as saying "please" and "thank you" create an illusion, but with no attempt to deceive. This is a crucial difference from a lie, which is an illusion with a clear attempt to deceive the other. In this ritual is much more like play, which is the joint entrance into an illusionary world (and which we shall explore much further in chapter 3).

By framing our interaction with the "illusions" of courtesy, the frame actually pulls us in after it, making the illusion the reality. And the reality will last only as long as we adhere to the illusion. So, for example, when we ask our children to please feed the dog and they refuse, we may get angry and shout, "DAMN IT, FEED THE DOG NOW!" At this point we both leave the illusionary world of mutuality and respect for the one of brute power. We fall back into a world from which politeness had saved us.

The continual possibility of falling out of the illusion does not make it a lie, no more than children's play is given the lie when mother calls the children home for dinner, or a play by Euripides is given the lie by the audience's exiting the theater and getting on the subway. Illusions are not lies—they are a form of the subjunctive. Illusion is what can be, as indeed so many different symbolic worlds can.[11] Answering "fine" to inquiries about how we are is usually a ritual pleasantry. We do not mention the nagging headache, the argument with the teenage child, or the overdue paper. "Fine" is untrue, but still not exactly a lie. "Fine" deceives no one; it simply establishes a certain kind of social relationship. One can pull it out of the realm of ritual interaction and treat it as a lie ("but your leg is in a cast!"), but that is a different form of interaction. Not true yet not deceptive—this is the joint entrance into an illusionary world.

Of course, by presenting our actions in this light—more precisely, by constructing a symbolic universe where our activities with one another can be understood in this manner—we are also in a sense actually denoting the construction of the illusion as the real nature of our interaction. The "as if" quality of the ritual invocation, its subjunctive sense, is also what makes it real. What is, is what can be.

This suggests that the rituals of politeness posit a possible, even plausible, mode of activity between interlocutors by building an illusion that pulls them out of a more Hobbesian world of the war of all against all. This works only so long as all accept that possible world (through sharing its mode of speech and approach), represented by the formal codes of polite invocation. This mode of speech (the please and thank you) is both signified and signifier in one. Courtesies point to a particular way of human social interaction (of mutual respect) and are at the same time an instance of that mode. By saying please and thank you, we are both symbolizing a fundamentally civil recognition of one another and actually acting out and instantiating such behavior in the world. Such civil modes of address are what Peirce called an "index," with the unique characteristics of being both about society and in a mutually creative relationship with it.[12]

We argue that what constitutes society—what makes the social a sui generis entity, irreducible to any other—is precisely a shared "could be," a mutual illusion of the sort that all rituals create. To a great extent, this is what symbols do more than anything else: they represent a "could be."[13] This shared "could be" (or, sometimes, "what if") is the nodal point where members of a society come together as symbol users. It is surely not coincidental that Terrence Deacon begins his important book *The Symbolic Species* by invoking the subjunctive as what distinguishes us from other mammals and primates.[14]

We could perhaps go one step further and postulate that much of what the individual ego experiences as a uniquely individual event (love, desire, hate, envy, frustration, etc.) can become social and shared only through its symbolic representation in terms of a "could be" or a "what if." What if we spent our life together, we slept together, he were dead and out of my way, I had her jewelry or beauty, I was boss and he worked for me, and so forth. We cannot actually share (as opposed to simply describing) our desire or hate or frustration with another soul; we cannot produce in another our own desires, hates, or frustrations. We can, however, attempt to evoke the same sets of feelings or experiences through a shared "could be." Our individual experience of an "is" (the very real feelings of desire, hate, or even hunger and poverty) can only become social through the imaginative act, the "as if." Such diverse phenomena as the thrashing of figures from the underworld by the priests of Demeter, the Muslim casting stones at Iblis during the hajj to Mecca, or Incas driving off evil spirits all involve this construction of (and by) a subjunctive universe, which creates a community of empathy at the same time.[15]

What we share as symbolic beings is potentiality. A community of fate shares a sense of what "could be" (if they rounded up all the Jews in Poland or Japanese in California or Muslims in Banja Luka, it "could" happen to you, even though you are a Jew in Toronto, a Japanese in Paris, or a Muslim in Islamabad), as well as, of course, a shared "once there was." The capacity to empathize, to share in the potential space of what could be, may be inherent in the human species as symbol users. Nevertheless, the specific forms of this cultural creativity, of the formation of this potential space, are not at all given or constant. They change as the historical context changes. The strong image of the barbarian as an other, for instance, only emerged in Athens of the fifth century BCE in consequence of the Persian conflict.[16] Thus the shared intermediary space of empathy can either contract or expand, and its structuring is a subject of conflict, often violent conflict, throughout history. Peasants in feudal society were beyond the shared empathy of the aristocracy. The bourgeoisie in Paris following the Commune of 1871 apparently did not see themselves as participating in the same "what if" as the defeated workers, and so on.

When we say of a culture that its members share a symbol system, or a set of values, or a common idea of the sacred, we are in essence asserting that they share the potential space of a shared "could be." The moral community that Émile Durkheim outlined in his *Elementary Forms of Religious Life* exists precisely because it shares the potential space of culture.[17] Much ritual action in fact provides this shared sense of empathy—sometimes even in terms of an explicitly shared "what if." When Jews sit around the Passover Seder table and are explicitly enjoined to fulfill the commandment to feel "as if you yourselves have been liberated from Egypt," they create that shared symbolic space where the communality of the "could be" becomes the very basis of the ongoing collective experience. The Shi'ite enactment of the defeat of Imam Hussein at Karbala and the Catholic participation in the Eucharist all have similar import.[18] Confucius, famously uninterested in the world of spirits, still insisted that when "he offered sacrifice to his ancestors he felt *as if* his ancestral spirits were actually present. When he offered sacrifice to other spiritual beings, he felt *as if* they were actually present."[19] Maimonides enjoins us to attend to our prayers "as if" we are standing before the Creator of the universe.[20]

While ritual activity carries its own form of intentionality, it is important to note that ritual is not necessarily concerned with what we term sincerity. In any ritual, as with saying please, performing the act marks acceptance of the convention. It does not matter how you may feel about the convention, if you identify with it or not. In doing a ritual the whole issue of our internal states is often irrelevant. What you *are* is what you *are in the doing*, which is of course an external act. This is very different from modernist concerns with sincerity and authenticity (including religious fundamentalist concern with such authenticity, as we address in a later chapter). Getting it *right* is not a matter of making outer acts conform to inner beliefs. Getting it right is doing it again and again and again—it is an act of world construction. This suggests the counterintuitive insight that in this world of ritual acts the self is left more "room to wander" (perhaps also to wonder) than in one where the self has to be firmly identified with its role—where the matrix of social order is in sincerity (for which there is never enough evidence, cannot be, anywhere, at any time). As ideal types the self *who does ritual* is very different from the self *who is sincere.*[21]

The creation of "as if" worlds is a central aspect of ritual action, which we see as necessary for human life. This subjunctive aspect of ritual is crucial to many forms of civil social behavior (though, as we pointed out, the codes of civility may be very different in different places). Thus, it is not enough for kings to be kings, they must act as if they were kings. Justice must not just be meted out, it must be seen to be meted out. There are any number of everyday examples that show the sometimes counterintuitive importance of this "as if." Imagine a family of five, two parents and three children—all love and care for one another, and any major event (when one falls and gets hurt, or when one wins a prize) will mobilize all of them to help or support or praise (as appropriate) the member in question. But, in daily life there is often much pushing, screaming, grabbing of hairbrushes, not helping with the dinner or feeding the dog, and so on. The parents then decide that everyone has to treat each other with a bit more respect, more civility, more use of please and thank you. Many of us have experienced this and know that it works—at least for a time, until the please and thank you begin to get lost. Ratcheting up the amount of love everyone feels, on the other hand, is not the way to make life more pleasant in the household. There is no need, and it is not even possible. Everyone loves the others. That is not the point. Instead, the problem is to get everyone to act *as if* they love one another. More real love (whatever that may be) is not needed, nor even reinstituting a feeling that has been lost. Not at all. What was missing was the behavior that would create a shared subjunctive— ritual. Erich Segal was wrong—love does not mean never having to say you're sorry. That is precisely what love does mean—at least if you want to share a life with the person you love.

Both self and other enter this world of shared action. Sharing the act, they both point to or index the shared world that is their relationship. Writ large, the social is this shared, potential space between separate egos. It is constituted by a common "could be," by a shared subjunctive that first and foremost parses out the lines and boundaries of empathy as shared imagination. Ritual enacts this shared space in a way not so different from the "enactment" of the potential space between ego and object in the form of transitional objects (such as the infant's blanket or special teddy, for example).[22] Ritual, in Margaret Alexiou's words, is critical in "keeping the metaphorical system alive."[23] Through their embedding in everyday life, "ritual systems carry metaphorical systems, each forming a treasury of associations transmitted over time."[24]

By emphasizing ritual as subjunctive, we are underlining the degree to which ritual creates a shared, illusory world. Participants practicing ritual act as if the world produced in ritual were in fact a real one. And they do so fully conscious that such a subjunctive world exists in endless tension with an alternate world of daily experience. Careful readings of Durkheim will show the differences of this understanding of ritual from his own, which sees ritual as the arena of collective effervescence that establishes the collective conscience. We, however, posit ritual action as a subjunctively shared arena, a space in between. It is not a place where individual entities dissolve into a collective oneness.

Since the practice of ritual creates its own illusory world, ritual must be understood as inherently nondiscursive—semantic content is far secondary to subjunctive creation. This is not, of course, to suggest that ritual has no words. It most certainly does—from invocatory language in religious ceremony to the use of "please" and "thank you" in contemporary American etiquette. But it is nondiscursive in the sense that it cannot be analyzed as a coherent system of beliefs. The meaning of ritual is the meaning produced through the ritual action itself. That is one reason that so many rituals include nondiscursive media like music or masks, and even language may be used in ways that defy discursive interpretation.

Moreover, the meaning produced through ritual action always exists in problematic tension with the nonritual world. This is why seeking to analyze ritual in terms of a larger vision of unity—whether found in the functioning of society or a meaningful system of signs—is so problematic, and so often misconstrues the actual workings of ritual. This has often been the case within Durkheimian tradition, broadly conceived.

In his own terms, Jonathan Z. Smith has made a convincing argument for this ritual creation of a subjunctive universe. In his famous study of bear ceremonial rituals among circumpolar hunters, Smith argued strongly against previous attempts to read the meaning of the bear ritual as an example of a nonrational, magical way of thinking. The ritual in question involved raising the bear from a cub, treating it as a guest in the village, and then slaying it only after it took actions interpreted as an acceptance of the necessity of its death. Interpretations of such a ritual as an example of sympathetic hunting magic saw it as an attempt to influence the natural world: by killing a bear according to proper forms of etiquette, the same would hopefully occur in the wild as well. Smith convincingly argued, on the contrary, that the ritual worked precisely out of the clear incongruity between the world of ritual and actual world:

> There is, I believe, an essential truth to the old interpretation of "sympathetic magic" as an "offensive against the objective world" but that the wrong consequences were deduced. It is not that "magical" rituals compel the world through representation and manipulation; rather they express a realistic assessment of the fact that the world cannot be compelled.[25]

Accordingly, Smith argues, ritual should be understood as operating precisely out of an understood tension between the world and what we are calling the subjunctive:

> I would suggest that, among other things, ritual represents the creation of a controlled environment where the variables (i.e., the accidents) of ordinary life may be displaced precisely because they are felt to be so overwhelmingly present and powerful. Ritual is a means of performing the way things ought to be in conscious tension to the way things are in such a way that this ritualized perfection is recollected in the ordinary, uncontrolled course of things. Ritual relies for its power on the fact that it is concerned with quite ordinary activities, that what it describes and displays is, in principle, possible for every occurrence of these acts. But it relies, as well, for its power on the perceived fact that, in actuality, such possibilities cannot be realized.[26]

Ritual, therefore, should best be understood as working precisely out of the incongruity of the subjunctive of ritual and the actual world of lived experience: "From such a perspective, ritual is not best understood as congruent with something else—a magical imitation of desired ends, a translation of emotions, a symbolic acting out of ideas, a dramatization of a text, or the like. Ritual gains force where incongruence is perceived and thought about."[27] As Smith properly points out, an emphasis on congruity has guided many theories of rituals—whether reading ritual according to a magical worldview, to a symbolic system of signs, or to the following of a myth. And, we would add, a functionalist reading of ritual is equally based upon an emphasis on congruity.

Smith's emphasis on incongruity and tension is an excellent starting point for a theory of ritual. But a friendly amendment to Smith's argument may also be called for. Smith's attempt to save ritual practitioners from being read as prerational actors may have led him to go too far in emphasizing the cognitive aspects of incongruity—that ritual works because it allows the practitioners to think about the disjunction between ritual performance and the real world. But it is important to note that ritual is not necessarily—or even primarily—something one thinks about. Indeed, if we take Smith's emphasis on incongruity seriously, it may actually help point us away from such a cognitive reading of ritual and toward one focusing more on the active, and endless, work of ritual.

Let us turn for an example to the practice of "secondary burial" among rural Cantonese of the New Territories, Hong Kong.[28] James Watson described how the goal of a family is to maintain the patriline. Marriage is exogamous, so women are brought in from other lineages in order for a patriline to continue. In reproduction, people consider the bones of the child as an inheritance of the father, and the flesh as an inheritance of the mother. Since the patriline is associated with the bones, the flesh that the females contribute is seen as bringing in a dangerous pollution to the family as well. While alive, therefore, a human being is inherently polluted. Only after death can this pollution finally be ended. The goal is to eradicate the polluting flesh and define the ancestor exclusively in terms of the bones. This is accomplished through a series of ritual actions. The corpse is first placed in a coffin. Just before the coffin is taken out of the village, the daughters and daughters-in-law of the deceased rub their hair against the coffin, thus absorbing the pollution of the decaying flesh. The coffin is then buried. Then, after the flesh has fully decomposed, the bones are exhumed, cleaned of every last scrap of flesh, and then placed in a ceramic urn. An auspicious location is determined, and the bones are reburied in a tomb. If this is done properly, the bones are then believed to bring fertility and good luck to the descendants. The continuity of the patriline is thus assured, freed from the pollutions of the flesh.

The subjunctive world created by these burial rituals only works in self-conscious opposition to an everyday world seen as inherently polluted. And, by definition, there is no possibility that such pollution can be eradicated in the real world: the ritual assumes that, for reproduction, a pollution of the patriline is inherent and necessary. Ritual, therefore, is an endless work of creating a subjunctive world in overt tension with the world of lived experience.

The Work of Ritual

Given an approach to the study of ritual that emphasizes tension and incongruity, it is interesting to explore the ways that ritual interacts with the world of everyday experience. Some of the most exciting work in this area has been undertaken by Robert Orsi, a scholar deeply concerned with the ways in which Protestant approaches to religion have led to misguided understandings of religious behavior. Orsi's ethnographic work on American Catholicism instead focuses precisely on the complex relationships that develop in everyday life via religious practices. As he states:

> Religious theories that emphasize meaning focus on the end-product, a story that is said to link heaven and earth, but the solidity and stability of this dissolves if you focus instead on the processes of religious meaning-making. What we see if we do this is the

wounding; in this devotional world, as in others, meaning making is wounding.[29]

Instead of the emphasis on systems of harmony, such an approach instead focuses on the tragic:

> I [have] suggested replacing the meaning-making subject with a more tragic figure whose engagements with the world, within particular circumstances of power, proceed through media that may embody meanings against him or her. Persons working on the world do so always in the context of the world's working on them. This leads to a more chastened view of culture generally and of religion in particular, one that steers clear of words like empowerment, agency (simply), and transcendence and instead moves in the register of the tragic, of the limited and constrained, or what I would think of as the real.[30]

Instead of focusing on the agency of the meaning-making subject, Orsi emphasizes the limited, and potentially tragic, relationships of everyday life.

For example, Orsi has explored the ways in which the relationships to saints that develop in ritual practice create a repertoire of orientations—a repertoire that in turn affects the ways in which practitioners respond to events in their everyday lives: "Religions have provided Americans in the turbulent and distressing circumstances of life in this society over time . . . with a repertoire of feelings and orientations with which to take hold of their world as it takes hold of them."[31] The focus of the analysis thus turns to the ways that everyday life comes to be reexperienced in response to the practices of devotion: "The narrative practices of the devotion do not represent the recasting of mundane experience in another "symbolic" or "religious" key, but the re-experiencing of everyday life in a new way."[32] The work of ritual, then, involves developing repertoires that operate in complex interplay with the world of everyday experience.

To quote Orsi once more, here in reference to his grandmother's devotion to Saint Gemma Galgani:

> What the saint seems to have offered was companionship on a bitter and confusing journey—bitterness and confusion to which the saint's own stories had contributed. My grandmother asked no grace of Gemma other than that of accompaniment, no miracle beyond the recognition of shared lives. But the sharing was costly. As Gemma's and Giula's stories teach, in between a life and the meanings that may be made in it, for and against that life is the wound. Meaning

making begins in wounding, and the process of meaning making is wounding.[33]

The interplay of religious practice and everyday life always operates, at least ultimately, in the realm of the tragic. We have finally left Radcliffe-Brown and Geertz well behind.

Ritual and the Tragic

These arguments imply that ritual always operates in a world that is frag-mented and fractured. Moreover, the subjunctive world created by ritual is always doomed ultimately to fail—the ordered world of flawless repetition can never fully replace the broken world of experience. This is why the tension between the two is inherent and, ultimately, unbridgeable. Indeed, this ten-sion is the driving force behind the performance of ritual: the endless work of ritual is necessary precisely because the ordered world of ritual is inevitably only temporary. The world always returns to its broken state, constantly re-quiring the repairs of ritual.

If the world is always fractured, and if ritual always operates in tension with such a world, then we need to think of ritual in terms of such an endlessly doomed dynamic. Ritual should be seen as operating in, to again quote Robert Orsi, "the register of the tragic."[34] Although the claims of ritual may be of an ordered, flawless system, the workings of ritual are always in the realm of the limited and the ultimately doomed.

Such an emphasis, needless to say, runs counter to much of twentieth-century and twenty-first-century theorizing about ritual. As alluded to ear-lier, most of these theories emphasize ritual in terms of harmony—in the sense of either interpreting ritual according to a harmonious worldview or see-ing the functioning of ritual as leading to harmony. Both of these views, we would argue, arose out of an evolutionary strain in twentieth-century Western thought—a strain that read ritual as belonging to a "premodern" world that had since been overtaken by a "modern" world in which ritual had become deva-lued. According to such a view, ritual was associated with more primitive cul-tures, where the emphasis was on conformity to and harmony with a larger social and cosmological whole. This contrasted with a modern world based on individualism and autonomy. Such an evolution was often presented in posi-tive terms, as the heroic release of the individual from conformity to a ritually based traditional order, and of the future freed from the fetters of the past. But it could also be presented in negative terms, as a shift away from a harmonious

world and toward one of alienation. Whether presented positively or negatively, however, the model was the same: ritual was associated with a premodern world and was accordingly read in terms of harmony and conformity
to tradition.

We would like to dispute this entire framework. In chapter 4 we will offer
our rereading of the issue of "modernity." Here, however, we would like to
stress that the reduction of ritual to harmony is simply false: it means taking the claims made within ritual (of systematicity, of harmony, of order) and
reading these as assumptions concerning the nature of the social and cosmic
worlds themselves. In fact, it is quite the opposite: ritual actions involving
order and harmony are only necessary among actors who see the world as
inherently fractured and fragmented. If ritual participants thought the world
was inherently harmonious, why bother with the rituals? Indeed, it is only
from a nonritual perspective (as, for example, among Protestant theorists of
the past century in the West) that such a reading of ritual becomes possible.
As we will see in the following section, indigenous theories developed within
ritual traditions hardly read the world as harmonious.

Let us make the point by referring again to the bear hunt rituals discussed
by Jonathan Z. Smith. The reading of the bear hunt as representing an assumption of a harmonious world, in which animals would willingly volun-
teer for their deaths, was only made by twentieth-century scholars who read
the ritual acts as representing the assumptions of the (primitive) participants. But, as Smith was able to show, the ethnographers who worked with
the natives clearly documented, both from the statements made by the ritual participants and from the actual hunting methods employed, that there
was no belief whatsoever that the animals would willingly give themselves
to the hunter. During the hunt, there were no rituals of respect with regard
to the hunted animals at all. Indeed, the preferred method for the hunt was
subterfuge—to kill the bear while it was asleep or otherwise unaware, so that
it would be unable to attack. In other words, the hunters clearly understood
that the bear would kill the humans if it saw them.[35] The ritual, therefore,
only makes sense in terms of the perceived disjunct between the ritual act and
the world of lived experience. The ritual cannot be read as representing a
worldview.

Instead of reading ritual in terms of a worldview of harmony, then, we
will emphasize ritual in terms of the tragic. From the point of view of ritual,
the world is fragmented and fractured. This is why the endless work of ritual
is necessary, even if that work is always, ultimately, doomed.

If so many scholars have misread ritual by placing it into a premodern/
modern teleology, it may well repay the effort to turn to indigenous ritual

theories to see how they read ritual action. We will see that they offer a very different picture than those emphasized by so many recent scholars.

Ritual and the Fractured World

The musings of Robert Orsi on contemporary American Catholicism resonate well with early Chinese discussions of ritual. This fact should not surprise. If contemporary theory has been overly influenced by Protestant readings of religious practice, then turning to theories that were developed outside of such a context may prove invaluable. So, to follow out the implications of our argument concerning ritual, let us return to these early Chinese texts on ritual, but now taking them not as pseudo-functionalist analyses but rather as themselves ritual theory. To deepen our analysis, we will turn to "Nature Emerges from the Decree" (*Xing Zi Ming Chu*), a recently excavated text from the fourth century BCE.[36]

Like many texts from early China, "Nature Emerges from the Decree" assumes a fractured, discontinuous world. It is up to humans to build patterns of relationships out of this fractured world and thereby create an ordered, ethical way of life. Ritual, for the text, becomes the repertoire of these patterns, a repertoire that is endlessly growing, constantly changing, and always in danger of becoming inadequate.

If we are to take the text seriously as theory, the argument deserves closer scrutiny. The text opens with a simple statement concerning human emotions: "In general, although humans possess nature, their mind is without a fixed purpose. It depends on things and only then becomes active; it depends on pleasures and only then is moved; it depends on repeated study and only then becomes fixed."[37] Humans by nature are simply pulled by the things they encounter in immediate situations. As the text elaborates: "The energies of joy, anger, sorrow, and sadness are given by nature. When it comes to their being manifested on the outside, it is because things have called them forth."[38] Humans are containers of emotional energies. These energies are constantly being dragged out by our encounters with things—and for early Chinese texts, the category of "things" includes humans as well.

Movement, therefore, begins when things, each with its own nature, affect each other in situation after situation. The ways that our natures are drawn out in situations are defined as our "dispositions": "The Way begins in dispositions, and dispositions are born from nature. At the beginning one is close to dispositions, and at the end one is close to propriety."[39] The Way—movement itself—starts with our dispositions, with the ways that, because of our natures, we interact with other things.[40]

At its basis, then, the world simply consists of situation after situation in which things, because of their respective natures, are banging against each other and reacting to each other—the reactions always being different in each situation because the things that happen to appear in each situation will always be different. Such are our lives.

As we are told in the opening line, however, this is inadequate: the goal is to achieve a fixed purpose through repeated study. Such a fixed purpose is defined as "propriety"—responding to things properly, instead of by immediate disposition.

Such a shift to propriety, however, does not consist of transcending a given context or imposing one's will upon it. It rather consists of refining one's responses to situations. And the repeated study that makes this possible is based upon ritual and related forms of practice. The text argues that a canon of proper behavior has been built up through past responses. This canon consists of the set of songs collected as the Book of Songs, the speeches collected in the Book of Documents, the rituals collected in the Book of Rituals, and the music collected as the Music. (The first three of these would later be joined with two other bodies of materials to become the Five Classics, which became a crucial part of the standard educational curriculum for much of East Asia until recent times.) "As for the Poems, Documents, Rites, and Music, their first expression was generated among humans. With the Poems, there were activities and they put them into practice. With the Documents there were activities and they spoke of them. With the Rites and Music, there were activities and they raised them."[41] Each of these arose in particular situations in the past. In response to particular moments, songs were composed, speeches were made, and activities were undertaken. Sages later chose some of these songs, speeches, and actions, put them into an order, and built an educational curriculum out of them:

> The sages compared their categories and arranged them, analyzed their order and appended admonishments to them, embodied their propriety and put them in order, patterned their dispositions and both expressed and internalized them. As such, they were brought back for use in education. Education is the means by which one generates virtue within. The rites arise from the dispositions.[42]

These rituals, then, arose from the dispositions themselves: they were simply actions taken in response to certain situations in the past. But the later-born sages deemed some of these actions exemplary, and as such defined them as part of a ritual canon that people in general should enact. The goal of such an enactment would be to refine one's own dispositions: by reenacting exemplary actions from the past, one trains one's responses so that one can achieve propriety.

Building a better society, therefore, is based upon ritualization: creating a canon of practices that everyone should follow. And the criterion for which actions from the past should become part of that ritual canon is simply based on whether a continued performance of them helps to refine one's ability to respond to others. Thus, one learns types of actions, pieces of music, exemplary speeches, moving poems, and so on.

The implication of this argument is that the world is inherently fragmented: there is no foundation, there are no overarching sets of guidelines, laws, or principles. There are only actions, and it is up to humans to ritualize some of those actions and thereby set up an ordered world. The resulting ritual canon is a set of practices that emerged out of previous responses.

Just as we saw with Robert Orsi's arguments, ritual is defined here not as a system of meaning but rather as a set of relationships. Some of these relationships come to be defined as ritual, and are to be enacted on a constant basis by the latter-born. An inherent tension is thus built up between ritual actions and those actions of the mundane world. In the ideal, the practice of the former will help direct the proper conduct of the latter. But the tension is never erased.

Ritual and Autonomy

Such a definition of ritual as subjunctive, with a full understanding of the inherent tension between ritual actions and their application to nonritual activity, will allow us to rethink aspects of ritual that have been misunderstood by those who tend to read ritual in terms of inner meanings or outer harmonies. In particular, we would like to turn to the issue of autonomy. From the point of view of what we have been calling a Protestant framework, ritual behavior often appears as a submission of humans to external norms—as a rejection of autonomy. Ritual, from such a point of view, consists of discipline and constraint, whereas sincerity is a turn inward toward the true self. From the point of view of a ritual order, however, this is not the case at all: a ritual order does not assume that all action is or even necessarily should be a repetition of rituals from the past. By definition, most action is not. The point is that, ideally, such actions should, in a sense, be ritual without ritual precedent.

Once again, we will allow our Confucian ritual theorists to guide us. The problem is very simple: if one is constructing a subjunctive world of "as if" through ritual, then what happens when one confronts a situation (as one does all the time—it is, after all, a fractured world) where there is no clear ritual telling one what to do, or where there are conflicting ritual obligations. This is a problem that confronts the most complex decisions we have to face in our lives, and it is also one that appears in common, mundane, everyday circumstances—if one is a parent and a child does something wrong, when does one speak sympathetically, and when does one speak harshly?

For our Confucian ritualists, the answer was clear: one of the goals of ritual is to train practitioners to be able to act as if there were a ritual telling them what to do. A contemporary example will help to make the point. When a child asks for butter at the dining table, one tells the child to say "please." When one then gives the butter, one tells the child to say "thank you." For the first few years of this, it is just by rote: one simply tries to get the child to repeat the words. And, if it stops at just this, then one has, to a minimal degree, created a subjunctive world of politeness. But the hope is clearly that it will not stop there: the hope is that the child, as she grows, will be able to express equivalent forms of making requests and expressing gratitude in situations where a simple "please" or "thank you" would be inappropriate.

This, of course, is the shift from emotional response to propriety discussed in "Nature Emerges from the Decree": ritual helps refine our ability to respond properly to situations. But perhaps the most powerful discussion can be found in the *Analects*, the text that purports to quote the words of Confucius and his disciples. The distinction made there is between ritual and humaneness. Humaneness is, essentially, simply behaving properly toward other human beings. For us, the crucial point is that this is not necessarily a sincerity mode (although many later followers certainly did read it as such). Instead, it is perhaps best understood as simply the way that one acts ritually when there is no ritual to tell one what to do: if one spends one's life doing rituals properly, then one gains a sense of how the subjunctive world constructed out of those rituals could be constructed in situations without a ritual precedent, or in situations where ritual obligations conflict. At a more mundane level: humaneness would be the ability to express gratitude effectively when simply saying "thank you" would be inappropriate or insufficient. Or it is the ability, to return to our earlier mundane example, of a parent to sense from the situation and the respective personalities involved whether at a given moment it is more effective to speak harshly or sympathetically to a child who has acted incorrectly. When ritual obligations conflict, the key is to have trained one's responses such that one can act as if there was indeed a clear ritual guide.

For early Confucian thinkers, there is an even higher level than humaneness: the highest example of ritual action was to become a sage. Here, too, it was certainly possible to define the sage as one who acts in individual sincerity, and many later figures did so. But one can also define it in ritual terms: a sage is simply someone who acts properly in any given situation—whether or not there is a ritual precedent to guide his action. As such, a sage would also be seen as exemplary, and his actions would therefore come to be defined as ritual for later generations.

Within ritual, therefore, there is indeed a mode of action that is in some ways akin to what a sincerity framework would valorize as autonomy. But it is an autonomy defined not in a Kantian sense but rather in a ritual sense— someone who acts without ritual precedent but does so as an extension of the "as if" of ritual. The point here is not that ritual does not constrain and discipline. It does. But, from the point of view of ritual, this is not a denial of autonomy but a means, at the highest level, of achieving its ritual equivalent. Sagehood, in other words, is only attainable through ritual—whereas a more contemporary framework would argue that autonomy is only achievable through a denial of ritual.

Intriguingly, it is in the Judaic tradition where one finds some of the most telling parallels. As Jonathan Schofer has argued about Rabbi Nathan: "The ideal sage is a man who is fully constituted through the Torah such that his most basic impulses are structured in accord with rabbinic laws and ideals. He attains this state by allowing himself to be trained, molded, planted, conquered, or governed by the tradition."[43] As in the early Confucian tradition, sagehood is the goal, but it is a goal that is to be achieved through a submission to ritual, not through a rejection of it. The inner comes to reflect the outer, and not the other way around.

Later thinkers in both traditions would take such notions to higher extremes. Maimonides held that the ultimate goal of submitting to ritual was to become not a sage but a prophet.[44] And later thinkers in the Chinese tradition would openly espouse practitioners becoming divine.[45]

Schofer himself notes the similarity of such positions to those found among Confucian thinkers. In drawing a comparison between the two, Schofer also points out the paradox of "their relatively similar views concerning the sage and tradition and their very different views at the level of theology or metaphysics."[46] The similarity exists because both are *ritual* orders, and both are therefore committed to the idea that autonomy can only be the result of submitting oneself to a ritual tradition, rather than asserting claims of sincerity against such a ritual tradition.

Again, from within the Jewish rabbinic tradition, we can find something similar expressed in the famous dictum: "All that a talmid chacham [sage/ student] is . . . to teach, was already given to Moses on Sinai."[47] The dictum can of course be read in different ways: on a simplistic level, it can be understood as severely circumscribing innovation—after all, all that is possible to be taught has already been given by the tradition (Moses on Sinai). More deeply, how- ever, the dictum actually legitimizes the ongoing cultural production *within* the tradition by extending the mantle of tradition to future generations of in- terpretation and exegetical prowess.

Ritual continues to provide an ongoing arena of creativity and tradition, acceptance and obligation. Ritual practice becomes the arena where the dy- namic of that third space, the potential space within which cultural creativity takes place, is worked out. Now this interplay allows different degrees of cre- ativity and acceptance. Ritual prayer in a synagogue or church tends to one end of a scale, text study to another.[48] The degrees of formalization, invariance of sequence, and encoding by actors are all different, with text study being, let us say, less formalized and invariant than liturgy. For that matter, text study itself can have differing degrees of formalization, invariance, and encoding by the actors within the same tradition, making a particular mode of study more or less ritualistic. The general point we are trying to stress is that creativity is always in tension with the tradition. Ritual provides the central space for play- ing out this tension. It is no surprise that both Jewish and Confucian ritual traditions strongly emphasized notions of autonomy. It is only from a more contemporary perspective that this would appear to be paradoxical.

Finally, we can learn something of the issue of autonomy and how it is structured in regard to ritual action from the laws of purity and impurity. These would seem, on first sight, to present the least autonomous, most "obsessive" ritual forms of engagement with the world that we can conceive. And yet, perhaps the case deserves deeper consideration.

We would like to argue that the play of intentionality within and upon the impurity of certain (material) matter seems to reproduce in ritual form the very play of creativity and tradition that is the source of all cultural production. Here of course the tradition is not a human, cultural tradition but the very stuff of the world. This is the creativity of human agency and intentionality as they act upon and transform the world. It is almost as if the categories of purity and impurity define a realm of meanings and significance (like a child's circle of play) within which the drama of humanity and the world—the cultural con- struction of categories—can take place and be invested with meaning. Impurity is always with us, if only because our categories can never in themselves fully encompass the world. To hark back to Mary Douglas's famous analysis, it is not so much boundaries violated that makes for impurity.[49] Rather, the play of impurity and purity itself constructs a cultural space where we need not query the origin of mankind (and its categories), in and out of the world.

Here too it is worth recalling how in early Israelite religion the rules of purity and impurity were critically connected to metaphors of creation and of *imitatio Dei*. The individual, entering into the state of purity (first at the Temple and, later, at one's own table) participated (first through sacrifice and then through ritualized prayer and eating) in the process of world construction. The congregant, as an adherent to the rules of ritual purity, participated in a process of cultural creation—the *as if* of world creation and maintenance.[50] In a subjunctive sense he was participating with God in the creation and maintenance of the universe through the construction of a space of ritual purity that was both inside and outside of the orders of the world being maintained. Boris Ostrer has, in fact, recently demonstrated how the Mishnah constructs the human body as analogous to the fallen Temple, or rather its altar, as a site of holiness.[51] Like the Temple, the body must be maintained in its purity, and his analysis of the alternating symbolic valence of red and white in the calculus of this purity is stunning. He shows how "the source of purity, the most pure and sacred place in the entire Jewish world [the Temple], is identified with the body, which bears the worst possible impurity."[52] Both, at different historical periods, mediate between the individual and the natural, social and supernatural worlds. By the rabbinic period (the time of the Mishnah) the rabbis had to replace the mediation of the ritual with the mediation of the text of ritual—but the dynamic is the same.

The psychoanalyst Arnold Modell identified a similar phenomenon in his analysis of Paleolithic art in the caves of Altamira and Niaux (representatives of an art form that existed, relatively unchanged, from 30,000 BCE to approximately 12,000 BCE).[53] Modell stresses how the Paleolithic artists made use of natural geologic formations (cavities in the floor, protrusions in the wall, formations of stalactites, etc.) as intrinsic components of their pictures. He analyzes this, which he calls "the interpenetration of reality with the artistic vision," as forming a transitional space of creative work, "a tangible expression of the mental process of creation itself."[54] Modell likens this to Winnicott's idea of transitional object—the teddy bear or favorite blanket—which plays the same role in externalizing psychic processes, "the child's first creative relationship with the environment."[55] Notions of purity and impurity play a somewhat similar if much more structured and complex role in mediating between humankind and the natural environment. Just as the cave art in Niaux makes use of natural formations in the creation of an object that (like ·

the transitional object) is neither fully human nor fully of the world, so too do ideas of impurity (at least in Judaism) create a space that is neither solely human nor solely of the natural world. In this sense they are akin to the transitional object that exists in a potential space between the individual and the environment.[56] With all the differences between the cases, the similarity is rooted in the appropriation of a space between the object world and the human one, partaking in both and, in the process, being transformed. Both take part in what Wilhelm Worringer called the "great process of disputation between man and the outer world" that will continue "to the end of time."[57] For Worringer, religion, no less than art, was one of the grand mediating structures of this disputation.

If we are willing to extend the object world to the existence of primary processes, as did the Confucian sages—specifically those drives of sex and death—laws of ritual purity center on creating a human space free from the overwhelming imperative of those drives.[58] The laws of ritual purity circumscribe a space between the social and the instinctual, a human space, not fully divorced from the overwhelming power of the instinctual but not fully succumbing to it either. These rituals construct a subjunctive space where some control over both death and sex can be at least temporarily and partially afforded.

Impurity is both always already there, in certain objects, and equally always only transmitted by acts of human agency and intentionality. It shares the characteristics of what Winnicott termed the "third arena of human living, one neither inside the individual nor outside in the world of shared reality."[59] This intermediary arena of living can constitute a potential space, which negates the idea of space as separation.

Rabbinic laws of impurity provide a clear example of this because they tie intimately to humanly constructed objects. Natural objects do not become impure unless they are the source of impurity. Houses can become impure, stone utensils but not stones, clay jugs but not mud. The Talmud presents examples of famous debates where the point in question was when in the creation of an object (an oven, a knife) does it enter the realm where impurity can adhere to it? The rules themselves create that space where the natural world can be mastered by its very distinction and separateness from the human endeavor. The impurity of menstruating women, lepers, or those with seminal emissions creates a human category out of a natural process (similar again to the Paleolithic artist who interpenetrates the creative/inner and the actual environment). In so doing it creates a space where mankind can approach and apprehend the world in a creative manner.

The laws of impurity in Judaism encompass both what scholars have come to characterize as ritual modes of impurity (involving bodily flows, scale disease, mold on houses, contact with certain animals and with death), as well as moral modes of impurity (revolving around the abrogation of injunctions in the realm of violence and sex).[60] Violations in the first realm pollute the individual and his or her body, violations in the second pollute the land and the community.[61] Each delineates a different type of space, between differentially defined entities. The first exists between the individual and the world of external objects. The second lies between the individual and the world of internal objects, which most threaten social order and the shared subjunctive of the community of empathy. Each form of pollution concerns the creation and maintenance of different "worlds." In each the consequences of its destruction are correspondingly different. Both, however, define a subjunctive space within which human existence can take place and, in so doing, a world can be constructed.

Crucially, both create a space for human action and praxis. They open up the very possibility of human agency by blurring the absolute dualism between world and humankind, allowing the latter to act on the former. This is true not only for the world of external objects but also for internal states, the chaos of drives and desiderata, demons and spirits that were the concern of the *Book of Rites*. Control over primary instinctual drives becomes the basis for an ordered human life in society and so for human life itself. Autonomy, in this reading, is in opposition not to heteronomy but to chaos—which makes any human action impossible. In contrast, ritual rules of (among other things) purity and impurity permit the very extension of human existence in the world.

Ritual and Its Dangers

Within their subjunctive worlds, of course, rituals may still lack real internal tensions. While ritual opens up the very possibility of cultural creativity and human praxis, it also carries its own dangers within that practice. To see how this is so, let us return to the Confucian tradition and to the "Nature Emerges from the Decree" text. Ritual, as defined in the text, is by definition openended. Any new set of actions that would occur in the ongoing accumulation of actions within a tradition would simply become part of what the latter-born would deal with, and any of those actions could come to be defined as exemplary and be entered into the repertoire that makes up a ritual canon. Since, in other words, the world is inherently fractured, the goal is to build an order, endlessly changing, through a constant process of ritualization. Such a theory assumes that there is an inherent tension between those actions that are deemed ritual and those actions that are not. Ideally, the practice of the former aids us in the practice of the latter, and the latter could always potentially be entered into the repertoire of the former. But the tension is always there.

Yet, of course, if such a tension is inherent, then it will always breed attempts to end the tension. There are several ways in which this can be done.

To begin with, there will be tendencies in a ritual order to close the canon, to declare that a given ritual order is complete and can allow no further additions or modifications. As such, no actions outside the current canon can be allowed in, and all such nonritual actions become radically devalued. In short, the lines between ritual and nonritual action become rigid and absolute. Once this happens, ritual can easily turn into pure repetition, being enacted more and more forcefully against what is perceived to be a complete disorder in the world of mundane reality. Ritual, in short, becomes endless, compulsive repetition—a cultural equivalent of the stereotypical compulsive-obsessive, constantly attempting to deny the fractured nature of lived experience through a turn to ever more purified repetition.

This danger always plays in relation to the opposite danger. If one of the goals of ritual is to create humans who are, to follow our Chinese and Judaic ritual theorists, sages, then we can potentially find a danger from the other end. Sagely action, by definition, is outside the dictates of ritual precedent, but it can and often does become precedent for new rituals. This means that a ritual order that allows too many sages can quickly cease to work effectively, because it would mean endless innovation and thus the end of a meaningful tradition. A canon that is closed absolutely can create problems; a canon that is too open can create problems as well.

Historically, both of these problems played out in the Confucian tradition, and, in fact, both constantly played off against each other. Indeed, one of the reasons that self-proclaimed Confucians in the first century BCE worked to close the canon was precisely in response to the proliferation of self-proclaimed sages over the previous two centuries. Their move was to proclaim Confucius as the last sage, and the Five Classics (mentioned earlier) as the final collection of ritual. The redaction of the Mishnah and the Babylonian Talmud followed a similar dynamic.

As we will detail in the chapter on ritual and sincerity (chapter 4), however, attempts to close a ritual canon tend to provoke a response of claims of sincerity—claims that rituals are simply rules of conformity that prevent sincere belief. There is thus an inherent dynamic in ritual systems to become too closed (to prevent the emergence of too many sages), and this in turn breeds a tendency to assert sincerity claims in opposition to ritual. As we will see, this is a recurrent and inherent tendency in ritual orders. The current situation—often and mistakenly referred to as a "modernity" standing in opposition to a "tradition"—is but one more moment in this dynamic.

Theoretical Implications

One of our concerns with so much ritual theory—whether of the functionalist variety or of the Geertzian hermeneutic variety—is that it has been overly concerned with reading ritual according to a vision of system, of totality, and of harmony. Whether that totality is read as a functional system or a system of meanings, it is always ordered and, when idealized, is always seen as either creating or exemplifying a static, harmonious world.

In contrast, we have argued here that ritual—particularly when it is effective—more often operates in the realm of the limited and thus the subjunctive. It is in practice (the only place that matters) imperfect to the situation at hand and in endless need of constant, if only minor, adjustment to make the disconnect less painful. With "Nature Emerges from the Decree," the claims rested upon a vision of a fractured, discontinuous world—a fractured world in which humans build out certain patterns. Ritual is part of a never-ending attempt to take particulars of these patterns and build an order out of them. Ritual, therefore, means never-ending work. It is a recurrent, always imperfect, project of dealing with patterns of human behavior—patterns that are always at risk of shifting into dangerous directions—or of unleashing demons.

Such a tragic view assumes there will never be a finality or a point of perfection. It is a fractured and fragmented world, and it will always be so. When it is effective, that effectiveness in part arises from the sense that one never creates a full unity, but one can, through ritual, develop more productive ways of connecting with other people and with the larger world. Although such a project is by definition never-ending, it can, for periods of time, create pockets of order in which humans can flourish.

Indeed, the biggest dangers for ritual orders tend to come from trying to end this fragmentation, leave the realm of the limited and the tragic, and achieve finality or perfection—either by turning to a purely closed system of endless repetition or by creating a totalizing system of sincere meaning. Radcliffe-Brown and Geertz, in a sense, mistakenly take each of these two alternatives respectively in their readings of ritual. The implication is not that they are fully wrong in their analyses—there would almost assuredly be moments in any given cultural history where one of these two forms would indeed play out. Their mistake was to take such forms as standard, rather than as moments in the cultural history of the workings of ritual.

2

Ambiguity, Ambivalence, and Boundaries

In this chapter we address those capacities of the human mind that allow the "as if" world of ritual to come into being and to persist. The "as if" quality in turn allows ritual to deal with the ambiguities and ambivalence of social life, as well as with the ambiguities and ambivalence in interactions with unseen and influential beings, especially deities. In dealing with ambiguities, ritual engages boundaries: boundaries are crossed, violated, blurred, and then, in an oscillating way, reaffirmed, reestablished, and strengthened. Among the paradoxes that attend the performance of ritual is the paradox that ritual plays out a completion, a closure that solves the problem at hand. Yet, at the same time the very nature of the repetitiveness of ritual implicitly shows that the problem is not solved once and for all, that all is not complete and perfect. There is, at bottom, a quality of "either-or, both-and" in the realm of ritual, paralleling those classic Gestalt psychology images—is it a jug, or is it two faces in profile, or is it really both? Here we shall examine some features of the mind in action and of the mind in development that are part and parcel of the capacity to create and live in the "as if" world of ritual.

Two streams converge in these discussions. The first is that of perspectives gleaned from studies and observations about the mind in development, the mind of the child, and the mind of the child in interaction with adults. The focus here is on the rituals and play of the developing child. The second stream is gleaned from clinical-psychoanalytic exploration of certain relatively exotic and ritualized forms of sexual gratification, loosely called "perversions," especially fetishistic and transvestite rituals. In both realms, the "normal" and the "abnormal," we shall highlight how ritual addresses ambiguity, incompleteness, and ambivalence.

In the first stream, we are in effect asking what is the nature of mind such that it can generate, respond to, and sustain rituals? There are any number of universal or near-universal "as if" activities and functions of the human mind. These include joking, riddles, playing, dreaming, daydreaming, storytelling, lying, mythmaking, as well as material artistic creation. These "as if" functions in turn overlap with the capacity to sustain ambiguity, such as the Gestalt perception experiments alluded to earlier show. The world of ritual, with its distinctive mark of repetition, is embedded in and dependent upon these other functions, and at the same time informs, shapes, and constrains their expression. In terms of child development, we shall address in particular (1) rituals of childhood, including the creation of symbolically meaningful forms and objects, (2) the capacity to invent and tell a lie, and (3) the embeddedness of ritual in bodily, nonverbal, registers.[1]

In the second stream, the abnormal, we shall deal with some of the particulars of these exotic sexual behaviors and also briefly deal with some extreme individual examples of lying. The two discussions of different ways of dealing with the "real-unreal," the "as if" and its inherent ambiguity, will converge in discussing two social and cultural phenomena, namely, the ritual nature of Greek tragedy, and the role in society of lying and deceit.

Before we begin this analysis, however, we must recall that ambiguity and ambivalence are built into the very structure of social relations in all social formations. That is to say, they are neither solely individual traits or proclivities, nor tied solely to certain developmental issues around ego maturation. Rather, the existence of ambiguity grows from the very nature of social structure; as such it served as a fundamental theme in the writings of Marx and later Simmel. More recently, it generated a vast outpouring of sociological studies of role conflict and what has been termed "sociological ambivalence" in the mid–twentieth century.[2]

On Ambiguity

The social scientific literature on roles and role conflicts written in the 1950s and 1960s, as developed by Robert Merton, George Homans, Lewis and Rose Coser, and other structural-functionalists brought insight into the social roots of ambiguity.[3] These studies, clearly distinguishing themselves from more psychological studies of ambiguity, relate the phenomenon to different forms of role conflict and ambivalences in the reciprocal structure of role demands and obligations—either of an individual caught between different role demands (teacher and mother), or even of different and contradictory obligations within the same role (the contradictory demands of teaching and research for a university professor).[4] The basic idea here is that the occupant of a particular social status (e.g., medical student, university professor) has different and often contradictory role sets. That is to say, she exists in complementary relations with occupants of different social statuses tied to but not overlapping with her own (a professor has relations with students, colleagues, and administrators, and sometimes students' parents as well). Moreover, these different role sets often have contradictory expectations (those of administrators and colleagues, for example). These constitute just one of many types of contradiction, different, for example, from that defined by Antigone, who simultaneously occupied different statuses with different expectations (sister of a dead warrior and loyal subject of her uncle the king).

Such ambiguities are to an extent built in to the social structure. Short of social revolution, and the restructuring of all role relations and redefinition of social statuses, there is no overcoming of such structural ambiguities. Even revolution, of course, sets us new social structures and new social roles and hence introduces new ambiguities tied to the newly defined postrevolutionary social order. Other work on "role strain" deals with similar and related phenomena.[5] So, too, does the aforementioned play of Sophocles'—which is simply to remind us that both the phenomenon and awareness of its existence are as old as human civilization.

This is crucial to keep in mind, because certain classics of the social sciences have instead come to see such ambivalence as an aspect of systemic dysfunction, and the corresponding types of behavior as forms of deviance. We refer specifically to Robert Merton's work on social structure and anomie, which sees aberrant, deviant, and nonconformist behavior as the result of a discrepancy between cultural goals and the institutional means of their achievement.[6] Merton specifies ritualist responses as one of these deviant forms. Our own perspective here, in contrast, is to stress the built-in nature of ambiguity in human social life. While we agree with the existing social scientific literature that the fundamental forms of ambiguity are not aspects of individual personality traits alone, but are in a sense structural, we disagree with their inherent assumptions of a possible stasis in the social regulation of such ambiguity. There is simply no way to regulate ambiguity or to define it away. The ever greater differentiation and delineation of social roles that characterize modern life and resolve certain forms of ambiguity only do so by creating multiple alternative realms of ambiguity.[7]

And it is here that an appreciation of ritual and ritualized action becomes relevant. Some preliminary work delineating the role of ritual in dealing with ambiguity has been done by Goffman in some very specific micro-contexts of certain forms of behavior in daily life.[8] More systemically, Max Gluckman identified jokes and rituals as ways of dealing with ambiguity in relatively undifferentiated societies, where there is little segmentation in time or place between people who interact within multiple role expectations (interactions between individuals who are both close kin members, fellow worshipers, citizens, trade partners, all in a relatively small and circumscribed physical setting, that of a village). As would be expected by Gluckman's research, modern society, with its ever-increasing social differentiation, does indeed tend to decrease the play of ritual in society (as roles become more segmented). Yet, and this is crucial, modernity does not do away with ambiguity or even, as far as can be measured, decrease its incidence.[9] It merely transforms the nature of ambiguity. Rather than being tied to the multiplicity of overlapping role sets, ambiguity emerges at the opposite end of the spectrum, that is, as a function of the elaborated role differentiation that brings in its wake the increasing ability of any role incumbent to hide certain aspects of her role from others. The more single-stranded social relations become, the greater the possibilities for differential attitudes toward role compliance, for negotiation of role expectations, for conflict and contradictions between role expectations, in short, the greater potential for different types of indeterminacy and hence negotiability within social relations.[10] In short, there is no "loss" of ambiguity in modern social formation, simply its displacement onto a different aspect of role incumbency. The tendency of modern societies to reject ritual and diminish its usage, however, leaves us bereft of a very useful mechanism with which to manage this ambiguity.

Thus, those premodern societies that were "high" on ritual had a relatively efficient way to deal with the ambiguity of human, social relations. Modern societies, on the other hand, no longer have ritual as such a resource and must rely on what we are calling a sincerity mode of interaction as a mode of negotiating ambiguity. In many circumstances this is simply not adequate to the task, as in fact many of Goffman's studies on the ritualization of discrete aspects of interpersonal relations have shown.[11]

We hope that by revisiting the problem of ambiguity through the lenses of ritual action we will be able to increase our understanding of its role in social life and, more important, of the different types of responses that exist within our repertoire to this most human of situations.

In the subsequent discussion, we emphasize in different contexts the capacity of the human mind to make multiple identifications, to imagine itself in different positions and in different "as if" relationships with various important personages in life. The small child, in her own developmentally appropriate way, imagines herself as a younger or older child, as a parent, as a nursemaid, as some public personage (astronaut, rock star) or herself as a parent with children. This capacity must go hand in glove with the social actualities implied by the concept of "sociological ambivalence," role ambiguities that may include contradictory and conflicting demands. We are thus crucially concerned with the relationship between two areas of ambiguity: that between these inner identifications and their role in forming "identity," and that of multiple roles and role demands. These constitute the interface between individual depth-psychological views and sociological views.

The material here suggests both that there is substantial "free play" in the multiple identifications made in development and also that taking on and trying out these multiple identifications is not without conflict and not without distress. Indeed, much of the day-to-day play therapy that child therapists do consists of noting how and when a child's particular experimental or play identification with someone (e.g., a parent, an older sibling) is seemingly free of tension, and at what point the free play is interrupted or blocked by anxiety about the implications of such an identification. For instance, a child can pretend to be his mother, bossing around the children in the family, but then an anxiety intrudes—as a grown-up, will I still have mommy or daddy there to take care of me? Clearly there is an interaction between "identification" and "role"—identification facilitates taking on a role, and the existence of the role facilitates the identification. Similarly, there is an interaction between conflicts among identifications, and role conflicts, or role ambiguities. In both of these arenas, we argue, ritual allows the coexistence and possibilities of resolution of these ambiguities—ritual allows the person or the group to live with the contradictions.

Rituals in Child Development

Let us turn to an example of a parent-child ritual.[12] A three-year-old boy is regularly put to bed by his father, after his mother has fed and bathed him. The procedure is ritualized, and the child greets deviations from it by strong protest, though the father might be more welcoming of a deviation that shortens the length of the ritual. The little boy sits on his father's lap, holding his favorite stuffed toy animal, while the father reads a story to him, the child having gone through the ritual procedure of picking which book to read (it always turns out to be only one or two out of a large number of possibilities). The father reads "Jack and the Beanstalk" and must read it the same way each time, but either father or child can make some variation if the other consents to it, usually done in a slightly teasing or playful manner.

The little boy and/or the father might accentuate in voice or gesture one or another of the characters, suggesting a partial imitation-identification with that character—the little boy can become the menacing giant, but it has to be in a particular way, with a particular verbal and nonverbal formula. A videotape would show also the repertory of bodily gestures, the alternating enfoldings and then separations of the bodies of father and son, the fidgeting and touching of different body parts at different points in the story, the variations in how closely the stuffed lion is held. There might then be one final good-night hug, and perhaps one song sung together, or sung by the father. With all of this, the child can go to sleep, and the father can leave the room.[13] If the child asks for one more story, or one more repetition, or begins to demand, not just ask, he is breaking the "ground rules," the frame of the ritual, just as surely as if the father announces that tonight they will read only part of the story.

If one were to observe and study this bedtime ritual over time, it would become clear how much is being enacted between father and son: issues of giants and little boys, tiny things that can grow big and straight and strong, little boys who can act like the father, mothers who encourage their little boy's efforts at "manhood," and the virtues of cleverness as a weapon of the weak. The father is reentering the childhood world of big and small, powerful and powerless, reverberating perhaps with some of his own childhood experiences of being read to by his father, the child's grandfather. While all these multiple issues are being symbolically represented, actual negotiations of role and power differentials are taking place between father and son, and in a setting of safety and familiarity, established and maintained in large part by the repetitiveness of the bedtime scene. The enactment and the negotiation require from both child and parent a capacity to relax and re-form boundaries; to shuttle back and forth between "is it really true" and "pretend"; to shuffle roles and role expectations; to imagine past, present, and future; and somehow to conclude, knowing all this will be repeated countless more times. In principle, what will allow variations and ultimately the evolution of new rituals is that the repetitions are building up certain structures inside the child, and that the father-son pair can move into a different orbit, as it were, in working on new sets of issues requiring imagination and repetition.

Erik Erikson, recognizing a current of psychoanalytic thinking beginning with Freud's early works, attempted his own approach to understanding the relationship between personal ritual and public ritual. Calling this approach "the ontogeny of ritual," he uses the example of the ritualized interaction when the preverbal child first wakes up in the morning and mother and baby engage with each other. His analysis can be applied to the example we have just given of the bedtime ritual. He identifies those elements that he suggests might facilitate seeing the relationship between personal rituals and public rituals:

> I will now try to list those elements of ritualization . . . emphasizing throughout the opposites which appear to be reconciled. Its mutuality is based on the *reciprocal needs* of two quite *unequal* organisms and minds. We have spoken of the *periodicity of developing needs* to which ritualization gives a *symbolic actuality*. We have recognized it as a highly *personal* matter, and yet as *group-bound,* providing a sense both of *oneness* and of *distinctiveness*. It is *playful,* and yet *formalized,* and this in *details* as well as in the *whole* procedure. Becoming *familiar* through repetition, it yet brings us the *surprise* of recognition. . . . the ethologists . . . tell us that ritualizations in the animal world must, above all, be *un-ambiguous* as sets of signals, we suspect that in man the *overcoming of ambivalence* as well as of ambiguity is one of the prime functions of ritualization. For as we love our children, we also find them unbearably demanding, even as they will soon find us arbitrary and possessive. What we love or admire is also threatening, awe becomes awfulness, and benevolence seems in danger of being consumed by wrath. Therefore, ritualized affirmation, once instituted, becomes *indispensable* as periodical experience and must find new forms in the context of new developmental actualities.[14]

Erikson's formulation thus alludes to the complex relationship between ambiguity and ambivalence. There is a power relationship, a clear power and role asymmetry between parent and child (or, in public ritual, between deities and humans or sometimes between priests and followers), but this is made more complicated, "ambiguous," as it were, by the human capacity for multiple and shifting identifications. The ritual setting thus allows the imagination of both father and son to flourish. It allows each to imagine himself in the position of the other—imagining forward for the child, imagining backward and forward for the father. Erikson refers to the intergenerational connection of certain parent-child rituals, suggesting the role of ritual in regulating ambivalence between the generations: "Thus, both infantile ritualization and adult ritual are parts of a functional whole, of cogwheeling, . . . of generations, and of a cultural version of human experience."[15]

What Freud would come to term the "Oedipus complex" (around 1910) is in effect a "bridge term" between the individual's struggle with generational implications of authority and sexuality and the ongoing societal efforts to regulate those intergenerational conflicts. The self and the continuity of the self are embedded in a generational continuum. In fact, the idea of generational continuity is the imaginative creation of culture, par excellence. Only the human species has grandparents playing a social role, let alone valuing ancestors and images of long-term generational continuity.

Following Erikson, we would not speak of *overcoming* ambivalence and ambiguity, but rather of ritual as expressing the ambivalence/ambiguity and allowing for the participants to manage the uncertainties and contradictions. The "ambiguity" in turn is a cognitive facet (though clearly a cognitive-emotional mix) of the ambivalence that each might and can feel toward the other. Exactly how all the analytic terms he cites—playful, formalized, detailed, mutual, periodic—interrelate is not easy to formulate in a systematic way, but clearly the right mix can be seen in what is a viable, stable (though not totally invariable), and gratifying ritual.

The work of D. W. Winnicott, taking place roughly in the same time period as Erikson's work, approached the relationship between personal ritual and cultural activities from a somewhat different perspective.[16] His seminal contribution in this regard is the notion of the "transitional object," like the baby's favorite piece of blanket or teddy bear—the baby's first "cultural creation." Modell, summarizing the import of Winnicott's contribution, writes:

Winnicott recognized that illusions are an essential part of living and not something to be depreciated as unreal. Illusions create a psychological space in which cultural experience occurs. It is a space that belongs neither to the subject nor to the object: it is a *potential* space, a third area of being that belongs neither to the self nor the other, it is a space in which we experience the illusion of shared imaginations. This *third*, a potential space in which illusion occurs, is also the psychological space in which playing occurs. Winnicott illustrated this by referencing the transitional object, the child's first plaything, a possession such as a blanket or teddy bear. A shared imagination is central to this concept of potential space. Winnicott (1971, p. 12) [writes]: "of the transitional object it can be said that it is a matter of agreement between us and the baby that we will never ask the question: 'did you conceive of this or was it presented to you from without?' The important point is that no decision on this point is expected. The question is not to be formulated." The parent accepts the fact that the baby has imagined the transitional object and by doing so shares in the baby's imagination and participates in the illusion of being part of the baby's construction of reality. It is important to note however that a shared imagination does not imply that individual differences are erased. Our thoughts remain solipsistic but an illusion of sameness is generated. Solipsism is preserved within an illusion of mutuality."[17]

Similarly, for this story-reading ritual, the question "did you conceive of this or was it presented to you from without?" is not raised while the ritual is ongoing night after night, yet at a certain point in the child's life, the ritual will be modified, changed, or radically transformed. Again, as this occurs, there might be negotiation between parent and child, some spoken but much unspoken, but it will not be about the motives or meanings of the ritual—performance trumps motive and meaning.

"Pretend," "make-believe" in imagination and in play are interwoven with "reality" in the developing child. A five-year-old boy was pretending to be a soldier with a weapon—a stick—fighting the bad guys. He was asked if he expected to win, and replied, "I don't know, this is my first time!" He was comfortably and creatively juggling fantasy and reality. We might also be witnessing here a game-ritual *in statu nascendi*—were he to play out this scenario multiple times, he would know the ending, and the onetime "experiment" would have become a more durable and stable structure.

Indeed, there is a developmental history of how children process in their own terms the spectrum ranging from the world of imagination to the world of solid reality, that messy mixture of harsh reality and fantasy with which we all live. Important cognitive landmarks in the child's linguistic development are words such as "perhaps," "maybe," "actually," that signal a growing capacity for dealing with ambiguity.

A five-year-old girl invites her grandfather to accompany her to the garage, where she wants to get something. She allows as to how the garage is a bit scary, and she appreciates his presence. He asks what she is afraid of. She replies that when she was little she did not have a clear idea of what was real and what was in her "'magination," and all kind of "pretend" monsters could be quite frightening to her. She sees her younger brother struggling with some of those same fears and confusions. But, she says, just the same, while she knows there are no real scary creatures in the garage, there might still be a few![18] We know well that the developmental process of sorting out the relationship between "as if" and "as is" continues over the lifetime of a person. "Superstition," for example, is an aspect of believing and not-believing simultaneously.[19]

Lying and deceit are certainly parts of the array of capacities to create imaginative worlds, "as if" worlds. An important developmental landmark occurs when the child first becomes able to lie: typically, the early lies are around toilet training, or other interactions that might involve shame. "I'm not doing something!" exclaimed a two-year-old girl, discovered grunting and straining, moving her bowels underneath the picnic table, when her parents and other adults had anxiously started looking for her.[20] The lie, as here, serves to make a separation from the parents, while it simultaneously recognizes their extreme importance to her. It gives her a measure of control and mastery over shame, while at the same time acknowledging that she has failed and is ashamed. It creates a wish-fulfilling state, while tacitly permitting her to acknowledge that her wishes for mastery and pleasing her parents have not been fulfilled.

Lying is certainly crucial for adult social interaction, and the capacity to understand and tolerate another person's is fundamental to sustaining the social fabric. Studies have shown how lying can be used to bolster one's own faltering ego, but also to protect other people from shame and exposure.[21] Lying also can be seen as experimenting with reality and with possible other worlds, and as such overlaps with daydreaming.[22] The role of daydreaming in "repairing" the past and soothing us at moments of injury is well known. We can recognize the phenomenon called, in French, *jeu d'escaliers,* and, in German, *Treppenwitz*—the great lines of repartee you wish you had come up with, as you are walking down the steps exiting the party. As any student of autobiography knows, especially each person as a "student" of her or his own autobiography, such replayings can subtly shade into "this is indeed what I did say."[23] At least as important, if not more important, is how daydreaming, under optimal conditions, represents a veritable laboratory in which all kinds of actions can be "tried out" and experimental outcomes can be imagined.

Ritual and Repetition

That ritual—whether private, personal, or public—implies repetition is a matter of definition. In terms of individual development, the role of repetition has been approached from several perspectives. The work of Piaget, based on observations of normal development, emphasizes the structure-building aspect of repetition of childhood games, at both the preverbal and verbal stages. Repetition in child development, through a cycle of assimilation and accommodation, accounts both for stability and for progressive change.

Freud's idea of a compulsion to repeat in the operations of the mind draws on both psychopathology and observations (unsystematic, but astute) of normal development.[24] It is a rather complex notion, encompassing ordinary conflict and the extraordinary situation brought about by trauma. In Freud's terminology, trauma represents a breaching of the "stimulus barrier," a basic shield for protecting the integrity of the person, of the psychic apparatus. He posits one form of repetition that is closer to the play of children—a response to a problem, and an attempt at mastery with the repetition. This is the example of his grandchild, aged eighteen months, playing with a string and spool, a game of "fort-da," "gone-come back," in response to his mother going off to work. This is repetition within the "pleasure principle," that is, within the realm of conflict among the several psychic agencies. The more extreme and constricted repetitions, which he terms "beyond the pleasure principle," are a feature of severe trauma—the World War I "shell-shocked" soldiers, with their repetitive, relatively fixed nightmares are his prime example. Contemporary thinking and research would still find some utility in this distinction but view it more as a spectrum, with the possibility of considerable overlap. But the play of children with a significant history of physical or sexual abuse shows significant differences from the play of children dealing with a problem, or trying to figure something out, though both have important repetitive elements.[25] It is as if the repetition has different meanings in the two situations, though both are aimed at achieving "mastery."[26] In ordinary play, repetition seems to move toward some resolution, and may indeed invite comment or participation by surrounding adults (or, say, older children). Thus, a nearly three-year-old boy, whose mother was quite visibly pregnant, and his little girl playmate of the same age repetitively built a house out of blocks, put a Fisher-Price person or persons inside, proclaimed something like, "Inside, can't get out," and then knocked the building down with great excitement. They then proceeded to rebuild it and repeat the procedure. When one of the mothers asked the children if they were unsure how a baby gets out of the mommy's tummy, they listened with great interest as she explained that the mommy has a special door, that looks small but can open quite wide, to let the baby out. Within the space of a day or so, the repetitive game was modified, and the building now included a door! Sometimes they would knock down the building, but sometimes they would place a person inside near the door they had built, and let the person come out. (After the baby was actually born, each mother reported a heightened curiosity on the part of the child as to exactly where the door was, what it looked like, and whether there was a doorknob.)

The repetitive ritual, or game, of the traumatized child seems more driven, more rigid, more prone to enacting onto others what has been done unto that child. A child traumatized by sexual abuse might have repetitive doll play, sometimes showing the abusive activity in fairly explicit form, but sometimes in some derivative, symbolic way. Such a child, under favorable circumstances (as in the movie *Forbidden Games*, discussed later), might find a playmate with whom to share the symbolic game, but under unfavorable circumstances might attempt to abuse another child in the same way he had been abused.[27]

What reinforces the repetition of ritual? Erikson's examples of a mother-infant awakening-in-the-morning ritual and the father-son bedtime ritual, presented earlier in this chapter, call attention to the importance of the nonverbal, the visceral, the rhythmic. While there obviously and usually is a verbal part to the mother's contribution, clearly it is not the denotative but rather the performative aspects of her words that are influential: the tone, the rhythm, the singsong, the associated smiles and gestures. The infant reciprocates, and/or initiates, with her or his own bodily rhythms, gestures, smiles, cooing, kicking, and the like. The father-son ritualized interchange likewise is marked by important nonverbal features, and even the reading of words has a performative as well as a more strictly denotative component.

The existence of "hard-wiring" for infant attachment and infant-parent bonding serves as a matrix, but the establishment of that bonding requires repetition, while also requiring room for maneuverability on either or both sides. Observations show how the negotiation can be derailed by one party not adequately responding and/or initiating (e.g., a seriously depressed parent or an infant who will later show clear signs of autism), and that it takes attention and investment to maintain the connection and the conjoint ritual. Each infant has his or her own set of unfolding bodily rhythms and sensory sensibilities, as does each adult, and there must be some conjoint molding of each to the other, while at the same time there remains the individuality of each. Clearly, in the performance of these personal rituals, it must "feel right," a complex enfolding of the bodily and the mental.

Ritual in Psychopathology: The Splitting of the Ego in the Process of Defense

As though in a parallel universe to the normal development of "as if" capacities, there is a realm of psychopathology, almost as a caricature of the normal. There, a driven repetitiveness and an array of mental devices for juggling real and unreal are combined in striking and puzzling clinical pictures. A particular form of this mental juggling, a kind of unconscious hocus-pocus, is seen in the so-called perversions, for example, fetishism, transvestism, exhibitionism, and voyeurism. These behaviors, mostly found in men, are remarkable for their intense sexual quality. Typically, such a practice constitutes the most important, the most exciting, and the most driven part of such a person's sexual life. At the same time, the practice might exist in a highly compartmentalized part of the man's life, with the rest of his life involving intense and close relationships. The mental mechanism involved was posited by Freud in his studies of patients practicing fetishism; he termed it "the splitting of the ego" or, as in the title of his germinal essay "The Splitting of the Ego in the Process of Defense."[28] In a decade when his other essays indicate a major interest on his part in the nature of illusion (e.g., *Future of an Illusion, Moses and Monotheism*), he published several pieces dealing with the capacity to devise and sustain a particular form of illusion in relation to sexuality. He had previously developed the concept of "disavowal" (*Verleugnung*), as part of his attempt to capture the various ways that an idea, a perception, a belief that is obviously true can be blocked out. He expanded disavowal into the idea of "splitting"—how to believe and not believe a perception at the same time. His main example comes from his studies of patients with fetishistic practices, published in 1927, and was later elaborated in 1938.[29] Fetishistic rituals are exemplified by instances of a man who must have at hand a woman's high-heeled shoe, or a corset, or a woman in a corset, in order to have an orgasm. The rituals are not experienced as warding off anxiety so much as for seeking pleasure and sexual satisfaction (though in fact there frequently is anxiety that pushes toward enacting the ritual). The ritual form of sexual gratification trumps the "ordinary" and "natural" process of sexual gratification, in Freud's view. But the case of the fetishist also reminds us of how much "ordinary" and "natural" sexual acts actually involve idiosyncratic rituals of all sorts.

There is a spectrum of mental "mechanisms" or "tricks" for knowing and not knowing at the same time, and the boundaries between these mechanisms are not always precise. The mechanism of "splitting of the ego" covers a range from repression at one end to florid denial of psychotic proportions at the other. All these mechanisms, in "small doses," or on occasions of great urgency are part of the repertory of everyday life, for dealing with situations that are conflicted, or difficult to fully acknowledge. (On receiving news of the sudden death of a loved one, a person typically cries out, "Oh, no, it cannot be true!") This splitting is thus a process we see in healthy people as well as in those with pathologies; it is a result of adapting to the world through the creation of subjunctives and thus related to the experience of ritual.

In repression certain contents are pushed out of consciousness. The husband, temporarily angry or dissatisfied with his wife, forgets that today is their wedding anniversary and does not bring home flowers or arrange for a special evening out. Psychotic denial is exemplified in the delusion of one paranoid schizophrenic man that there are no women in the world, except that, perhaps, there are some men who are dressed up as women. The person practicing a fetishistic ritual, by contrast, cognitively knows quite well about the differences between men and women and between male and female genitalia, but the fetishistic ritual allows a subjunctive disavowal of the differences. That these rituals appear in the context of sexual acts points to the immense complexity and ambiguity of sexuality, *tout court*, a complexity and ambiguity that virtually demands ritual. Normal "splitting" verges into the world of creative illusion and culturally held illusions, so the question arises what makes the splitting in the fetishist so persistent and one component, the fantasy of a female penis, so unconscious?

A Fetishistic Ritual

A young man in his late twenties, behaviorally heterosexual, though often preoccupied with whether or not he is homosexual, had a practice that was indeed ritualized.[30] He would see a man on crutches, or with a cast on a leg, or with some obvious impairment of a leg waiting at a bus stop, and looking as if in need of a ride. As he passes this injured or deformed man, he stops his car and offers the man a lift to his destination. If the offer is accepted, and it usually is, he drives the person to his destination, chats with him, drops him off, accepts the thanks of his passenger, and then returns to his own home (or office). There he will have an intense sexual fantasy about the man, almost always accompanied by masturbation. He has never consciously tried or even intended to seduce the man into a sexual involvement, and indeed almost never has anyone he picked up ever proposed such involvement to him. This practice persisted from early young adulthood, through several long heterosexual relationships, punctuated by an unsuccessful attempt at a homosexual relationship. It was deeply gratifying, deeply exciting, in fact, the most exciting part of his sexual panoply in act or fantasy, but also a source of discomfort and shame. When unable or unwilling to engage in the ritual, he might become extremely uncomfortable. While much of the significance(s) of this ritual was initially out of his awareness, or affectively muted, gradually multiple components emerged.

His earlier history, as it unfolded in treatment, involved a grandfather, severely impaired in walking, often incontinent, whom as a young boy he tried to help. But also as a young boy he was made anxious by the grandfather's physical state and obviously could not do all he wished to help him. At one level, the repetitive nature of his symptom-ritual was a reenactment of "I can help him—I can't help him," "I love him—I'm terrified by his condition." He felt similar conflict over the ongoing bitter dissension between his parents, and between them and his grandparents; the ritual had a component of trying to repair those several breaches. Over time, his associations and dreams contained material to substantiate the role of the existence of an organizing, *unconscious,* fantasy about the "detachability" and "movability" of penises, from male to female and back. As it were, one could not count on who owned the penis, who owned the power that went with it, and how permanently one could hold onto this organ and all it represented. This illusion and fantasy were also re-presented and enacted in his ritual. There were abundant examples of a con-fusion of male and female genitalia, and confusion between injured limbs (especially legs) and injury to or amputation of the penis. His imagistic version of the female reproductive organs was of a tangled mesh of ropes and pulleys, littered with broken eggshells, quite dangerous to an inserted male organ. Themes of the power of women and the power of adult sexuality vis-à-vis the powerless small child who was exposed to the tangled consequences of sexu-ality were also condensed into the ritual.

Other highly charged issues included a dread of separation from core family members, especially his mother. Similarly expressed and symbolized were deep altruistic yearnings to save and rescue injured and disadvantaged people, including grandparents, and indeed acts of altruism and generosity were an important part of his relationship with others. But there was also a sense of powerlessness, deep despair over whether he could ever really make a difference. And there was a profound concern with holding his "self" together in the face of a variety of threats coming from his internal persecutors, or from problems with actual people in his life.

His history revealed enormous imaginative capabilities, evincing them-selves even as early as age two. With these capacities he could be creative in his play and later in his work life, and simultaneously spin out and contin-uously reenact this symptom ritual. Even as a young child he could engage others in parts of his imaginative play and the imagined worlds he created, but as the ritualized symptom developed in his young adult years it was definitely not shared. Insofar as it was enacted with actual injured people, they were incidental, selected for cameo appearances, as it were, in his private drama, though treated quite kindly.

The performative aspects of this activity were indeed impressive. Careful attention to details of the scene, of the way he and the other participant behaved, what they said, was far more important in capturing his attention than the underlying meaning of the enactment. In short, there was typically a gap between the performance and the meaning, with the performance be-ing by far the more important. Exploration and elucidation of the meanings represented and condensed into the ritual did not adequately explain the

"ritual," that is, the repetitive aspects of the behavior. In other words, eluci-
dating the motives and meanings does not necessarily elucidate how and why
it is ritual in nature.[31] But how and why was the ritual so tied up with sexual
excitement? Perhaps the sexualization of these childhood experiences contributed a visceral reinforcement to what for him were adaptive and useful
defenses, disavowal and splitting.

A modern exploration of the nature and function of this mechanism
focuses on the interactional aspects of disavowal and splitting. For this man,
the childhood atmosphere was marked by oscillations between overexposure
to parental sexuality, infidelity, each parent's gratuitous undermining of the
other parent, and "underexposure" to truthful discussion, to interactions helping the young child clarify the muddle in which he found himself. Goldberg
suggests that "disavowal . . . cannot be achieved by the singular activity of the
child, but is a product of a mutually made-up world."[32] The child buys into or
accepts, as it were, the parents' own split, their own inability to tolerate differences and separations—to see the child as a particular person and not as their
fantasy creation—in order to maintain the bond with the parent. Goldberg
further elaborates that the person practicing, for example, a cross-dressing
ritual "does not impose his illusion on another to have it accepted as true, as
much as he asks the other to 'be of two minds,' just as he is . . . the wish is not to
blind the other to reality but to cause the other to tolerate the two supposed
realities; not to suspend disbelief permanently but to balance belief and disbelief; and not to embrace the unreal world but to satisfy the split in reality
visited upon the child by the parent or parents, who lived in two worlds."[33]
Goldberg provides an example from his practice:

> A transvestite male who reports that his mother, before marriage to
> his father, gave birth to a baby girl fathered by another man. The
> illegitimately conceived child died shortly after being given up for
> adoption. Soon after, the mother married the patient's father, and
> they had a son. Years later, when the mother began a longing and
> reverie for the baby girl taken from her, the patient saw his mother as
> ever searching for that lost girl in him. He recalled her depression
> when he was a child and likewise recalled the experience of joy that
> came to him (and perhaps to her as well) when he was dressed as a
> girl by an aunt and later, when he dressed as a woman. His con-
> sideration of himself either alternatively or sporadically as man and
> woman seems likely to be a result of a divided vision of himself as
> now of one sex and now of another, a vision of mutual construction of
> parent and child.[34]

Goldberg grounds his explanation of what the person who splits needs from the other person in an incident where this man brought in a photo of himself in women's clothing and asked Goldberg, did he not think that he really looked wonderful. Goldberg reluctantly said yes, while maintaining another thought—that the man simply looked overweight and ridiculous. He felt "had," that he'd been co-opted into the process by which his patient maintained the various splits in his ego. The splitting, socially constructed and socially maintained, therefore has the capability of being contagious.

The role of such private rituals in maintaining a fragile integrity of the self, not just of the genitalia, is an issue elaborated in contributions of self psychologists like Goldberg. For Arnold Modell, public rituals may provide a way of dealing with the paradoxes of selfhood. By virtue of the ritual originating from outside of the self, the ritual allows the self to recognize difference and otherness, and simultaneously to perpetuate and reinforce self-sameness and continuity of self.[35]

But the continuity of the self is also embedded in generational continuity. As discussed earlier, the idea of generational continuity—including grandparents and ancestors—is entirely a cultural construct, unique to the human species. It is perhaps similar to sexuality: generational relations are so complex that they virtually "demand" ritual.

Generational and transgenerational issues are symbolically encoded in these private rituals. As treatment deepens and the symbols are further explicated, the role of several generations of family may become clearer. Suppressed and denied family narratives come into focus, and the role of ancestors as "ghosts" pervading the life of the patient becomes clearer.[36] Personal change and growth in these situations, whether with the help of psychoanalysis or not, involve some process of moving from one orbit of "splitting" to another orbit, with a different quality of the mix of reality and fantasy, of that "ordinary" mix of perceptions of one's parents, siblings, and ancestors, involving both realistic appraisal as well as a certain amount of fantasy-driven misperception and misunderstanding.

Maurice Apprey, in a study of "transgenerational haunting" and "transsexualism," laid out some possible links between public rituals, such as tribal rituals involving cross-dressing, and the private rituals of cross-dressing.[37] Both, at different levels of explicitness, involve transgenerational linkages, conflicts and disruptions and attempts at restoration. The self as fractured, the self as divided, the self as whole, and the oscillations among these versions and experiences of the self are played and replayed in the private rituals involving splitting. Analogously, the public rituals may play and replay the group as fractured, the group as divided, and the group as whole.

Comparable to the development of the capacity to lie in the mind of the ordinary child, there are a variety of psychopathological conditions involving one form or another of driven, compulsory lying and even imposturing. So-called pathological, or compulsive, lying also involves complicated acrobatics to deceive oneself and deceive another in the service of warding off a too painful traumatic reality. One man who sought help for his compulsive lying had a background of four or five male relatives, including his father, who had died in the past few years of gastrointestinal malignancies. He was experiencing ulcer pains and intermittently was quite panicked. Lying was reflex and ritualized; the more he could lie about anything and everything, the better and calmer he felt. The therapist recounted to his own colleagues that discussions with the patient were nothing short of vertiginous, since it was impossible to know when the patient was lying and when telling the truth. But one day it was clear he was telling the truth: on the morning of the day of a scheduled meeting, he had had a serious industrial accident, almost lost a finger, and was rushed to the hospital. The finger was saved, and when he next came to see the therapist, he allowed as to how the only benefit from the accident was that he did not have to come to therapy that day. Since the therapist was (with the patient's ambivalent consent) trying to help him stop lying, the therapist was also exposing him to unbearable conflict and dread. Better to sacrifice a part than the whole—the risk of losing a finger was preferable to facing the unbearable anxiety about death and annihilation. The "vertiginous" nature of the discussions with the patient represented a successful defense on the part of the patient, to get the therapist to live with him in the tolerable world of "it's true/not true."

The lie, as we indicated earlier, is a particular form of the subjunctive, of the "as if," a functional equivalent in some sense to the ritual act in framing a contradictory state, mood, or action that could not otherwise be articulated. Psychoanalytic perspectives on lying, overall, suggest the communicative role of the lie—the lie tells a story in disguised form that could not otherwise be told. That the lie could be telling a story of serious trauma of abuse or neglect is an idea that slowly developed in the psychoanalytic literature but became more solidly grounded in the last few decades with a greater interest in serious childhood trauma.[38]

Thus, pathological lying and the "splitting of the ego" may at times have a common underlying meaning and cause—that is, severe childhood trauma of abuse and/or neglect. As such, the lie or the personal fetishistic ritual may be both a defense against remembering and a form of remembering, a blighted narrative of the early trauma. It is well known by now how much severe trauma predisposes to the coping mechanism of dissociation, a more severe form of disconnecting than "splitting" of the ego. Trauma, with its dissociative potential, also restricts the free play of imagination and does predispose toward more repetitive, limited play, not easily amenable to innovation and growth. Hence, the rituals in question are relatively fixed and fixated, and the wishes and fears represented more elemental, less modified by time and maturation, and less amenable to communal sharing and hence communal modification.

A Public Ritual: Greek Tragic Performance

Let us consider Greek tragedy and its performance—a cultural institution with major ritual aspects. Its contents explicitly portrayed the traumatic, the forbidden, and, most painfully, that web woven by divine actions (often malicious or capricious) and human self-deception. Yet the Greeks not only watched these plays but clearly were nourished by them. The power of the tragic performance/ritual depends upon the cultural availability of a willingness and ability to enter the "as if" realm of crafted deception. "Tragedy, by means of legends and emotions, creates a deception in which the deceiver is more honest than the non-deceiver, and the deceived is wiser than the non-deceived."[39]

The functions subserved by the tragedies and their performance included presenting in public the forbidden, the unacceptable, the socially destructive, and in a form that allowed the audience to both accept and deny the existence of imperfection, pollution, malice, and catastrophes human, divine, and natural. The plays in performance thereby allowed transient crossings and blurring of boundaries between licit and illicit, the speakable and the unspeakable, the real and the imaginary, and by the nature of their capacity to evoke "the willing suspension of disbelief," much could be negotiated. As Aristotle wrote in his *Poetics*, the best tragic plots are those involving a few prominent families, where terrible things happen within the family. Stories of children killing parents, parents killing children, incest taboos violated, a spouse murdering her spouse were the basic fare. Ambivalence and ambiguity in the realms of intergenerational tensions, divine/human tensions, or sibling issues could be performed and enacted, allowing the audience transient identifications with various characters and situations, but not obligating either actor or audience to remain permanently enchained in any particular role. In many of the Greek tragedies, the chorus occupied an ambiguous and ambivalent position, sometimes sympathizing with, sometimes blaming the hero or heroine, but typically presenting a gamut of emotional reactions. The chorus was a link between the audience and the main characters/actors and, in essence, cued and permitted the audience to view the action with an ambivalent mixture of emotions toward the heroes. Members of the audience could "be moved," and move closer, empathizing with the hero/heroine, or move farther, distancing themselves.

Motives in their purity and impurity were explored and dissected, and issues of sincerity, hypocrisy, "real reasons," and self-serving rationalizations could be represented and enacted. Intergenerational identifications (intergenerational cogwheeling), in all their complexity, were presented, represented, and brought to some sort of conclusion—the curtain must come down at some point. But there was never a total resolution of the issues.

The formal frame of a ritual—acting, dancing, music, evocations of the divine origins of the ritual—all contribute to the communication *and* containment of what is, in life, "radioactive material." The Greek performances were an annual event, lasting three days, with a kind of agonistic competition preceding—a set of judges picked three playwrights, each of whom had a day to present three tragic dramas and a satyr play (satirical and bawdy). Then judges decided who won first place, second, and third. The competition element was an important part of the ritual, a kind of artistic contest-of-arms.

The illusion of the theater was (and is) socially constructed, socially sanctioned, indeed revered—Dionysus, the patron god of theater, was also the god of illusion. In the terms suggested earlier of "splitting of the ego," the actors and audience were not asked to choose between radical alternatives but rather to have the experience of terms of the polarity, simultaneously or in an oscillating manner. Splitting the ego can be as much part of ordinary life as of psychopathology.

Lying and Deceit

The subjunctive character of "as if" in public and private ritual is akin to lying and deceit. It is possible—though a risky generalization without more data—that cultures where ritual behavior is deeply embedded are also those that have a somewhat different valuation of certain forms of lying and deceit than cultures that emphasize sincerity and authenticity. We can at least begin to point out some sources for the social construction of lying and deceit among the sources of Western culture.[40] This is exemplified in the importance accorded to deception and cunning in the Hebrew Bible and in early Greek texts.[41] The Muses in Hesiod's *Theogony* and the Sirens in Homer's *Odyssey* claim they know how to make deceptions seem like truths. Plato, most notably in the "noble lie" and other "fictions" he devises in *The Republic*, self-consciously and deliberately plays with lying and deception.

In the Hebrew Bible, God deceives (e.g., 2 Kings 22); wisdom, cultivating "deceits," was present at the creation of the world (e.g., Proverbs 8:12). The patriarchs and matriarchs, Abraham, Isaac, Jacob, Sarah, Rebecca, Leah, and Rachel, all engage in important lies and deceptions, which are clearly, within the texts, valued.[42] In Greek texts, the language of deception and falsehood is associated with poetic inspiration and creativity. It seems that such language in the ancient texts overlaps with, among other things, some of the psychic experiences that psychoanalysts have been trying to capture with the language of "splitting of the ego," and creative use of transitional objects, individually and culturally.

Deceit/cunning/*metis* are ways of dealing with the flux and shifting complexity of the social world (and also of the physical world). They also turn out to have implications for the complex process of getting to know another, as well as to know oneself. Deceit in the *Odyssey*, for example, has multiple meanings and multiple determinants. Odysseus is characterized in the opening lines as *polutropos*, "polytropic"—a man of many turnings. Along with its "practical" side, to fool, deceive, or decoy an actual or potential threatening other, there are powerful "psychological" motives at work. These motives are both to influence the other, including enlarging the other's empathy and the self-awareness, and influencing the self to a wider empathy and self-recognition. In modern language, some of these motives are conscious and some are unconscious. In a work like the *Odyssey* we might add the dimension of "socially expectable deceit" and "socially unacceptable deceit." Odysseus tells a number of false stories about himself to test out his audience, to influence them, and, indirectly, to highlight for himself certain issues of his own identity. Thus, paradoxically, disguise and deceit are pathways toward truer and fuller recognition of both self and other. The story of King David being confronted by the prophet Nathan about his sin with Bathsheba illustrates the use of a "deceit" or "cunning" by Nathan. David had clearly used terrible deceit to win Bathsheba away from her husband, and when Bathsheba told David she was pregnant, David arranged to have her husband, Uriah, killed in battle. Nathan presents David with the "situation" of a rich man with many sheep, who wants to entertain a traveler at a feast, and who takes the only sheep of a poor man who is his neighbor. David becomes indignant and says that of course the rich man deserves to die and must make abundant restitution. He then gets David to realize the import of what he has done—he, the king, with multiple wives, stealing the wife of another man, and to boot, arranging that the other man should be killed in battle (2 Samuel 12). Thus, indirection and "counterdeceit" can be used as a way of holding up a mirror.

Socially acceptable deceit, "cunning," is a virtue to be respected, feared, and even cultivated. Such deceit is adaptive insofar as one experiences the world as shifting, unpredictable, and always liable to be turned topsy-turvy, sometimes by divine caprice, sometimes by the unexpected-expectable turns of ordinary human life. In a sense, cunning as a virtue, the ability to disguise oneself, dissimulate, and deceive, implies that the world out there is often turning up in disguise. You cannot always know whether something really means what it seems to be or not. Hence the crucial importance of ritualized activities such as reading omens, of interpreting dreams and oracles correctly. If you can pierce the disguise of things, read the meanings as they truly are, you also find out more about yourself. From a modern perspective, cunning and ruse, and learning to read the world's disguises, may be part of learning how to read oneself, one's real intentions.

Further, the emphasis on the value of certain kinds of deceit in these older cultures also highlights the nature of the maturation and development of conscience in the individual in nontraditional societies as well. Over the course of development, one learns the rules, the lines, and also how to read in between the lines. "Cross at the green and not in between" is a good idea for teaching six-year-olds about traffic, but not flexible enough for all the more complex demands of life.

The relevance of these latter considerations to ritual is that ritual involves a certain kind of shared "deceit" or "self-deception." "Yes, Virginia, there is a Santa Claus" represents an attempt to reintegrate the growingly sophisticated child into the world of culturally shared illusion. In that world, one has the flexibility not to insist on the morally correct need to establish once and for all if there is or if there is not a Santa Claus. Socially organized deceit is another way of looking at ritual, but not entirely pejoratively. Public ritual, then, also temporally stabilizes the flux and unpredictability of the world. Erikson's and Winnicott's formulations, each in his own idiosyncratic terminology, suggest how the formation of these "personal" (but not "private" in the sense of the person with an obsessive neurosis or a fetishistic ritual) rituals can be a model for understanding aspects of public or communal ritual. The ritual established between two people is at the least a conceptual bridge to communal rituals, and more likely actually intertwined with the complex history of the origins and functions of communal ritual.

We now shall turn to this complex story.

Private, Personal, and Public Ritual

Is the child's capacity to devise ritualized behaviors at least in part a function of the availability in the culture of ritualized activities, of public or communal practice of rituals in the "as if" space of the world? An intriguing example of the intricate nature of this question is to be found in the photographic essay by Margaret Mead and Gregory Bateson on childhood in Bali.[43] There are photographs of the well-known Balinese dance-trance state, with the dancer's hand held limp and the fingers splayed in a particular configuration. What is striking is a photograph of a six-month-old child, nursing at the mother's breast, with the child's hand appearing in that same characteristic pose.[44] Bracketing for the moment the question of whether there is some genetic predisposition to that hand position, we must consider that the baby is very early on being prepared for participation in the culture's ritual life. The child's capacity for trance (innate in most people in varying degrees), for some kind of identification-mimicking of the parents, for beginning to develop an "as if" capability—all these intersect with the culturally valued dance-trance rituals.

Or consider the classic World War II film *Forbidden Games*.[45] Two young children, a boy and a girl (around five or six) develop their personal rituals around death and burial—disturbing in their frankness to the adults around them—amalgamating the available Catholic rituals and the horror of the little girl having witnessed the Nazis killing her father. Here, too, it is easy to say that there is some confluence of the personal and the public, the personal and the communal, and ritual formation prompted by severe trauma.

In discussing Greek tragic drama performance, we must consider what it means for a child to grow up in a society (and a family) that values this public ritual. That child's developing capacity for "splitting," for developing creative "as if" realms, interacts with the familial and cultural atmosphere that cultivates, indeed enjoys, the ritual of tragic drama.

These examples help frame the question about what is the nature of private rituals, whether those of everyday life (all of us have some) or of the more exotic rituals associated with psychopathology. These ritualized behaviors, as we have argued, reflect attempts to deal with issues of pressing concern to the individual, but at the same time issues of pressing concern to the culture(s) at large—separation and reunion, the succession of generations, gender differences and their import, including the power relationships entailed in gender differences, the nature of permissible and forbidden pleasures. The existence of these private rituals depends upon the mind's capacity to split, to repress, to symbolize, and to express in symbolic terms and action. They tend to be invariant, often more strict in requirements of enactment than most formal religious rituals. Nor do they invite, by and large, participation by others. Others may be included, but they tend to be somewhat impersonalized, perhaps used as objects or players in the ritual, whose meaning is not necessarily shared by the enlisted other. When, at times, the private ritual goes "public," there is a major transformation of its essential nature. Clubs or groups organized around fetishism or transvestitism are subject to a totally different dynamic, where each member of the group can make claims as an individual, asserting and inserting his or her own demands for shaping the exact form and spirit of the ritualized behavior.[46] In sum, private ritual requires the construction and maintenance of a private world, allowing the illusion of control over the imaginary presences, whose identity must be kept mysterious and hidden, including (or especially) from the person constructing the fantasy.

In contrast, public ritual invites participation from a defined group, and even if the ritual is conducted by a person who is alone, say praying alone at the appropriate time of day for a Jew or a Muslim, there is a keen sense of participating in a larger group. Further, in public rituals the unseen presences are often identifiable and identified—such as various ancestors, ghosts, demons, or deities. Public rituals, at times self-consciously, but so often implicitly, are intended to serve as intergenerational connections. The Passover Seder is explicit in this regard, and many other rituals in various cultures entail the participants reminiscing (or painfully remembering) about what the ritual performances were like in their own past.[47] Private rituals may be just as concerned with intergenerational issues, but these must remain covert.

The public and private rituals we have discussed each have their own rules and rhythms of change and variation. However seemingly stable and invariant a given ritual may be—indeed over generations—there are often changes in relation to shifts in historical pressures and cultural concerns. Certainly the interpretation of the ritual may shift over time, and there may be subtle changes in performance and audience-participant relationships. But these changes, however fraught with tension and anxiety, are "consensual," that is, communal, and are agreed-upon shifts in how the culture applies "as if" significations and to what elements of the ritual.[48] For private fetishistic rituals, there may also be changes, though the specifics of how and when "natural" shifts occur have not been studied in any systematic detail.

Meaning and Significance

Part of the difficulty for an investigator of ritual, whether public or private, is the nature of the search for the "meaning" of the ritual. For discussion purposes here, we distinguish between the *significance* for the agent in private, personal, or public rituals and the *meaning* of the ritual. The significance is more or less accessible to the inquiry, "Why do you do it?" For a private sexual ritual, the answer might be, "I have to, or I go nuts." Or, "I may be ashamed of it, but it's my main source of pleasure, and it gives me so much and takes away so little from anybody else." For a public ritual, the answer might be, "We have always done it this way," or, "Our dead cannot rest unless we do this rite and do it properly," or, "If we do not do this, our people will wither away;" or, "How else can our sins be forgiven?" Its significance may also be in part encoded nonverbally, viscerally, and indeed in the nervous system. What may be difficult for the subject to describe, let alone explain, is the depth of feeling and of what we might roughly call the "psychosomatic" aspects of ritual performance. Consider the crucial role of music and rhythmical chanting or music in so many rituals, elements that have a deep emotional import not necessarily translatable into words but entraining the body and brain. A man involved in a transvestite ritual, for example, could feel terrible, psychically and bodily, if not able to perform the ritual. When performing, he might enter into states of excitement and occasionally something approaching ecstasy. The !Kung dancers, to take an example of a public ritual, if prevented from dancing would experience extraordinary and even intolerable tension, and when performing, could experience something that can be called transcendence.[49]

In contrast to "significance," "meaning" implies something beneath the surface, something other than what the participants or observers can immediately know. Fundamental to Freud's psychoanalytic approach to ritual was the assumption that the ritualized behaviors described—private and public—have *meanings* in this sense, and further, that in principle these can be discerned by the work of interpretation, a deciphering of the symbolic code of the behaviors. That deciphering is work, and as such it encounters resistance. Historically, this Freudian framework was enormously influential in what later came to be termed "psychological anthropology" and the whole schema of looking for the contending forces and conflicting pulls that are symbolically represented in public rituals. It is not a coincidence that Clifford Geertz recalled Freud so clearly in the title of his influential essay collection, *The Interpretation of Cultures*.

Yet the search for hidden meanings and disguised motives can also turn out to be endless and bottomless. Psychoanalysis has been divided between those who assume that the method can yield "explanation without remainder" and those who assume that whatever end there is to explanation is a more or less agreed upon resting place (cf. Hume, "Explanation is where the mind rests"). At another time, or in the hands of another interpreter, new and different meanings might be discerned. In this regard, the psychoanalytic search for meanings can parallel the quest entailed in sincerity, the quest for the truest moral or immoral motivations of the actor(s). The search for a final psychoanalytic explanation or a final determination of the measure and degree of sincerity can be not only endless but finally thankless.

3

Ritual, Play, and Boundaries

Our broad definition of ritual has the combined advantages and disadvantages of pulling our attention out to behavior well beyond intuitive understandings of the term. The key formal features we have identified—like creating a subjunctive world or crafting a performative order through repetition—put watching *Romeo and Juliet,* saying "please," or playing cops and robbers on the same analytic plane as Daoist rites to renew the structure of the universe itself. Our hope in doing this is to reveal more about the workings of a crucial social phenomenon, but we also recognize the danger in stretching a term so broadly that it loses any analytic rigor. The first part of this chapter takes our argument to the general category of play, with the goal of deepening our understanding of ritual through the comparison. The exercise also leads us to suggest that ritual offers more than one way of crossing into a subjunctive world, and that each mechanism has potentially different social consequences, including different possibilities for the creation of empathy. The second part of the chapter focuses on the boundaries that must be crossed in the creation of empathy—the ways they frame our social and personal categories, and the ways that ritual allows us to play with them.

We are hardly the first to be tantalized by the apparently close connections between ritual and play, or to find that the many similarities force us to think hard about where the differences might lie. Many of anthropology's most creative thinkers about ritual, for instance, also felt the need to explore its relation to play. This was at least in part because each of them found extremely playful aspects of ritual (or perhaps ritualized forms of play) that jarred the commonly held assumption that ritual, as religious ritual, lies in the realm of the earnestly serious. Radcliffe-Brown thus wrote about social relationships where scatological joking is required, Max Gluckman struggled to differentiate between ritual and sport, Mary Douglas wrote a classic article on ritual jokes, and Victor Turner analyzed a trick at the core of a key Ndembu ritual.[1] These thinkers push us beyond just comparing play and ritual to examine how playfulness is somehow inherent in ritual. Playfulness, as we will discuss, ties intimately to the negotiation of boundaries (which is central to ritual acts), to the issues of ambiguity raised in the previous chapter, and thus to the very construction of subjunctive worlds. Ritual's ability to create subjunctives allows for the possibility of empathy as much as it creates social boundaries, and its loss can pose serious social problems. We will begin with the playing of games, though, because playfulness is not entirely the same thing as play—just ask any child who is losing at chess.

Comparing Ritual and Play

Play, like ritual, deals with the subjunctive, with the "as if." It presents us with a mode of assimilating both physical objects and social relations into the experiential world of the individual—and ultimately of society. In this, ritual and play share some strongly salient features that set them both apart from the world of work, of instrumental calculation and other modes of integrating self and world. In a strong sense, then, our inquiry into ritual and play continues the concerns of the preceding two chapters. Our analysis of the subjunctive as well as of ambiguity (both sociological and psychological) is all about the interface of self and the worlds of material objects and social relations.

This is where our project intersects, at least in part, with some of the perspectives on play, especially those developed by such a thinker as Piaget, who saw play as an evolving stage in the coordination of self and world. Piaget works out an idea of play as providing a crucial moment in our developing capabilities to re-present, that is, in the widest sense, to symbolize the world.[2] He argues that a child begins developmentally with imitation, simple repetition (which affords the pleasure of mastery), and slowly progresses through half a dozen stages to child's play and make-believe. Make-believe already requires the ability to symbolize, to dissociate signifier from signified and so to create the illusionary world of play where the rocking chair is the mountain and the lamp shade the damsel in distress. At its final stage, full-fledged symbolization (beyond play) provides the crucial means to move from what Piaget calls "assimilation" (of world to ego) to "accommodation," that is, the construction of symbols and symbol systems that allow the self to change in response to the world. Play for Piaget thus takes us beyond imitation, which is but the ego attempting to reproduce the object world, but not yet all the way to symbolization—where we already begin to accommodate to that world. Hence the particular character of the ludic in assimilating reality to the needs of the ego: it is neither pure imitation nor pure symbolization. As we shall see in the following discussion, however, ritual also includes both imitation and assimilation. It reproduces an "as if" world (imitation). Yet this is not the infant's imitation of the "as is" world of raw experience. Instead, it imitates (re-presents) the highly symbolic subjunctive world that ritual itself posits.

One of the most influential attempts to merge the categories of ritual and play in the twentieth century came from Johan Huizinga's *Homo Ludens*, in which he placed play as a primary building block of civilization, viewed "culture *sub specie ludi*," and saw archaic ritual as sacred play.[3] Nearly all critics agree that his concept of play is too ambitiously broad, and his style of argument too fast and loose. Nevertheless, his definition gets at so many of the core features of play that no one writing on the topic can avoid him. We also find the definition as illuminating as it is frustrating, and we take it up here because it touches on so many of the features we have emphasized for ritual. It helps clarify just why games and rituals seem so similar.[4]

First, play for Huizinga is free. It is never imposed by biological need or moral duty, and the players can always suspend the game. Play, in other words, stands apart from the world of coercion. If politics is ultimately the legitimated control of coercive force, then play always lies outside its realm. Second, play is disinterested. It is not about satisfying needs or maximizing life interests. Play does not make life possible by providing food or shelter; instead, he writes, it "adorns life."[5] That is, play is not economics any more than it is politics. It epitomizes the sphere apart from our mundane needs, and we can see how this would lead Huizinga to the idea that play undergirds human civilization, which he sees primarily as high culture.

Third, play is somehow separated from ordinary life. It has its own time and place, its own course and meaning, secluded from the rigors of the everyday. Finally, play creates its own order within its delimited time and space; it is order. These last two points lie at the core of our own discussion of the subjunctive nature of ritual, its construction of an "as if" world that is bounded apart from ordinary life with its own sets of rules and its own space and time. Huizinga himself is quite explicit and bold with the comparison:

> Just as there is no formal difference between play and ritual, so the "consecrated spot" cannot be formally distinguished from the play-ground. The arena, the card-table, the magic circle, the temple, the stage, the screen, the tennis court, the court of justice, etc., are all in form and function play-grounds, i.e. forbidden spots, isolated, hedged round, hallowed, within which special rules obtain. All are temporary worlds, within the ordinary world, dedicated to the performance of an act apart.[6]

This resonates, of course, with much anthropological discussion of ritual, like Mary Douglas on the role of boundaries, or Maurice Bloch on the way that ritual contexts encourage cyclical concepts of time in which nothing permanent ever changes.[7] Bloch in particular argues that ritual creates a "social structure," that is, an image of society as rule-bound and changeless, systematically ignoring the strategizing and improvising that make up so much of life as we really live it. This can work completely, for Bloch, only within the ritual context. If we think about it in these terms, Huizinga is arguing that this bounded realm of constructed order constitutes that most human world that falls between coercion and physical needs, politics and economics: society itself. His definition frustrates because he calls all of this "play," but it has continued to inspire because it points to such important features of our social world.

Hans-Georg Gadamer provides a far more systematic account than Huizinga when he explores the relationships among play, festival, and art.[8] All these realms, for Gadamer, require us to enter into their alternate worlds, to join a "community" that they both typify and create. All bring us into "traditions," even if those traditions renounce earlier ones and require us to accept a new one, like much avant-garde music or art. His use of "symbol" in this context pulls us away from meaning as representation to meaning as action—he reminds us of the etymology of the term in the ancient Greek token, split in half, by which one party could identify another. Its significance lay in its ability to mesh with its other symbol-half, rather than in its allegorical reference to something else.

In the same way, children playing imaginative games are not so much representing superheroes or puppies as being them for the moment. They are not even "playing," in the sense that they have momentarily put aside self-consciousness of play. That is why an adult presence can so ruin the fun—it forces attention on the fact that this is play and thus breaks the subjunctive world. Jokes are like this too. Any joke that has to begin or end with "I'm just joking" will fail. Within the world of the game, those children simply are superheroes and puppies, just as a wafer is the Body of Christ. The children do not need to be able to fly or wag their tails any more than the wafer needs skin and hair.

Play, ritual, art, and festival each thus creates its own bounded community and world of action. Each is a shared and bounded human construction with a rhythm (usually called "repetition" in ritual studies), rules of understanding and action, and powerful performative effects. Each deals with the dynamics of boundaries and boundlessness, maintaining a tension that is built into human existence. Ritual and play are both, to borrow a term from Brian Sutton-Smith, "enacted subjunctives."[9] Both construct a third space (similar to Winnicott's transitional space or object) where we create, experience, and share alternative realities and orders.

Gadamer works through festival and play to develop a theory of aesthetics, but like Huizinga, he leaves us wondering how we can distinguish ritual from play, if indeed we should. What exactly is the difference between making a pun and saying grace, waving around a rubber chicken and sacrificing a real one? We have learned something by putting these things together, but surely we run the danger of losing sight of some important distinction in the process.

As a beginning, we can recognize that all of these acts create subjunctive spheres, but the particular "as if" worlds differ from each other in important ways. Some subjunctive worlds claim to be true and eternal, while others are ephemeral and ad hoc. In play we can create worlds of cops and robbers, goalies and forwards, or pawns and knights, but we can choose to abandon those worlds at any time. On the other hand, we must always return to purification rituals, because living a human life means becoming polluted, and the only way we can adjust is through periodic returns to another world of possibilities.

Note that this is not the same as saying that play is voluntary but ritual is compulsory. Sometimes the social pressure to play is overwhelming: no one feels more isolated and lost than the child kept out of game. And many rituals are voluntary, although some are clearly constitutive of their traditions (like baptism for a Christian). Rather, ritual's worlds—performed or not—are eternal, while play's are ephemeral. Hockey (not to mention more obviously ad hoc play like tickling) could disappear forever from the universe, and while some few hockey players and fans would feel that the world had fundamentally changed, most would probably shift their sports passions elsewhere. Remove communion, however, even for a Catholic who rarely takes it, and everything is different.

This has some important further implications. Ritual's evocation of a more permanent truth encourages greater predictability and repetition in ritual than in play. We know how a ritual will end because it always comes out the same way. Eternal truths demand it. This is not true for play. Even when we know there will be a winner and a loser, we cannot know in advance who it will be. Other kinds of games just stop rather than ending—playing house suddenly seems less interesting, or tickling starts to become annoyance, and we move out of that world and on to other things.

We know in advance how rituals end, but because rituals create worlds of unending truth, there is also a sense in which they have no end. The ancestors receive incense smoke every day, the witch Rangda and a magical animal called Barong in a Balinese festival always battle to a stalemate, Easter comes every year.[10] Weddings and funerals, in which each of us may play the central role only once, are just as endless when seen from the society as a whole. Even petty etiquette like saying "please" is more like ritual than play in this sense. We cannot say "please" just once and then forget about it. We repeat these niceties eternally because the social conventions they enter must always be renewed. Play, on the other hand, never has to be repeated at all. So when we play, the ending is unknown but its world can easily end. Ritual's world, however, is endless, even though we know the ending of every performance. This also means that ritual always incorporates its past in a way that play does not. Because ritual is endless, it continually makes the past into the present. Play, however, continually defers the present into a future when the ending will become clear.

Thus we can see clearly that while ritual does indeed share certain characteristics of play, especially those focused on the subjunctive nature of their engagement with the interaction of world and self, it also differs from play in certain critically important features. Like child's play (according to Piaget), it has a strongly developed subjunctive sense and an emphasis on repetition and indexicality (all of which characterize child's play). Yet at the same time it also shows an extremely high degree of symbolization, quite unlike what can be found in any type of play, children's or adult's. Adult play (of which we shall have much more to say in the following) of course involves a degree of symbolization (the rules of tennis, or golf, etc.), but the scale, depth, and elaboration of that symbol system is nothing compared with what one finds in ritual. Scratch a ritual and you will find a virtual library of meanings, interpretations, teachings, historical events, symbol systems, visions of perfection, and so on. Not so in the rules of tennis, which can be summarized in a brief notebook. Thus the scope of significance given to the system of symbolization differs markedly between ritual and play.

Pieter Brueghel the Elder managed to capture many of these dynamics of games and ritual in two of the paintings from his *Theatrum Mundi* series,

FIGURE 3-1. *The Fight between Carnival and Lent*, Pieter Brueghel the Elder (Kunsthistorisches Museum, Vienna, with permission).

depicting the absurdities of human life. His famous *The Fight between Carnival and Lent* was painted in 1559, and *Children's Games* was completed the next year (see figures 3-1 and 3-2). It is no accident that both are very similar in style, each showing myriad figures scattered across the canvas. Color, composition, and even the sense of internal tension in the two paintings greatly resemble each other.

Nevertheless, the differences in composition resonate with the points we are making. Both, for instance, take place within the enclosures of city squares, but the space of *Children's Games* opens up to an unbounded realm of a winding river and the sea beyond, while the scene in *Carnival and Lent* leads only to the further enclosures of the town's streets. The games recognize the broader world in a way that the rituals do not. An even more crucial difference lies at the center of each painting. The action in *Carnival and Lent* focuses on the meeting of the two ritual moments. Emaciated Lent on his bare cart, drawn by two bent-over penitents and followed by various piteous beggars and self-satisfied burghers, meets the jolly and rotund Carnival, riding on a wine barrel and trailing his own troupe of gourmands, drunks, and entertainers. *Children's Games*, on the other hand, is quite uncentered, letting our eyes wander at liberty from one to another

FIGURE 3-2. *Children's Games*, Pieter Brueghel the Elder (Kunsthistorisches Museum, Vienna, with permission).

of the little groups playing at their separate games. While *Carnival and Lent* concerns the moral battle between moral license and utter restraint, *Children's Games* is not about anything at all.[11] It has been called the only one of Brueghel's paintings with "no recondite allusions or moral innuendos."[12] Ritual is centripetal, bringing people together in a concentrated act that creates society (or, in this case, society as seen through two different ritual lenses). Play instead sows its seeds across the field of the canvas. Ritual defines boundaries even as it posits wholeness. Play instead opens us to the limitless, even as it organizes its own rule-bound activities.

Forms of Ritual, Forms of Play

Let us return to the insight that ritual and play create subjunctive worlds that shape social structures. A close look at different types of play will ultimately help us differentiate among types of rituals, clarifying how they relate to the creation and crossing of boundaries, and thus to the delineation of self and other, in-group and out-group. Roger Caillois pushed the study of play significantly beyond Huizinga, and his categorization of play into four types is particularly helpful.[13] We will use this typology to explore some of the differences in the ways we can make the transition into a subjunctive world—there is more than one way to split an ego. Caillois uses the following categories:

- *Agôn* covers the competitive games in which external conditions are equalized in order to measure the innate skills and talents of competitors directly against each other—racing, football, chess, and the like.
- *Alea* (dice) includes all games of chance. It is almost the opposite of *agôn*, in the sense that victory and defeat come entirely from external causes, and the players have no control—from flipping a coin to casino roulette.
- *Mimicry*, Caillois writes, is the acceptance of a "closed, conventional, and, in certain respects, imaginary universe."[14] This is the world of simulation, from children imagining themselves as dragons to a performance of *Oedipus Rex*.
- *Ilinx* (from the Greek for "whirlpool") is the pursuit of vertigo, of what Caillois calls "voluptuous panic."[15] It includes children's pleasures like spinning in circles or tickling, but also the more adult thrills of noncompetitive skiing or white-water kayaking.

Each of these categories has some obvious ritual correlates: ritual competitions like the early Olympics, divination through a randomizing process like drawing Tarot cards, ritual dramas of many kinds, or ecstatic trance. The comparison becomes much more than just an exercise in classification, however, if we identify general patterns behind the four categories. We suggest that two critical processes underlie Caillois's categories, and that they reveal some important features of rituals and "as if" worlds in general: First, are set social roles affirmed or subverted? And, second, does the self remain in control or lose control? Making these distinctions helps disaggregate rather different behaviors that we sometime lump together under the single rubric of ritual, and to spell out their different social consequences for empathy and pluralism.

Agôn and *alea* affirm set roles. In their different ways, they reveal the identity of the players. They show us as we are in other contexts: boldly aggressive or cautiously defensive, brilliant strategists or opportunistic tacticians, lucky or cursed, winners or losers. This is quite obviously different from mimicry, in which we utterly abandon the roles and behaviors of everyday life for something new. Actors are, for the moment, someone else, just as children are superheroes or puppies. *Ilinx*, too, removes us from our usual roles, but more by dissolving all roles than by substituting temporary ones. The "voluptuous panic" of dizziness, hilarity, or ecstasy takes us out of ourselves but does not put us into any other selves. While Caillois does not make quite this generalization about roles, the latter half of his book suggests it by claiming that *agôn* and *alea* together constitute one close, fundamental relationship, while mimicry and *ilinx* constitute another. He argues that the *agôn*/*alea* pair comes to dominate in all the great civilizations, even though mimicry/*ilinx* may survive in marginal contexts like Carnival. He does not offer much empirical support for this correlation, but it is consistent with the possibility that states (a hallmark of "civilization") would discourage practices that subvert roles.

The other distinction—does the self retain or give up control—cuts across Caillois's two "fundamental" pairs. Mimicry and *agôn* allow the player to keep her self-control; *alea* and *ilinx* give it up. That is how playing the part of a god differs from being possessed by the god. The child pretending to be a ninja warrior has a form of self-control that her brother, tickled into gales of helpless giggles, has given up. Self-control is also the fundamental difference between *agôn*, where the players control the outcome, and *alea*, where the player is at the mercy of outside forces.

Identifying these processes lets us move beyond just classifying types of play and then pointing to those rituals that seem to fit, at least in part. Instead, we can focus on the forces that both share, and thus clarify a broad range of different kinds of rituality (or even subjunctivity more broadly). Table 3.1 illustrates our reworking of Caillois and some of the ritual associations that follow.

To begin with the upper left quadrant of the table, we can see how these underlying ideas broaden the utility of a concept like *agôn*, which can include ritualized competitions but also much else based on self-control and role affirmation. There are, of course, ritualized games that fit in easily. We are lucky to have good documentation of several cases where clear-cut games have

TABLE 3-1. Types of Play and Ritual

	Self Retains Control	Self Gives Up Control
Affirm Roles	**agôn** ritualized battles/games purification magic sacrifice	**alea** divination votive ritual followers of charismatic leader
Subvert Roles	**mimicry** rites of reversal ritual drama Pesach (recalled sacrifice)	**ilinx** spirit possession intoxication *communitas*

become ritualized in relatively recent times. In the Trobriand Islands, just off New Guinea, for instance, British cricket after the colonial period rapidly evolved a highly ritualized form with ties to earlier patterns of warfare and of the intervillage feasting that was a key to local power.[16] A visiting village would bring a team of any size, but always far larger than the standard cricket team of eleven. The hosts would create a team of the same size. Bats and faces were painted in the colors and ornaments of warfare. Trobriand cricket did not lose its playfulness—teams had magical chants to help their play, which grew out of both old war magic (for power throwing a ball instead of a spear) and popular culture (like one for catching balls based on the advertising jingle for a popular brand of gum). Yet we can recognize this as ritual in part because the final score was less important than the play itself and the feast that followed. Scores were expected to be close and hosts to win. Like ritual, but unlike pure play, the end is known in advance.[17]

The incorporation of competitive games into ritual occurs because so much ritual is already self-controlled and role-affirming, just like *agôn*. In fact this category seems to get at the heart of the most prototypical rituals, the ones we often see in monographs on ritual in anthropology or religious studies. When Maurice Bloch, for instance, identifies ritual language as something that cannot carry semantic meaning because it is invariant, he sees it as a kind of pure form that can only reinforce patterns of traditional authority—an *agôn*-like affirmation of role and control.[18] His critique of Clifford Geertz's discussion of cyclical time is similar: such concepts of time, he argues, come to the fore only in ritual contexts where worldly change is denied in favor of an image of eternal power, of a naturalization (or supernaturalization) of the current roles and their occupants.[19] This sort of ritual reaffirms roles and leaves the self (or rather particular selves) in control.

Nancy Jay comes from quite a different theoretical direction than Bloch, but she also sees ritual—epitomized by sacrifice—as a way of reinforcing priests' power, affirming their control and enhancing their roles. She argues, for instance, that different depictions of sacrifice in the three major sources of Genesis (known as J, E, and P) vary with the source's view of patriarchal power. The voice least interested in sacrifice (J) is the one most willing to discuss women's contributions to the lineage, while the most enthusiastic about sacrifice (P) is also the most thoroughly patriarchal.[20] Using data from around the world, she claims more generally that sacrifice appears in situations of strongly hierarchized power. Purifications also tend to reinforce existing roles, boundaries, and norms of behavior. Even etiquette, which creates and re-creates a subjunctive world in its own way, shares these features of the self retaining control and affirming roles. Addressing someone by title and last name, for instance, establishes a social distance or hierarchy, reconfirmed with every address, that can pervade the relationship in all contexts.

The role affirmation and retention of self-control in the *agôn* quadrant of the table thus get at the heart of the usual categories of ritual (which need not be agonistic at all in the literal sense). This is ritual at its most social, setting up clear categories and boundaries that define and create a social structure—the ritual of Bloch's analyses of Madagascar or Geertz's of Bali.

Expanding our view to the other quadrants, however, helps clarify the penumbra of ritual-like acts that we also often include, but which differ in some important ways. *Alea*, in the upper right, retains *agôn*'s emphasis on proper roles but cedes control to forces beyond the self. This is gambling for Caillois, but it is a very short leap from there to divination through some kind of randomization procedure like throwing yarrow stalks or looking for ravens in the sky. For some Chinese, gambling itself is a kind of divination, as winning or losing is viewed as a sign of one's general fortunes at the moment and can influence business or other financial decisions.[21]

Votive rituals, in which we beseech the gods to give help, are less obviously like gambling but fit squarely in this category as behaviors that affirm us in our roles while acknowledging that our fates are in the hands of the deities. As mothers we ask for children, as traders we beseech profit, as patients we pray for healing. If our wishes are granted, we give thanks by leaving an effigy of the baby conceived or the knee healed, donating money for an opera to entertain the gods, or giving gold medals and cash donations to build the splendor of their temples.

Even something like following a charismatic movement falls in this category, although the leaders themselves usually would not. Followers retain their roles, or sometimes occupy newly defined roles within the movement, but either way those roles define them both within and beyond the "as if" moment. As with votive supplicants or diviners, though, they have ceded control over their own fates to an outside figure, in this case the charismatic leader.

This analysis clarifies why "aleatorical" rituals seem to fall somewhere near the boundaries of ritual proper. Like games—but quite unlike agonistic rituals of sacrifice or purity—we do not know the results in advance. The gods or saints may grant or refuse our requests, the divination may be encouraging or horrifying, and the charismatic leader might do anything at all. These quasi rituals also tend to be more ad hoc than other forms of ritual, again like games. Thus engaging in the rituals of purification is part of the life of Hinduism, as is venerating ancestors for life in China, but no Indians or Chinese are compelled to pray that their new car will avoid accidents or that they will win at mah-jongg. The rhythms of repetition also apply less here, in part because the absence of a known ending makes genuine repetition impossible. One can repeatedly divine the same question, of course, especially if the first answer was undesirable, but at least in China the gods have been known to give false information to people who keep annoying them like that.

Aleatorical rituals tend to slip more easily out of their subjunctive world than other forms. They typically start like other rituals in establishing a boundary to mark entry into the "as if" world, for instance, by burning incense before choosing lots in a Chinese temple or shuffling the Tarot deck three times. The ending, however, always involves the world "as is," a replacement of the subjunctive mood with the indicative. The disease is cured, the baby is born, the tall dark stranger appears…or not. No wonder, then, that such rituals can often easily devolve into games proper in some contexts. Divination, in a Chinese temple as much as in a carnival booth, can be just for fun. Even ritual curing, while never a game, often becomes just one optional step in a much broader strategy of healing that might involve votive prayer, spirit mediums, local herbalists, and Western-style doctors.

On the other hand, these rituals are just as role-affirming as the agonistic ones. A supplicant hoping for a god's divination in Taiwan, for example, must first burn incense to show respect for the god, and announce in his heart, "My name is XXX, I live at such-and-such address, and I was born on X date in Y year at Z time. Will you allow me to perform a divination by drawing lots?" This, modern informants say, is so the god can consult the right file. Roles are affirmed with shining clarity here, even as control is handed over to the divine world.

Moving to the bottom row of the table, we come to mimicry. Like *agôn*, mimicry leaves the self in control, but unlike both *agôn* and *alea*, it overturns the roles of our everyday lives. We are someone else, but only within the subjunctive limits of the pretense. Scholars have long noted the close relations between dramatic performance and ritual. Among all of Caillois's forms of play, theater most closely resembles ritual. It claims to deal with ultimate truths, at least sometimes, in a way that playing tag or checkers never does. It is repeated, and we always know the ending. Part of the power of a play like *Oedipus Rex*, after all, lies in the audience knowing exactly his horrific situation and ultimate doom even as the play opens and Oedipus seems on top of the world. Hamlet always dies, Godot never arrives, over and over, the same way every time.

Dramatic performance becomes indistinguishable from ritual especially where its performative functions are accentuated, and where the actor's temporary role appears to be more than artifice. Chinese folk opera, for example, typically takes place on a stage facing a temple, and occurs especially on ritual occasions where it is said to be for the enjoyment of the deities, and only incidentally for the masses of living humans who crowd around to watch. The stage itself defines a ritual arena, complete with its own cosmic orientation (male dressing rooms on the yang side and female on the yin side, for instance) and its own backstage altar. The content of the play also matters: auspicious occasions need auspicious plots, just as people must say only happy things and avoid even accidental puns with negative connotations at the lunar New Year. This is performative, as the words uttered shape the future.[22]

Such transformations involve changing roles, but always into new and clearly defined roles. In a way, Jews do this when they re-create the freedom from bondage at Passover, as Muslims do when they commemorate Ibrahim's sacrifice. Mimicry appears much less like our classic ideas of ritual, however, when its roles become loose, flexible, and improvised. Under these circumstances we no longer know the ending in advance, and true repetition is impossible. Children's imaginative play is like this, and so, to an extent, is something like Carnival. This is why a game of imagined kings and knights can degenerate into an actual fistfight, while *Camelot* cannot. In Carnival, the edge of excitement lies not so much in turning normal roles upside down (as in any dramatic play), but in the possibility that the players may let the role run away with them. All the participants know that the roles reversed today will be back to normal tomorrow, but no one knows for sure what will happen if the King of Fools leads the masked mob to riot instead of ritual, carnage instead of Carnival. Such things happened only occasionally, but the possibility was always there. The subversion of roles via mimicry always hints at the threat of a dissolution into chaos, in both play and ritual. Donning the mask can dissolve the old self sufficiently that anything becomes possible, and the alcoholic enhancements of Carnival can further collapse both old and new roles.

These possibilities bring us finally to the last category, *ilinx*. Ilinx is giddy play and ecstatic religion in all its forms. We give up self-control in a way quite different from mimicry's embrace of a different self through an alternate role. Instead, all roles dissolve and anything becomes possible. Caillois's example of spinning around until we fall over captures these dual instabilities of lost self-control and abandoned role definition. We are in the realm of mystical transcendence, ecstatic rapture, and inspired vision.

The utter freedom at the extreme of this kind of experience opens up a world of new possibilities, but we should recall that "anything can happen" is a recipe for horror as much as delight. This is why most social worlds in which *ilinx*-like ritual is important place great barriers around it, trying to keep it under control. Thus Victor Turner writes about *communitas*— the variant of *ilinx* created in the liminal periods of rites of passage or pilgrimages—that when it becomes normatively recognized "its religious expressions become closely hedged about by rules and interdictions—which act like the lead container of a dangerous radioactive isotope."[23]

When spirit possession becomes institutionalized, for example, the mediums are either carefully trained in advance (as in many African cases) or subjected to interpretation by unpossessed intermediaries. The oracle at Delphi thus gave responses only through the intercession of the Prophetes and Hoisoi, rather than directly from the mediums.[24] Spirit-writing cults in modern China and Taiwan similarly rely on a respected community member to interpret the writings of the gods. Another alternative is to allow such cults to thrive only at the social margins, as in a whole range of groups from the Zar cult in northern Sudan to the Korean *kut* ritual, both of which feature women, and are looked down on by men as cults appropriate only to the margins.[25]

Without these lead containers, societies face the constant threat of chaos or worse. Anything from charismatic leaders to mass forms of spirit possession can crack open the container. The results can lead to rapid periods of social innovation and experimentation, which are sometimes reinstitutionalized but also often collapse. China's worst conflagration of its generally awful nineteenth century was the Taiping Rebellion, which began under the charismatic leadership of Jesus Christ's younger brother (Hong Xiuquan) and spread rapidly when it opened space for a massive spirit possession movement in the mountains of the southwest.

Hong had come bearing his monotheistic message, but the movement really began attracting a massive following when the leader was away for some time, and his teaching combined with local traditions of spirit possession. Soon God himself was speaking directly to followers through the mouth of a medium. So was Jesus, alongside a whole host of Chinese popular deities and star spirits. These innovations allowed the movement to grow rapidly and to attract people from ethnic groups that would not otherwise have cooperated. Yet, according to a contemporary European observer, they also "brought disorder and dissension among the brethren."[26] The chaos decreased only when Hong returned—he really was Jesus' brother, and so did not need to be possessed—and rebuilt the "lead container" by determining that only one close follower spoke with the voice of God, and another with the voice of Jesus. All others were false, and they were crushed. This was not so much Weber's rationalization of charismatic authority as the creation of charismatic authority out of ecstatic anarchy. It worked, and the group went on to conquer China's economic heartland for a while, and to cause perhaps 20 million casualties.[27]

Ilinx is often surrounded by ritual, which helps shape the lead container that is always part of the experience. Yet ecstasy and trance always contain that seed of the possibility of breaking all their boundaries. *Ilinx* as pure play is not so different. It usually ends in collapse—panting exhaustion, a dizzy fall, giggling immobility. And it often contains the possibility of exceeding its boundaries, as when tickling escalates into shoving or into lovemaking.

Of these four categories, only the one we have called agôn affirms a fully stable social world, where participants remain in control and use that control to affirm their roles. The chart also lets us recognize, however, the other modes of rituality—or more broadly of subjunctivity—that let us enter subjunctive worlds under different circumstances, and that imagine society in different ways. Each constructs the frame of ritual or play differently. Each creates a different sort of tension between boundary maintenance and boundary transcendence. Each points us toward the vital importance of the boundary itself.

Frames and Boundaries

In fact, all forms of ritual and play bring us to the problem of boundaries. They do this both internally, by assigning people to categories (polluted or purifying, knight or dragon), and externally, by setting boundaries around their own "as if" worlds. Much of our preceding discussion in this chapter has been about the categories internal to the ritual, like self and other, or the reaffirmation of predefined social roles. It has shown how various forms of ritual can maintain or undercut internal social boundaries and distinctions, from the most boundary-conservative form of agôn to the boundary-dissolving ecstasies of *ilinx*. Here let us turn to the important problem of the external boundaries, the frames that let us know we have entered a subjunctive world, where even agôn must be able to cross boundaries. This, as we have been arguing, is central to the social consequences of ritual.

Boundaries both join and divide, bring together and distinguish. Even more important, they constitute the very existence of an object. As Martin Heidegger pointed out: "A space is something that has been made room for, something that is cleared and free, namely within a boundary, Greek *peras*. A boundary is not that at which something stops, but, as the Greeks recognized, the boundary is that from which something begins its *presencing*. That is why the concept is that of *horismos*, that is, the horizon, the boundary."[28] Distinctions and boundaries are inherent to the very structure of thought and to our use of symbols in thought.

The boundaries or margins define the center, and the center holds only so long as it organizes its margins. This is as true in politics and society as it is of ourselves. When the margins fail (and these can be the margins of a discrete realm of knowledge, a building, a species, metaphor, empire, or individual ego), the center's collapse is not long in coming. The somewhat paradoxical result of this insight is that we are constituted on our boundaries, that is, on a plane that we do not fully control. Our boundaries, precisely because they are boundaries, are the point of distinction: the point where self and other meet. The power of the center still organizes these edges, but they also open to something beyond the center's control—the other. This creates a vulnerability, but thus also the need to tolerate what is on and even beyond those margins.[29]

Marginal states and statuses are precisely what represent the identity of society and express the solidarity of the group as a whole. This gives margins or boundaries the potential to provide an ongoing challenge and critique to society and its received knowledge. Margins embody the skeptical consciousness that is necessary to a life meaningfully led with other people. Precisely this existence on the boundaries is what led Sigmund Freud to his concept of "the narcissism of the small difference." It is not the totally or far-off other who challenges me, my way of life, values, and goals. Instead it is the one who is similar but yet different—whose very difference thus constitutes a continuing critique of my way of being. These others are not so far removed from me as to preclude interaction and dialogue, but far enough distant to provide the crux of that definition and critique of self by other.

Yet, to have another patrol one's boundaries is inherently unstable; it involves a great expenditure of psychic energy to maintain. There is thus often a tendency to do away with the other who has such power over us. We see this all too often in the fate of minorities within majority cultures. Doing away with the other, either by elimination or by incorporation into ourselves is so tempting because it appears to allow us to patrol our own boundaries. Doing so, however, destroys the other who is necessary for the very constitution of self. It turns the other into a slave (to borrow loosely from Hegel) from whom no recognition is possible or worthwhile. The move to incorporate the other appears to grant us safety and control, but not recognition. Living with the reality of the other's control is thus fragile and uncertain. Having our own boundaries in the hands of an other presents us with a frightening situation: less than total control over our own constitutive terms of ordering, meaning, and integration. This danger leads to ritualization. Yet, ritual also allows us a way to mediate the danger and to transpose the constraints of external control into potential openings toward the other. Empathy, we argue, emerges from the very particular interpolation of boundaries that ritual affords.

All boundaries by definition impose constraints. They differentiate, limit, restrict, define, and break the flow of the continuities of the universe (of thought, emotion, sensuous perception, or physical reality). Such frames appear as givens in the world, imbued with the authority of the past. Yet, the future often brings new frames, and reorders what is in existing frames. That is precisely the inherent risk in the future and in future-directed action. The future represents as well the possibility for creativity, which is very much about breaking apart and reordering what is already framed in one particular way. Boundaries are reframed, limits are broached, constraints are torn down, clichés are unpacked, and new meanings emerge. This is always a risky business— but a necessary one, for individuals as well as for all systems, whether institutional or symbolic. Roles in the family can be rethought and reframed, as can the meaning of the Catholic Mass and the role of the church in the lives of the congregants. Both are creative processes, both risky, both bring pain to some and liberation to others. Both break with old constraints and impose new ones, unpack existing meanings and infuse new ones.

The openness of the future thus carries the potential to question existing categories and the boundaries through which they are constructed. Though given, boundaries are never uncontested, and the inherent open-ended nature of this contestation makes the negotiation of boundaries an endless project, part of the continuing human enterprise. Lasting social order rests on some integration of this future orientation (replete with its strong element of change and risk), with a perception of a shared past, of ties that limit, circumscribe, and define—and hence give meaning. Communities cannot be totally future-oriented affairs. An openness to the future—which is at its most basic an intergenerational one—always balances (to different degrees) commitments tied to a shared past. Clearly, the relative valence of each is different in different traditions. Christianity is, in these terms, more future-oriented than Judaism. A liberal capitalist social order is more future-oriented than a feudal one. But some mix is always present.

We would like to argue that this dual movement between past and future, this "playing" with the loss of boundaries but never totally succumbing to it, is similar to social empathy. Empathy rests on a temporary elision of self, a renunciation of ego's central place in its own symbolic universe, on a reframing of the boundaries of meaning, trust, and power. Ritual, with its movement between subjunctive worlds, is one way in which we accomplish this.

Thus when Marion Milner discusses the ability of ego to perceive the other as external object, she comes back again and again to the fusion of ego and object, to the loss of ego boundaries, that is, of boundaries between ego and object as one necessary stage in the development of such apperception. The very "confounding of one thing with another, this not discriminating, is also the basis of generalization," she says.[30] Critical to this process is the role of symbols, which act as mediums, intervening substances (transitional objects) that, in blurring boundaries between ego and object, make possible as well the eventual possibility to perceive object outside of ego. Symbols, as transitional objects, are the critical link that allows us to perceive the other, through a process of not quite incorporating the other within our internal space. Thus, the ability, says Milner, "to find the familiar in the unfamiliar, require[s] an ability to tolerate a temporary loss of sense of self, a temporary giving up of the discriminating ego which stands apart and tries to see things objectively and rationally."[31] Generalization—which is a necessary component of empathy— itself rests, as pointed out by Ernst Jones, on a prior failure to discriminate, a prior tendency to note identity in differences.[32] Again, boundaries are blurred and reconstituted.

Empathy, which rests on a decentered self, on an ability to generalize out beyond one's own experiences, thus implies a very particular attitude toward boundaries. Boundaries, while they must exist, must also be porous and less than fully discriminatory. That is, empathy must rest on the very type of duality between boundaries and their dissolution that we argue occurs in both ritual and play. The balance between continuity and creativity occurs through accepted conventions of movement across subjunctive boundaries, not through the denial of boundaries (and a concomitant ideal free of limits and constraints), nor through totalistic assumptions of self, other, and society.

This duality of boundaries—the need to recognize them but also recast them, to erect them but also cross them—bears on a further and central aspect of empathy: the ability of the human actor to construct shared, subjunctive universes within which their ties, bonds, desires, and obligations are projected (as we discussed in chapter 1 on the subjunctive and chapter 2 on ambiguity and the splitting of the ego).

As a way of further exploring the relations between ritual and empathy, and between erecting and crossing boundaries, let us start with some of the borders around both play and ritual. "Let the games begin" draws a clear, bold line around the Olympics. It is a classic performative—words that act—along the lines of "I now pronounce you man and wife." Throwing out the cere- monial first pitch at a baseball game accomplishes the same thing. Other games have much softer boundaries, as when a group of children at a picnic spontaneously evolve some game that resembles football, or when children playing imagined roles constantly break the frame to renegotiate ("I'm tired of being the robber all the time!" or just "Wait until I get back from the bath- room!"). Even at the most rule-bound extreme, though, play always takes us across a boundary into the play-world, and eventually back out again.

Similar crossings happen in all kinds of contexts beyond play. The cry of "Court is now in session" takes us across the boundaries into the judicial arena. Formal meetings work the same way: "I call this meeting to order," and "I hereby declare this meeting adjourned." In particularly formalized contexts, we further mark the crossings with noise. In these cases it is the bang of a gavel, in Chinese rituals it is fireworks, and at concerts it is applause. Rodney Needham noted this correlation between percussion and transition almost half a century ago but left it unexplained. [33] We suggest that this common use of percussive noise marks boundaries even better than formalized speech acts because the impossibility of reducing noise to discursive meaning meshes neatly with the act of moving between disjunctive subjunctive worlds. Noise (or sometimes words so formalized as to carry very little meaning at all) is an ideal marker of the moment when we are caught between discursive worlds.

Views of ritual as boundary definition and maintenance, as a reinforcer of hierarchy, are thus too simple. Even the rituals we have compared to agôn, those most concerned with rules and ranks, must transcend boundaries in order to take place, and must be willing to cross back over those boundaries at the end. As we have been arguing, purification rituals—which are agonistic in affirming social roles and maintaining self-control—are not really there to make us pure. True purity, a unity with the divine, would leave us with no need for ritual. Instead, purifications allow us to continue living in a broken world where real life is a series of difficult compromises, where pollution is inevitable. Purification is like brushing teeth in the sense that we do not expect them to stay brushed—living a human life means getting them dirty again. We just try to keep them from rotting completely away. The ordered beauties of the ritual world exist only because we cross into and back out of them. A true utopian, imagining an uncompromised world where we all stay pure, needs neither ritual (nor toothbrush) nor any form of crossing between subjunctive worlds. This crucial sense of boundary has been missing from much of the anthropological work on ritual, for instance, when Geertz sees ritual spectacle as the heart of the Balinese "theater-state." The rituals he describes indeed celebrate the glories of hierarchy above all else—they are pure agôn—but it is much more difficult to see them as the primary purpose of the state if we remember that they are circumscribed by their own boundaries. [34]

Gregory Bateson's innovative work on play is especially useful here because it leads us to concentrate on the frame itself, on the dual creation and crossing of boundaries that is so important for social life. [35] Saying "we are playing now" is not the same thing as playing. The statement marks the boundary, just as a frame does for a painting. It is what Bateson calls a meta-communicative act—a communication that tells us what kind of communication we are undertaking. As he points out, the act of play itself, even in nonhuman mammals, implies the ability to accept different communicative contexts—different subjunctives. How else would a young dog know whether to take a nip as play or battle? We use such signals constantly as we switch between worlds.

By realizing that switching into a new "as if" reality requires a signal of a different logical order, Bateson encouraged us to look at the frame itself, and not just at what happens within the frame of ritual or play. What is involved when we step on the clutch to change from one gear to another?[36] The suspension of disbelief required by our entrance into a subjunctive world always means accepting the social conventions that define how we get into and out of that world. In many cases, those conventions are clearly etched, defined by clear convention. We do not walk on the concert stage, even during intermission. We applaud after arias but not between movements. We are otherwise silent as long as the conductor stands on stage. When composers (artists, fullbacks, priests) challenge those conventions, as when John Cage wrote a piano piece consisting of four minutes and thirty-three seconds of silence, we tend to find it very difficult to cross the boundary. The silence that normally helps form the boundary around the beginning and end of the performance became the performance itself. The composition dissolved into its frame, in a way reminiscent of the tendency to deny all boundaries that we have discussed. The audience at the premiere was annoyed, and many walked out.[37]

Maurice Bloch makes a particularly strong case that ritual means accepting social convention and existing lines of authority.[38] For him, as we have mentioned, the utter formalization of ritual can do nothing more than reinforce traditional authority, and the only way to avoid acceding to the system is to refuse to take part at all. This observation recalls Caillois's claim that the spoilsport is far more of a threat to play than the cheat. The cheat works within the conventions of the game, but the spoilsport dismisses the entire exercise by refusing to enter the frame. Worse, the spoilsport shatters the "as if" world by denying its existence and insisting on the world "as is." Taken to extremes, the "spoilritual" can undermine crucial structures of society and mechanisms for dealing with others.

Mary Douglas makes a similar point, asking when talking about sexual organs or feces is funny and when it is instead obscene. What is the difference between a joke and an abomination? For her, the key is that an abomination denies basic categories of experience, and so threatens both reason and society. A joke instead "represents a temporary suspension of the social structure, or rather it makes a little disturbance in which the particular structuring of society becomes less relevant than another."[39] This was precisely the point recognized as well by Rose Coser in her study of laughter among the staff of a mental hospital. There she quoted Henri Bergson, approvingly, that "laughter corrects men's manners. It makes us at once endeavor to appear what we ought to be, what some day we perhaps end in being."[40] A joke, in other words, brings us briefly into a subjunctive world, and back out again. In contrast, an abomination is, like the spoilsport, rejecting all the rules. We recognize which one we are dealing with, says Douglas, by the power of the social conventions that define the genres: jokes mirror social forms, but obscenities reject them.

A view of ritual as highly bound by rules, controlled by authorities, and utterly inflexible is probably useful as an exercise in ideal types, but it ignores the vast penumbra of rituals that are not "agonistic." More than that, it ignores the boundary crossing that every ritual, every subjunctive, requires. We do not always cross over into the subjunctive world as a mechanical reaction to some conventional trigger. We can see this most clearly outside of ritual. We can, for instance, view art as wallpaper or wallpaper as art. The difference lies in whether we focus the mind on the object in a certain way, that is, whether we choose to view it "as if" it were art. This is quite a different way of crossing a subjunctive boundary from when the conductor steps on stage or the dean declares a meeting in session, thereby compelling us to change our behavior. Instead, we have a choice about whether and how to frame our viewing.

Informal and optional transitions like this are especially common in some kinds of play. Many children's games, as soon as they move away from the highly rule-bound pole of checkers or organized baseball, constantly cross in and out of the frame as the players renegotiate the rules and roles of the game. What exactly constitutes "moving" in a game of freeze tag? Can the robbers capture the cops? The game continually pauses and restarts as rules are invented or adjusted for the contingencies of the moment. This is just the kind of oscillation we saw in the previous chapter, with the father reading to his son. The extreme perhaps is the sort of card game where the older brother stops between almost every turn to explain ever more elaborate rules, until the younger sister eventually realizes that he is just inventing the entire thing on the spot for his own benefit. Adults also negotiate such informal boundary crossings in our own forms of play, when, for instance, we begin to spell out elaborate and impossible fantasies as if they were truths and then switch back to the world of ordinary honesty and dishonesty. We do this when we speak ironically and expect others to follow; we do it when we flirt. These more negotiable boundaries are very different from the clear and straight lines we usually imagine surrounding ritual. Nevertheless, these behaviors are still ritualized, as the cases of flirting and courtship clearly indicate. They are important indicators of how ritual allows us to play with boundaries, interpreting past and future in the formation of new modes of empathy. Ritual mediates boundaries even as it posits them.

Certainly ritual tends more toward the rule-bound, but there are two senses in which ritual is open to change, and in which its frames must always be negotiable. First, as we argued in chapter 1, all ritual has to deal with the contingencies of the world. No set of ritual rules (or legal rules, or any other kind) can ever be complete, no matter how much we elaborate on them. Jewish women in the ritual bath must not have any impediment, like clothing, that would block the purification. But what exactly is an impediment? Does food caught between the teeth count? What about a filling or a false tooth? Does a tear count? Is a dried tear different from a wet tear? There is no end to these issues, and any ritual in practice must find its compromises, as Jewish purification does for teeth and tears. What shall we do if the sacrificial white cock turns out to have a brown feather? There are all kinds of possibilities, from adding an extra prayer to just plucking the feather out, but in the end there is always some element of improvisation, and thus always some breaking in and out of the frame as the ritualist decides what to do.[41]

The second way in which rituals are open to renegotiation is when the rules themselves are changed, or even when new rituals are invented. There is little room for this in what we have called the agôn-like rituals, but we see more innovation especially where roles are less powerfully predetermined. Like adjusting the rules to the exigencies of real performance, this also requires metacommunication—stepping outside the ritual, however briefly, to reconsider it. Let us give a few quick examples, all touching on the more open-ended categories of ritual beyond *agôn*.

First, many Daoists write magic talismans (*fu*) almost every day for clients suffering from some kind of illness. This is votive ritual of a sort, where the charm has a ritual structure of its own, but the empirical result is not known in advance. In one case, a Daoist asked one of us to check up on his patients. He explained that if patients got better, they usually did not come back. And of course they did not come back if they got worse either. With no feedback of his own, he wanted a researcher to find out which of his charms worked best. When asked what he would do if he found out a charm did not work well, he said he would change it. The kind of innovation possible can be seen in figure 3-3, which shows a sort of postmodern talisman (written by a different Daoist) created by cutting a charm in half vertically and pasting the two halves on either side of a second charm. Such a thing is possible thanks to the photocopying machine. The charm within a charm contains its own broken frame—visual evidence of its maker's creative reframing—boundaries are broken and created at the same time.

Finally, much ritual innovation around the world has origins in *ilinx*-style rituals, where direct divine inspiration lends itself to new creations. The New

FIGURE 3-3. Innovative Daoist charm (Taiwan, 1978, collection of Robert P. Weller).

Guinea taro cult, for example, introduced new gardening rituals, featuring songs filled with "foreign" words.[42] The Taiping Rebellion, which we mentioned earlier, also innovated rituals based on the statements of mediums, like congregational worship at flag-raising ceremonies.[43]

Cell Walls and Brick Walls

All of this suggests that crossing into a new subjunctive space may be more complex than just stepping over a line, and that the nature of the boundary itself is worth a closer look. Such boundaries, after all, are key to the understanding of self and other, and to the ways that groups identify with and separate from each other. Even boundaries that look like simple lines may not always work that way. We may, for instance, frame the beginning of our classes—a transition from the less formal register of chatting or looking at notes to a more formal one where students are silent and at least apparently attentive, and where the professor holds power over any interactions—by saying something like "Let's get started." There is nothing more frustrating, though, than saying those performative words and having them get lost in the general babble. Professors thus face the problem of how to let the class know that they are about to cross the boundary, of how to frame the frame. Usually we do this by waiting for silence before beginning. Yet the problem just recedes...how do we make people fall silent? In this case the answer is usually positional. We walk up to the podium, for instance, from some other place. Even this very simple and everyday transition can thus easily have many layers surrounding it, with position framing the silence, which frames the performative announcement, which frames the lecture itself. In principle, these frames could recede forever. In practice, however, they do not, because we have a prior social understanding of what counts as a boundary, and of the proper contexts for crossing it.

On the other hand, the cases of ritual change remind us that metacommunicative work must take place even during the course of a ritual, as we adjust it to the contingencies of any particular performance. Our image of a boundary should be more like a cell wall than a brick wall. That is, it must be possible to send certain kinds of signals across the boundary, even as it remains impermeable to others. The ability to step out of a context and then back in again is crucial to both ritual and play, and ultimately to empathy. We can deal with other people only by creating a boundary between self and other, and then by being willing to cross it. Bridging the gap between subjunctive worlds always requires the ability to create a certain ironic distance that allows us to recognize and enter the "as if." The same sense of distance, the ability to meta-communicate, also encourages us to toy with the boundaries themselves.

Umberto Eco's discussion of the comic reveals some of the difference between boundaries as cell walls and as brick walls. Attempting to reconstruct an Aristotelian definition, Eco sees the comic as the violation of an unstated rule (usually a minor one) by an unsympathetic and animal-like character, allowing us to enjoy both the rule breaking and the humiliation of the character. Thus he writes that the "comic is always racist: only the others, the Barbarians are supposed to pay."[44] The boundary between us and the other is impermeable in this version of the comic, and there is no opening for empathy, that most fundamental way of crossing a boundary. Eco distinguishes this sort of comedy from what he calls "humor" or "irony," in which we sympathize with the ridiculous character, laughing at him but also sharing his plight and becoming aware of the structures that create it. When we read Cervantes, we do not just laugh at Don Quixote's foolishness, but through him we begin to question the nature of society itself. "Humor is always . . . metasemiotic: through verbal language or some other sign system it casts in doubt other cultural codes."[45] Here is probably the most significant similarity between play and ritual. By taking us across boundaries, both make us aware of the structures within which we live—not just by reinforcing them but by allowing us to step above them for a moment, to see how and why we have constructed them, before stepping back inside them.

Tickling is a convenient metaphor for this play with the frame itself. Tickling is a clear form of *ilinx*, but one that plays primarily with personal boundaries between self and other, my skin and your fingertip, never quite penetrating and never quite withdrawing, flirting with the edge of sensation. Tickling the boundary can be more or less explicit in ritual, as in play, but the possibility is always there.

We can often see this role visually by looking at ornament in architecture or textiles. Ornament tends to occur just at the boundaries—doorways, rooflines, hems, collars, seams of all kinds. The repeating abstractions that occupy such spaces, even something as simple as dentil molding, elaborate the boundary through their infinite repetition, like ritual itself. They avoid the boundary as a simple line, embroidering on their mediation between either side. Ornaments also often create an ironic self-consciousness by referring back to earlier ornaments, as when postmodern architects use exaggerated roof ornaments that recall nineteenth-century neoclassicism, which recalled the Renaissance, which recalled Greece, and so on (see figure 3-4).[46] We will return to this in chapter 5.

When Radcliffe-Brown published one of the first anthropological studies of ritualized joking, where people in certain relationships are required to tease

FIGURE 3-4. Harold Washington Library, Chicago (ornamentation designed by Kent Bloomer, photo by Andrew Stott, with permission).

each other, he saw it as exactly this kind of boundary play.[47] In this case he argued that joking relationships occur when people must simultaneously transcend and maintain boundaries, for instance, with members of an allied clan or with their in-laws. When the boundary is absent (as with siblings) or total (as with enemies), jokes are unnecessary. Jokes tickle the boundary.

In many places around the world, humor also plays an important role within funeral ritual. Funerals in northern Taiwan, for instance, include a period when a ritual specialist, dressed in Buddhist robes, performs elaborate and esoteric mudras to help the dead soul through the underworld. At the same time, he keeps up a steady monologue of jokes at the expense of both the dead person and the society around him—certainly not excluding visiting anthropologists. A small audience watches and laughs. Later on the day of the burial, the entire troupe of ritual specialists will save the soul from the perils of the underworld by acting out its escape from various tortures through a combination of acrobatic prowess and skillful petitioning of spirit officials. A large audience of relatives and neighbors watches for the pure entertainment value as the ritual experts turn somersaults, eat fire, and tell more jokes.

We could certainly see this as part of a broad dramatic ordering of the mourners' emotions over the course of a day that begins with wailing over the coffin and ends in quiet contemplation. Yet, following Mary Douglas's work on Africa, where we also find funerary joking, this appears as part of a more general pattern where jokes tickle the boundary between life and death, permanence and dissolution, cosmological universals and human particulars. She writes that "by the path of ritual joking these African cultures too have reached a philosophy of the absurd. By revealing the arbitrary, provisional nature of the very categories of thought, by lifting their pressure for a moment and suggesting other ways of structuring reality, the joke rite in the middle of the sacred moments of religion hints at unfathomable mysteries."[48]

As an example, Margaret Thompson Drewal described a masked dance performance that occurred as part of a Yoruba funeral.[49] Several of the masked figures depicted and ridiculed foreign groups living among the Yoruba. One was dressed as a Hausa meat seller with fingers and teeth red from the raw meat he had been nibbling on the side. A lumbering Dahomean warrior followed, with boils on his face. Still another satirized the Bariba, another northern neighboring group. All this is comedy, in Eco's pejorative sense. In this case, however, the wife of the dead man added another layer of meaning by improvising her own dance—boisterous, teasing, obscene, and generally scene stealing—although she was not part of this masking troupe. As Drewal says, "She effectively subverted the comic discourse on foreigners, creating another one on top. Playing the situation, she transformed . . . an undesirable foreigner into an ironic object of her own desire."[50] In a ritual tradition that Drewal describes as particularly open to play and improvisation, comedy became irony, and the ritual was reframed. To rephrase her case a bit, the intolerance of the comic was replaced by the pluralism of the ironic.

This ability to play with and elaborate frames is inherent to any form that both recognizes boundaries and crosses over them, as any pluralism must. It is implied by the metacommunication that changing frames requires. Ritual epitomizes this kind of situation, although the literature in anthropology and religion has tended to pay little attention to such boundary play.[51] After all, even the liminal period in rites of passage could be seen as a sort of play at the boundary between the stages of child and adult, bachelor and husband, or commoner and knight. So also are the entrepreneurial ritual changes we see all around us, from insisting that only free-range chickens are kosher to Hindu priests blessing trucks.[52] Games and rituals encourage us to explore boundaries by accepting both their social reality and our ability to penetrate them.

The ability to recognize and toy with boundaries is crucial to human society. Metaphors, for instance, simultaneously accept and transgress the boundaries of the words that make them up. They are crucial to the human imagination but also constitute much of our ordinary speech.[53] Poetry relies on us being able to read between the words, as diplomacy requires us to read between the lines.

Subjunctive worlds and the boundary play they require have much broader consequences, though, than just opening the imagination. At the level of individuals, the potential space of the shared subjunctive is crucial to our ability to empathize, and hence to our potential to develop trust and solidarity. Viewing a Greek tragedy, for example, was supposed to broaden our empathy, to expand our hearts by allowing us to enter the shared space of the mimicry.[54] Sitting in the audience thus became as much a part of the mimicry as acting a role. The "as if" of the tragedy lets it apply as much to us as to the characters on stage. Empathy requires accepting the structures and boundaries of the "as if" space. It is not possible if we either deny all boundaries or if it cannot penetrate the boundary of the self.

We can share all kinds of things in the world—subways, soccer teams, grocery stores, fear of the police—without ever coming together as a moral community, much less accepting the existence of other moral communities. Moral communities require sharing empathy, not just spaces, times, and objects. We share empathy (what the classical sociological literature calls trust) only when we share the potential space of the subjunctive, and when we recognize that its boundaries can be crossed. Just by showing that other worlds exist, rituals may well offer us an image of a society with room for an other. If we somehow removed such subjunctive worlds, it is difficult to see where we would find the grounds for either empathy or pluralism. Certain forms of mimicry, like serious drama or serious comedy, can be experienced or interpreted either as enhancing empathy or as sharpening differences. The history of interpretation of plays about war, such as Shakespeare's *Henry V*, shows how they can be seen as showing the humanity of the enemy or demonstrating his complete "otherness" from us.

Not Playing

Not all ritual invites as much play as the Yoruba funeral, but the possibility is always there. Much ritual includes—even requires—a sense of synesthetic fun that academic analyses of ritual have tended to downplay. Ironic dances at the center of African funerals or the Chinese insistence that community temple ritual be loud, colorful, and boisterous (*renao*, literally "hot and bothered") surprise us perhaps only due to the post-Protestant assumptions of our understandings of ritual. Our intellectual technology for understanding ritual, after all, developed at a time when dominant religious traditions have downplayed much ritual in favor of the idea that what really matters is our internal state, not mere external convention. We will take this up in detail in the following chapter, but for now let us take a brief look at the dangers of losing the sense of play—the ability to recognize and negotiate boundaries—that both rituals and games require.

The ability to play with boundaries disappears under two circumstances. First, playfulness dies when social boundaries are denied. Individuals become private, atomized selves, each identical in its core characteristics, and everyone merges into a great mass. This is roughly the contemporary image of a market society.[55] Bakhtin points out how this process denuded the representational function of games over the past 200 years: "Having been absorbed by the sphere of private life, the images of games lost their universal relationship and were deprived of the meaning they formerly conveyed. The Romanticists sought to restore these images in literature . . . but they understood them subjectively, within the structure of personal destinies."[56] This is part of the triumph of the modern, individual trope and of the primacy of internal reality. Today, it is often this atomized individual who imagines that there is only one possible world—a world *as is* instead of one of the multiple *as if* worlds that ritual allows.

Second, and just as deadly to the sense of play, is when boundaries become impossible to cross, when a single moral community becomes the only acceptable community, when the cell wall becomes a brick wall. Either way there is no more movement into and out of a subjunctive world. We have only the world "as is." This leaves no significant room for ritual, or even for games. We can watch them deteriorate for all four of our classes of games and rituals when boundaries freeze up or become invisible. With games the collapse happens so often and easily that we have all seen it; with ritual such events are unusual, and the consequences can be severe. We have suggested in the previous chapter that severe trauma can constrict or even destroy the child's capacity to play, that the play ensuing from traumatic events tends to be more rigid, less imaginative, and more stereotyped. "Playfulness" is restored when more flexibility appears in the child's play.

Agonistic games can collapse when they are no longer "as if," that is, when the competition overflows the boundaries of the game—hockey players who punch each other bloody, soccer hooligans who attack the fans who surround them and the cities that host them, chess players who sweep the pieces to the floor in angry frustration. In each of these cases the antagonism of the game spills over into other kinds of interaction. Often we try to patch this back up by resurrecting the boundaries of the subjunctive. "It's only a game," we say, and hope for the best as the participants go off to tend their bruises. As the close ties between ritual and play show, however, it is never *only* a game. Social life depends on the ability to change frames, to enter subjunctive worlds, and to recognize and cross boundaries.

Like agonistic games, some rituals reaffirm conventional roles and leave the self in control. The sense of boundaries is very strong, unlike the open-endedness of votive ritual or the unpredictability of spirit possession, although the sense of competition that defines agonistic games need not be present at all. These rituals occur in a kind of pure subjunctive, and it is hard to imagine them at all without boundaries that can be crossed. And indeed they disappear in moments of utopianism, when all boundaries seem to dissolve. What use are food taboos if we live in a world that is not inherently polluting, if it is not broken but complete? What is the need for sacrifice as a way of communicating with the divine if the divine already exists within us? Buddhism thus removed the Hindu sacrifices because the Buddha-nature is inherent in every individual, just as Protestants moved away from Catholic sacrifice because each follower needed to take God directly into her own heart without intermediation. This is why utopian movements so often also tend to be antinomian, denouncing all conventional rules.

In *alea* the boundaries are weaker to begin with, because the end result is usually measured outside the ritual itself. They begin to break down, for example, when diviners (or poker players) are accused of manipulating the results for profit, or when Chinese worshipers throw a god image in a river for failing to grant a wish. Charismatic movements wreak the greatest havoc when they completely dissolve the boundary of the subjunctive world. People die when, like utopians, they try to force their particular "as if" world onto every world. The Taiping Rebellion ended in a horror of massive casualties and interior decimation because Jesus' brother dissolved the boundary between subjunctive and indicative, and because he created another line that could not be crossed, between his followers and the "imps and devils" who could only be slaughtered.

Even mimicry can end badly when it exceeds its proper boundaries. Take, for example, the story of the Scythian king Scyles, as Herodotus relates it in book IV of his *History*.[57] King Scyles loved Greek ways and would sometimes leave his army in the suburbs of the city of Borysthenes. He would enter the city alone and change into Greek clothes, walk around the market, and even make offerings to gods following the Greek rituals. He left his bodyguards at the gates to make sure that no Scythian would see him, and would stay as long as a month at a time. Eventually he even built a house, took a local wife, and was initiated into the Bacchic Dionysian rites. Disaster struck, however, when the locals taunted the Scythians, who looked down on their Dionysian rites, by bragging that their own Scythian king was a participant. The Scythians then saw their king in his Bacchic frenzy and angrily described the scene to the army. A rebellion followed, finally enthroning Scyles' brother, who beheaded his too-Greek sibling.

King Scyles here overstepped the bounds of play itself. A Scythian king must act *as if* he were a Scythian king. This might include studying Greek houses but not moving into them, admiring Greek women but not marrying them, and knowing Greek gods but absolutely not losing his very self to them. Mimicking the Greeks would have been fine, but adopting their essence by living in Greek space, creating Greek kinsmen, and perhaps worst of all, worshiping like a Greek could not be borne. Scyles was doomed when what should have been play became ritual. Worse still, the most damning rituals were his participation in frenzied *ilinx*, where he gave up his self. Rather than playing with the boundary between Scythian and Greek, self and other, Scyles tried to pretend there was no boundary, and lost his head.

Ritual mimicries like Carnival could also occasionally burst their boundaries. This almost inevitably happened on the small scale of drunken vandalism, petty theft, and fistfights, as we have mentioned. Yet the possibility of full-scale riot or even insurrection always loomed, as in the case Ladurie documented in Roman in 1580, where Carnival became rebellion.[58] That lead container around Turner's "radioactive" *communitas* experience could break down, as masquers became marauders, or pilgrimage became Crusade. In many of these cases we can see a move toward *ilinx* on the way to chaos. This is no surprise, since *ilinx* is the category that least recognizes boundaries—it dissolves both externally created roles and the self. Anything can happen with *ilinx*, and that is a recipe for disaster as much as for creativity.

We began this chapter by comparing ritual and games to create a simple classification scheme based around two kinds of boundaries: the self and its ability to control action, and roles as defined by social convention. Each of the four categories shows a different kind of subjunctive world, with different relations to boundaries. While boundaries are especially clear in agôn, the realm of many prototypical rituals, all the categories address them. As we have seen, it is not enough to say that such rituals require or reinforce boundaries, or even that they create the boundaries. Even more important, they tell us how to negotiate across boundaries in different ways, in part because undertaking a game or a ritual itself requires crossing a boundary into a subjunctive world. Ritual teaches us that boundaries are both conventional and necessary, whether we think of the convention as God's creation (like Jews) or as ours (like early Confucians). This same ability to step outside of a world and see its boundaries for what they are also encourages us to play with them and explore their fractal complexities. Losing that sense of play—by denying that boundaries can be crossed or by denying that they exist at all—undercuts all ritual, and perhaps society itself.

If we are right, then periods of reaction against ritual may pose a unique set of social problems. Such reactions have occurred throughout history, but modernity in general has brought us into a particularly long and powerful such period. With the current emphasis on sincerity over "mere" convention, on internal states over outward behavior, the problem of boundaries no longer has a clear solution. We explore this dynamic of ritual and sincerity in the next chapter.

4

Ritual and Sincerity

This chapter explores how ritual as a mode of thought and practice relates to a second, typically antiritualistic mode, which we call "sincerity." As we have seen, in ritual we subject ourselves to externally given categories of order. These categories can be rooted in anything from a transcendent deity (as in Judaism) to the ordering of the physical and social world (as in Confucianism). The performative nature of ritual is typically more important than its denotative meaning. That is why its formal qualities tend toward repetition and nondiscursive media like incense smoke, spirit masks, or half-heard chants in unknown languages.

Sincerity often grows out of a reaction against ritual. It criticizes ritual's acceptance of social convention as mere action (perhaps even just acting) without intent, as performance without belief. The alternatives it often suggests are categories that grow out of individual soul-searching rather than the acceptance of social conventions. Sincerity thus grows out of abstract and generalized categories generated within individual consciousness. The sincere mode of behavior seeks to replace the "mere convention" of ritual with a genuine and thoughtful state of internal conviction. Rather than becoming what we do in action through ritual, we do according to what we have become through self-examination. This form of thought emphasizes tropes of "authenticity," and each individual thus takes on an enormous responsibility.

A life of pure ritual or pure sincerity would be absurd. Both modes of thought coexist in all of us, though not without tension. From the point of view of sincerity, ritual is mere hypocrisy and convention. Viewed from ritual, however, sincerity can threaten the very existence of society by refusing its conventions. Though the tension between the two usually remains under control, it can also lead to shifts in the balance between ritual and sincerity, as nearly any of the world's religious traditions shows: the Buddhist critique of Hinduism, Christian critique of Judaism, Wang Yangming's critique of neo-Confucianism, and so forth. As these examples also imply, reform movements based on sincerity tend to be tamed over time with new creations of ritual (as the Catholic Church illustrates), just as highly ritualized historical moments tend to be challenged by sincerity (as in the Reformation). Extreme forms of sincerity discourage all ritual-like behavior, all subjunctives—not just ritualized religious practice but music, adult play, dance, even humor.

These theoretical considerations lead us to explore here the idea that ritual and sincerity offer alternative modes of framing social thought, action, and interaction. Furthermore, the "balance" between them and differentiation of realms that each addresses in society have critical consequences for the ways that individuals experience the world and, significantly, for civil order.

The Terms of Sincerity

Lionel Trilling begins his famous study *Sincerity and Authenticity* by quoting some of the best-known testaments to the sincere mode of thought. He includes Polonius's speech to Laertes, "This above all: to thine own self be true" and Matthew Arnold's dictum on "the central stream of what we feel indeed" (as opposed to what we merely say we feel). He goes on to quote Schiller on the harmonious unity of each man's human ideal and discusses the central role of Puritan "plain sermons" on the developing idea of sincerity in our tradition.[1]

Indeed, the Calvinist influence goes well beyond its sermon form, for the widespread practice of diary keeping and spiritual soul-searching—the search to find the workings of grace in one's soul—was a central aspect of Puritan religiosity. It presupposed a self that could be fully grasped, a whole and complete inner state that could be judged for what it was: saved or damned, regenerate or unregenerate.[2] The spiritual writings of Puritan divines take us on a trip inward, on a search for the self that, given the very length of these works, puts paid the notion that such a search for the sincere inner man can be easily completed. Lacking any external referents, any anchors in the world outside the self, such an inward search for sincerity is truly never-ending. It is sincerity all the way down, which means, ironically, the never-ending search, all the way down, for the sincere.

Civilizations or movements with a diminished concern for ritual have an overwhelming concern with sincerity, which we can see in forms as widely varied as those Puritan sermons and the Buddhist concern with uncovering the Buddha nature hidden within each of us. In some sense, then, sincerity works as the social equivalent of the subjunctive, which we discussed earlier. If there is no ritual, there is no shared convention that indexes a possible shared world. Instead, social relationships have to rely on a never-ending production of new signs of sincerity (though of course there can be ritualized forms of the search for sincerity).

We have seen how the subjunctive mode constituted a shared reality, a world that allowed the projection of a shared future through stories of a common past. A community of fate shares a past and is thus destined to share a future as well. Fate straddles both past and future. Without such a shared subjunctive space, without a common origin in a pre-given and authoritative reality (authoritative precisely because it is assented to collectively), individuals must project alternative sets of bonds to connect to each other. If we are not bound by a shared subjunctive, we can only be bound by the depths of our own sincerity. Sincerity of feeling comes to replace the subjunctive world of shared "illusion" as the new ground of personal commitment and interpersonal bonding. The establishment of a stable and unquestionable *as is*, rather than a common *as if*, becomes the projected basis for the intersubjective world.

We have been arguing that we can model two ideal typical forms of intersubjective behavior and attitude that correspond to two rather different modes of social existence and interaction. Unlike ritual, the sincere form is characterized by a search for motives and for purity of motives, reminiscent of Immanuel Kant's privileging of the purity of the moral will. Sincerity morally privileges intent over action. This concern with intent has become the touchstone of much of our moral reasoning, for instance, in Kant's writings on the workings of the "good will."[3] As Kant stresses: "The good will is not good because of what it effects or accomplishes or because of its adequacy to achieve some proposed end; it is good only because of its willing, i.e. because it is good of itself."[4] Thomas Nagel and Bernard Williams cogently delineated the limits of this view by showing the insufficiency of a morality that totally eschews consequences and the external world of action in making moral calculations. As Nagel clarified: "However jewel-like the good will may be in its own right there is a morally significant difference between rescuing someone from a burning building and dropping him from a twelfth story window while trying to rescue him."[5] Nonetheless, from the Puritans of the seventeenth century to the talk shows of the twenty-first, a concern with the inner wellsprings of action and sincerity has become almost an icon of modernist culture.

The need to establish society and morality on the basis of sincerity, though, runs into a deep problem. How can we express true sincerity except by filtering it through the social conventions of language? How are we to know if people's professions of sincerity are genuine or just acts of hypocrisy, representations of their true self or just what they would say "as if" they were sincere? Worse still, even our own private thoughts can work only through language, and thus can never fully reveal our innermost sincerity (or lack of it). We can accumulate great quantities of discourse, but never dispel the suspicion—even within our own minds—that it is all just artifice. This is why the Puritans produced such an enormous quantity of written self-examination, like Cotton Mather's famous autobiographical writings. It is just as evident in our teenage children's endless concern with establishing the truth of feelings—their own and those of their peers. The Calvinist's "Am I really saved?" and the teenager's "Am I really in love?" are at heart similar kinds of questions. After three decades of marriage, kids, laundry, mortgages, funerals, fights, and in-laws, the relationship tends to be sustained by a shared "as if" rather than a continued "as is." Relationships that fail to construct a shared subjunctive over the long term tend to fall apart. It is not enough to love each other sincerely if people fail to act as if they love each other; and acting as if they love each other includes ritualized forms of expressing concern, verbally and in concrete deeds of helpfulness.

Antiritualist attitudes deny the value to this subjunctive of play, convention, and illusion. They seek to root interaction in some attestation to the sincerity of the interlocutors. If our love for each other is registered only in what we say, then we are caught in the perennial chasm between the words (of love) and the love itself. The words are but signifiers, arbitrary and by necessity at one remove from the event they signify. Hence the attempt to express love in words is endless, as it can never finally prove its own sincerity. Ritual, by contrast, is repeated and unchanging, a form of practical wisdom (what the Greeks called *phronesis*) rather than symbolization. We can in the end distinguish two forms of the words "I love you." The emotionally wrought confession by the starstruck young man appeals to the sincere mode. Of course, like all the language of sincerity, we have doubts—perhaps he is just trying to get her into bed. Or perhaps he is indeed sincere and, having established this "as is" of his love, will never feel the need to say those words again, even through decades of marriage. He may also fail to say those words ever again because he is not sincerely experiencing the same kind of love as when he first "fell in love."[6] On the other hand, we also have the ritual "I love you," whose performative aspect is more important than its denotative function. This is why one can repeat it for years and years to the same person. In so doing, one is not adding any bit of hitherto unknown information, but instead acting out a ritual, rather in the manner of a prayer.

In the continual search to renew the "authentic" sources of sincerity, there is little room for ambiguity. All ambivalence and ambiguity threatens the attempt to arrive at the "true" self. That true self can of course be very different in different times and historical periods. But in each case, sincerity tries to resolve all ambiguity to forge a "pure" and "unsullied" consciousness. Fifty years ago in Russia or China it was the search for a "true" revolutionary consciousness. In the mid-nineteenth-century springtime of the peoples it was to be at one with the spirit of one's folk, as exemplified in the epic poetry of Adam Mickiewicz in Poland or the Russian orientalist music of Glinka or Borodin. The particular model of the "true" self may change, but the dynamic of ascertaining its presence is everywhere similar. This is a dynamic that leaves little room for ambiguity, for mixed motives, and for the complexity and contradictory character of most human striving.

Sartre's characters as depicted in his *Iron in the Soul* illustrate these contrasting ideals well by showing the attraction of the workers' movement in Paris before the outbreak of the Second World War along with the self-loathing of those who could not master such unidirectional sense of self-purpose.[7] Variants of this occur in the literature of all peoples and epochs. In this context we can recall how Puritan rule in England was followed by a Restoration comedy—a ritualized, playful, illusionary antidote to the rigors of Calvinist sincerity. Pascal's Jansenist strictures against the theater also remind us of the grave difficulties of the sincere approach: "All great amusements are dangerous to the Christian life; but among all those which the world has invented there is none more to be feared than the theatre. . . . [W]e make ourselves a conscience founded on the propriety of the feelings which we see there, by which the fear of pure souls is removed."[8]

The drive to be at one with oneself and with the world, Polonius's model of the true self, in fact plays false with the reality of existence. A measure of hypocrisy complements any notion of a true self because we can never fully express an inner being and because any social interaction is mediated by language and other conventions. Shakespeare apparently shared some of this assessment, as we can see from the character of Polonius, in whose mouth Shakespeare puts those lines about "to thine own self be true." He is after all a meddlesome buffoon, not above lying and spying on his betters, full of bombast and self-importance and deceit: a model hypocrite, except for his great capacity for self-deception.

In many cases—in life as in literature—the almost childlike fascination with authenticity, with uncovering the "real" motives for action, the "uncorrupted" fount of feeling or the "pure" state of experience gives way over time. It evolves into a much more somber and realistic vision of just how complicated, contradictory, and ambiguous the sources of action, feeling, and intent really are. Going one step further, true understanding and creative growth ultimately occur only by coming to grips with this rather unromantic and severely compromised nature of our lives. Single-minded adherence to the "sincere" model of existence in the world does not allow for this realization. It results in a continual production of a hypocritical consciousness that holds up as a model a deeply compromised, narcissistic, and unrealizable ideal. It adheres to a vision of wholeness that is not of this world and is lost with the very earliest stages of differentiation.

Totalizing Boundaries and Overcoming Them

Cognition continually establishes boundaries between entities. It disaggregates the world and defines its component parts. The ability to distinguish between discrete objects, temporal events, and spatially positioned units, which ties to the human reliance on language, forms a fundamental aspect of our way of knowing the world. Such distinctions—and the need for such distinctions—exist in the social world as well. We must distinguish between different social roles and types of relationships. We mark the sets of responsibilities and obligations to each, to keep track of our complex and multilayered relationships to a myriad of others, whether within kinship units or civil society—or, for that matter, increasingly in a global world order. On the simplest level we achieve this by distinguishing between roles and role obligations (cousins are not brothers, fathers are not uncles, students are not appropriate sexual partners, fellow citizens are not slaves, and members of our golf club should not be predatory targets). This uniquely human capacity, advanced through our linguistic competence, lies in our ability to maintain this knowledge over almost infinitely complex networks of role relationships.[9]

On the most fundamental level, the ordering of social life requires us to make distinctions, to posit differentiations, and, in the most elemental way, to separate out the different units of our social world. Social order, as all order, rests on distinctions and on separation. Logically, the separation of different units requires the positing and maintenance of boundaries between them. It is not mere coincidence that the creation myths of different peoples typically begin with a process of differentiation, whether in the book of Genesis or Hesiod's *Theogony* or the Akkadian *Enuma Elish*. They also go on to show how a concomitant process of dedifferentiation threatens the newly divided world, as with Chronos swallowing his children or the stories of the Flood, both Babylonian and biblical.[10] Differentiation and hence order are won only at great cost and sacrifice and maintained with great effort and wisdom.

Much of the work of culture—precisely the repressive capacities of civilization that Freud made so much of, the cause of our discontent—is bound up with this process of differentiation.[11] Freud speaks of violence and sexuality as the two primary instincts that must be channeled—directed into differentially specified and civilizationally approved venues. In other words, violence and sex are bound to certain roles and role obligations and removed from others. The yearning to go beyond order and its repressive, differentiating demands, however, is always present. Different disciplines and different thinkers have approached this yearning differently, but something similar is at the core of Freud's idea of the polymorphous perverse, Émile Durkheim's idea of the effervescence of the sacred, Max Weber's idea of pure charisma, and Victor Turner's concept of *communitas*.[12] All register the strong pull, from which we are never totally weaned (and the image of infant narcissism is not irrelevant here) to get beyond the distinctions and differentiations of social order. We must forever posit boundaries, even as we deeply desire to abrogate them (at least partially, symbolically, and within contexts that can "contain" the effects of such abrogation).

Following Owen Barfield, we can trace this tension in the very workings of language and of the poetic:

> In the whole development of consciousness, therefore, we can trace the operation of two opposing principles, or forces. First, there is the force by which . . . single meanings tend to split up into a number of separate and often isolated concepts. . . . The second principle . . . is the principle of living unity. Considered subjectively, it observes the resemblances between things, whereas the first principle marks the differences, it is interested in knowing what things are, whereas the first discerns what they are not. Accordingly, at a later stage in the evolution of consciousness, we find it operative in individual poets, enabling them to intuit relationships which their fellows have forgotten—relationships which they must *now* express as metaphor. Reality, once self-evident, and therefore not conceptually experienced, but which can *now* only be reached by an effort of the individual mind—this is what is contained in a true poetic metaphor; and every metaphor is true only in so far as it contains such a reality, or hints at it. The world, like Dionysus, is torn to pieces by pure intellect; but

the poet Zeus, he has swallowed the heart of the world, and he can reproduce it as a living body.[13]

Barfield is drawing our attention here to two separate but interconnected phenomena. The first is the dual tendency of consciousness to seek both differentiation and unity, disaggregation and reaggregation, separateness and totality. Many have remarked on this aspect of human cognition and emotion (akin to Freud's Eros and Thanatos, the love and death instincts), and it also forms part of the philosophical study of symbols and symbol systems.

The other insight Barfield brings to our attention is that cognition itself implies the loss of a unity that exists only when that unity is experienced in a "self-evident" manner. This is just as true for all forms of communicative competency, and hence for the institutionalization of any system of ordered rules and regulations. Unity is lost as soon as we conceptualize reality, only to be reclaimed through poetic metaphor. As Ernst Cassirer noted, "The One Being eludes cognition. The more its metaphysical unity as a 'thing in itself' is asserted the more it evades all possibility of knowledge until at last it is relegated entirely to the sphere of the unknowable and becomes merely an X."[14] Or Laozi: "The Way that can be spoken of is not the eternal Way."[15] Communication, social order, and the organization of experience require differentiation, hence boundaries between entities, and hence too the loss of unity. The search to reclaim unity or totality that Barfield finds in metaphor (which has the important caveat that it knows itself to be but a facsimile of totality) can be found in other phenomena as well. This search to dissolve boundaries and so realize an order of totality beyond all distinctions lies at the core of many different forms of social action that are not characterized by this reflective knowledge of their own limitations.

The challenge of reaggregating a differentiated universe, of the search for wholeness and totality, involves erasing the boundaries that constitute any given, real empirical order. We seem incapable of ridding ourselves of this search, either individually or collectively, even though the real, historical attempts to return to wholeness and unity have been fraught with horror and destruction. In the end the boundaries and distinctions make life possible. They define, and hence permit, the separate existence of individual entities, and they are intimately bound up with ritual, as we have argued throughout this book. There is no escape from this world of differentiation, no matter how painful we find its inherent artifice, and in spite of the continual search for such an escape. It is no coincidence that Freud's *Beyond the Pleasure Principle* identifies this urge to escape with Thanatos, the urge to destruction, that is, a return of life to an inanimate, inorganic state.

Historically, this tension has sometimes been expressed as the quest for utopia, for the overcoming of all order—that is, of all boundaries. The idea of utopia is as old as civilization itself, and all civilizations have partially institutionalized it. Clearly, then, we have at best an ambivalent attitude toward boundaries. We need them to exist collectively and individually, but we continually strain against them. Perhaps it is this strain that has led philosophers and religious thinkers, such as Martin Buber[16] and Paul Tillich, to claim that utopia is "rooted in the nature of man himself."[17]

The utopian impetus is rooted in an underlying vision of the ideal and perfect society—whole and untainted—posited in contrast to the fractured and imperfect reality of human existence. There are utopias past—Garden of Eden, Hesiod's Golden Age, and individuals' fantasized blissful childhood—and there are utopias yet to be. The former involve some divinely organized and ordained realm of bliss, but even then, there are rules and constraints, and the reigning deity or deities must not be ruffled. The utopia to be created involves both the perfect realization of all rules and the boundary-defining laws of order, even as it proposes a world where boundaries would be meaningless. In a sense it posits an order beyond order. This idea unites the different modes of utopian thought, which extended not only back in time to Plato and earlier Greek literature but beyond the Western tradition, to include Japanese, Chinese, and Indian thought.[18]

We can understand utopian orientations very much along the lines developed by Karl Mannheim, as a state of mind embodied in actual conduct seeking "to burst the bounds of an existent order."[19] The utopian propensity embodies a "rage for order," an "impetus to save the world from as much confusion and disorder as possible."[20] And the "rage" may well entail violence in setting up the conditions deemed necessary for the utopia. Such a utopia always needs a kind of "specialist," or "professional," some kind of purist, who has the knowledge, the power, and the means of coercion. The need to order combines with the desire to overcome all boundaries by acclaiming a "true" order, to dissolve artificial distinctions and ritual conventions in favor of a genuinely sincere Truth. Utopias totalize: they seek to dissolve all the markers of concrete empirical (and hence fragile) order in an ultimate order beyond all change and partiality. As pure order or as the transcendence of order, utopias leave no room for the ambiguities, compromises, and ironies of life.

Our own world, we must note, is far from free of similar impulses to overcome distinctions and dissolve boundaries. In fact, the greater the social differentiation and the more the processes of social and economic distinction progress throughout the world, the more people feel a need to reintegrate those distinctions at a higher order of meaning. This need cannot be met within the terms of differentiation and distinction. The result is a greater and greater push to reintegrate, but using symbolic orders that no longer define the terms of distinction and disaggregation. One example, as we will discuss later, is the ascendance of those particularly dangerous forms of religious sentimentality most often termed "religious fundamentalism," which are in fact massive efforts at reintegration, with all their attendant dangers and dislocations.

The Limits to Uncertainty

The realization that our boundaries are only artifice, that the world is fundamentally broken, allows us to accept and even play with their inherent ambiguity, as we saw in the previous chapter. The sincere boundaries of Truth, in contrast, root out all ambiguity. We are thus arguing that the ritual mode has a built-in ability to abide with the inevitable ambiguities of life, even within an equally inevitable impulse toward an ever delayed—yet also never abandoned—desire for wholeness and totality. Sincerity, in contrast, seems by its very definition to exclude ambiguity. Recall that its dictionary meanings include "being without admixture," "free," "pure," "whole," and "complete."[21] Samuel Johnson lists among its cognates "unhurt," "uninjured," "pure," "unmingled," and "uncorrupt." Sincerity, carried to its extreme, is the very search for wholeness, for the overcoming of boundaries and the positing of a unitary, undifferentiated, uncorrupted reality. It is the utopian impulse itself.

Ritual does something very different, because many of its forms incorporate a degree of ambiguity within its very practice. In moving between differentiation and unity, ritual recognizes the ambiguous nature of reality and registers it, rather than denying it. While in some senses ritual searches for a wholeness like that of sincerity, it does so through a recognition of difference and ambiguity, rather than by denying them. Ritual does more than posit a reality. Rather, its pattern is often the classic dialectic of positing a reality, negating it, and ending up with a "truer" reality.[22] Ritual's opening to subjunctive worlds allows this play with different versions of reality, unlike the singular approach of sincerity.

An excellent example of this negation, built into ritual, is in the first Islamic Shahadah (profession of faith), "La illa ha illa 'llah" (There is no god but God), which posits the existence of God only after it has posited the nonexistence of other gods. As William Chittick notes, this Shahadah discerns between the Real and the unreal, or between the Absolute and the relative, or between God and "everything other than God," which is the universe. Traditionally the Shahadah is said to be divided into two halves, the negation ("no god") and the affirmation ("but God"). The first half denies the inherent reality of the world and the self. The second half affirms the ultimacy of the divine reality. The Shahadah means that there is "no creator but God," "none merciful but God," "none knowing but God." In sum, it means that there is no reality but God and that all the so-called realities of our experience are secondary and derivative.[23]

This structuring of ritual is no simple rhetorical device. Instead, it allows for a recognition of the ambiguous nature of empirical reality, in a way that the sincere mode would find threatening and overwhelming. The very structure of ritual—its performative nature, reiteration, and even the fact that not all of the meaning of the ritual is fully encoded—allows one to recognize the complicated nature of reality as it stands, rather than to deny it in a vision of wholeness that can never stand in the relations between two people.

Once we reject the view of ritual as the nonessential husk of something else that is "more" real (the visible sign of an invisible grace, as it were), once we return to an appreciation of ritual as a language in which the medium is very much the message, we come up with something counterintuitive to most senses of Enlightenment thought and sentiment. Ritual acts and practitioners are not after all hypocritical because they give external signs for an internal state that may not be present. The very external, performative aspects of ritual—especially their repetition and recollection of places not given to purely rational or instrumental computation—give it a unique lability. As structured duality, ritual encompasses the ambiguity of life much better than sincerity can. It allows one to "play" with such ambiguity in a manner precluded by sincerity's undue concern with the authenticity of one's actions and beliefs. Instead, practitioners of sincerity must contend with a degree of internal hypocrisy as part and parcel of their existence, because the desired wholeness of such sincerity is, in the final analysis, impossible. This is counterintuitive to say the least. It goes against the grain of most of our thinking about ritual and what is meant by it.[24]

Ritual, then, may help us develop a new appreciation of ambiguity and of the variability of borders and categories. Ritual unshackles the mind from a need to *believe* in a dogma of our choosing, as long as we act properly. This can leave us much more open to the complex and hence necessarily ambiguous nature of reality, while still retaining the possibility of acting within and upon it.

This aspect of *acting upon* the world is critically important in understanding how ritual functions in the cognitive ordering of reality. As we know, the addition of a bit of information to an unclear conceptual field both clarifies the area of the informational bit and, at the same time, problematizes the area around it. In the same way a new rule or law clarifies old ambiguities but always opens up new ambiguities at its edges. These in turn can be clarified by adding more bits of information, more rules, more laws—only to problematize further areas, and so on and on in endless progression. Every time we add clarifying bits of information to a conceptual field, we problematize the surrounding areas, which beforehand had been blank, neither clear nor unclear. There is no way, within the limits of reason, or the frames of sincerity, "to get it right," because ambiguity is built in to any and every conceptual field. The usual solution is simply to mark off, and reject what cannot be clarified, but the invariable result is a further problematization of the relevant definitions.

There is no final solution to this problem, only the creation of temporary and contingent spaces where we agree (and this is crucial) to eschew final understanding and just *do* what has to be done—the pragmatism of practice. This is essentially the role of the umpire in sports. The umpire resolves ambiguities by making a call. The call may be problematic—it may even be "objectively" wrong—but for all that, it must be accepted for the game to continue. The politics around the legislative decisions bearing on the Florida count in the 2000 U.S. presidential election were, in this sense, precisely over who would make the call that allows the game to continue even in a situation of hopeless ambiguity.

The nature of cognition means we must eventually lay aside the search for ultimate understanding to progress with the project at hand. Sooner or later we have to stop asking why, and simply act. The etiology of a particular dementia may be beyond my understanding, but I know what has to be done for the patient to better her life, or at least make her condition somewhat less painful or dangerous. As we know from the theoretical inquiries of Alfred Schutz, this is not ancillary to the problem of knowledge but stands at its center, because all knowledge is knowledge of an object in-order-to. This is what he termed the "problem of relevance," which he saw as central to all areas of human knowledge.[25] The knowing is intimately bound up with the doing. In our terms, we can never relinquish the performative aspect in favor of some "pure" understanding (which is what we aspire to in more sincere modes of experience).

The dual moment of both realizing and accepting the limits of understanding—the ability simply to move on with a life short of the ultimate Truth—brings us immediately back to issues of ritual. Ritual is a critical device that allows us to live with ambiguity and the lack of full understanding. The presentation of ritual's "as if" universe, the subjunctive, requires neither a prior act of understanding nor a clearing away of conceptual ambiguity. Performance simply and elegantly sidetracks the problem of understanding to allow for the existence of order without requiring understanding. In this way it is similar to kinds of decision we must make to take any concrete action, where we accept that we have as much understanding as we are likely to get and even though it is incomplete (as it always must be) action must be taken. This is true for a medical intervention, a financial investment, a marriage commitment, a declaration of war, or the planning of a highway—for virtually all forms of human endeavor.

Ritual and Sincere Prayer

Our analysis thus far suggests a continuum of orientations to order, or perhaps to the categories of order, that exemplifies the different admixtures of sincerity and ritual that can be found in the social world. Ritual orientations stress the performative, repetitive, subjunctive, antidiscursive, and social. Sincere orientations, on the other hand, tend to privilege the indicative, unique, discursive, and private.

These categories are not just psychological types, but rather structural alternatives to action. These two modes of response, with their internal tensions and interactions, have existed at all times in all civilizations. We can find them in the Israelite prophets as well as in Confucian commentaries on texts of ritual instructions. They exist in Shi'a instructional manuals and in Buddhist practice. They may even be "hardwired" in the very structure of our symbolic capacities.[26]

One typical feature of sincerity is the proclivity of people to reflect deeply on their ideas, to make them explicit and orderly, to place their categories of thought directly under the "mind's ray," as the phenomenologists would put it. They thus constantly question and justify their motives for action. At other times, however, people simply act following long habitus.[27] When asked why they do what they do, people may simply be at a loss for how to explain themselves because they have never before been motivated to think this through. This attitude typifies much ritual behavior, where the act itself is the most important thing. Chinese children, for example, learn at a very young age to make the appropriate motions for offering incense, but there is no explanation of why. Similarly, some orthodox Jews compare fulfilling the obligation of morning prayer to brushing one's teeth—these actions require no particular internal cognitive or emotional state. The ability to create explicit explanatory discourse can thus serve as one indicator of a sincere as opposed to a ritual attitude.

With ritual, the basic categories of action are given. All ritual (at least in the sense we use the term here) relies on the social acceptance of authoritative understandings and procedures. Sincere understandings, however, rely far more on internally generated knowledge and motivation. The Protestant (or Sufi or Hasidic) direct approach of the individual to God is an example of this more sincere approach. Authority in the ritual case lies in the acceptance of social institutions (a Catholic priesthood, or society itself for some Confucians), while for sincerity it lies instead in the individual's inner states.

While we see the tension between ritual and sincerity as built into the human civilizational enterprise at all times, its particular articulations are epoch specific. There are sincere reactions against ritual and ritualizations of sincerity. Sometimes both occur concomitantly and in very different mixes. Let us illustrate with an example. The Anglican communion can certainly be considered ritualist within the horizon of Western Christianity. It is the most ritualist of all Protestant communions and is no different from the Catholic Church in its stress on the importance of ritual. Under certain circumstances, however, there may be enormous pressures to move in the sincere direction. The ordination of an avowed gay bishop in the Anglican communion in October 2003 was just such an event. It evoked two general types of responses that mixed ritual and sincere attitudes in different ways. The very act of this ordination meant that ritual itself could no longer be taken for granted (as it would be in the "pure" form of ritual). Instead, people were forced to respond through self-examination and the production of new discourse, that is, through the mechanisms of sincerity.

The result for one faction was an explicit embrace of externally given normative imperatives—biblical injunctions against homosexuality. This faction hoped for a complete rejection of the ordination and may yet lead to a split in the church. This response to the break in ritual caused by the gay ordination is an explicit attempt to regain a sense of wholeness through returning to the earlier taken-for-granted ritual. Yet there is a crucial difference, because it must now rely on the discursive and indicative to make its case. That is, this faction has no choice but to embrace sincere tropes in defense of the old ritual ways. At the same time, however, there was a countermove from the other faction. This group, which favored the ordination, combined ritual and sincerity in a different way, arguing that homosexual bishops are fine because they are natural (taken-for-granted) and self-given categories. Thus, they claimed, gay bishops do not violate transcendent or externally given norms. The point is that events in the world (in this case a bureaucratic decision taken in a hierarchical institution) compel a response. Church members cannot simply remain unmoved when faced with events such as the ordination of a gay bishop. Their responses can be usefully understood in terms of these categories of the ritual and the sincere.

Prayer provides a further useful example of how this exercise in naming provides the means to make important distinctions and so to disaggregate social phenomena. Social surveys of such topics typically ask people questions such as when was the last time they prayed, how often they pray, and so on. The responses then become a crucial variable in determining the degree of "religiosity" of the populace. Yet, such surveys make no distinction in types of prayer. They conflate supplicatory prayers, whose time and content are not mandated by tradition, and those prayers that have been set for centuries or millennia, such as the daily prayers of Jews and Muslims.

The Protestant housewife, mixing her cake batter while praying for a good visit with her friend, with whom she has had some difficulty and to whom she will serve the cake, receives the same "sociological" significance as the Jew praying *ma'ariv* (evening prayer) or the Muslim at *jum'a* (Friday prayer). Aside from the ideological aspects of such categorization, it is simply poor social science. The Christian is, phenomenologically speaking, doing something very different from her Jewish and Muslim counterparts. She is engaging in a voluntary, discursive, indicative, and very private act. She is sincere. The Jew and Muslim instead undertake a performative, repetitive, subjunctive, sometimes antidiscursive, and social (even when done alone) act. They are doing ritual. To conflate all these acts as "prayer" misses the point of the different actions and denudes them of their significance to the people involved.

Of course, both Islam and Judaism recognize supplicatory and private prayer as well. In Islam, for example, a menstruating woman can engage in such private and individual prayer, but not in the daily prescribed prayer (mandated five times a day). Judaism has lengthy discussions of the whole issue of "intention" in prayer, that is, of its "sincere" aspects. The greatest of Jewish legal decisors and philosophers, Maimonides, makes very clear in his *Mishne Torah* (twelfth century) that the only prayer that demands such sincere attention and intention is the Shema ("Hear O Israel the Lord our God, the Lord is One" and its attendant three brief paragraphs). The whole Jewish phenomenology of observance attends centrally to the distinctions between times when intention is mandated and when (almost all other times in daily prayer) one can pray without such attention and still have fulfilled one's daily obligations.

Interestingly, Maimonides presents a "theory" of declension from what we would term sincerity to ritual in matters of prayer.[28] He suggests that originally, at the time of the First Temple, prayer had been spontaneous and individual, each praying in his or her own fashion. The destruction of that temple and the exile led to a "confusion of languages" that then necessitated (in the time of Ezra) the codification and formalization of prayer. This ritualization of prayer would have to ensure equality for all, so that the prayers of the "verbally challenged" would be at the same level as those of the most articulate. Here is an original, almost transhistorical vision of perfect spontaneity, of sincere prayer. The intrusion of history and catastrophe (i.e., a broken world), however, necessitated the introduction of ritual.

The distinctions we are drawing between ritual and sincerity get lost when all are subsumed under the general and undifferentiated rubric of prayer. Such an undifferentiated rubric, we hasten to add, is not ideologically neutral. It carries its own historical and cognitive baggage—of a Christian (more precisely Protestant) stress on sincerity as defining what we have come to understand as religion. The distinction is important precisely for the ritualist, who defines her existence in terms of practice and performance, and thus distinguishes intentional prayer from other forms of observance. We can understand this only when we fully recognize the salience of both categories and do not continually (often unconsciously) subsume ritual to sincerity. When we lump all together under the general rubric of prayer, we lose not only the specificity of the phenomenological acts performed by our contemporary respondents but also the specificity of different civilizational encounters with transcendence and its demands. We end up with much less of an understanding of what is and what was, and more of a projection of our own categories unto the outside world (itself an exercise in the sincere).

Our own categories for the world we inhabit (that of liberal academia in the United States) are very sincere. Indeed, the entire world of liberal modernity can be usefully understood in terms of the tropes of sincerity. The centrality of the individual and the valuation of the private are after all central to the normative program of liberal, enlightened modernity. From this follows modernity's extremely discursive character, its cultural stress on the unique and singular, and in this country anyway, its privileging of individual choice above repetitive action. Certain aspects of this cultural code, of course, go back to the very foundations of the European and Western civilizational endeavor. The importance given to individual will as an explanation for social change has, for example, been a critical trope in Western political thought for centuries. The workings of the individual will of course are singular, unique, discursive, and indicative to the highest degree. It is the sincere written on the course of history.

We can usefully compare liberal tropes of sincerity with Mohist tropes of universal love (bo'ai). Mozi was a Chinese philosopher of the fifth century BCE whose ideas were the main competitors of Confucianism for many centuries in China's early history. This was a period of constant warfare among the various states that would eventually unite to form China. Confucius's answer to the discord was ritual, as we discussed in chapter 1. Mozi, however, consistently ridiculed ritual as artificial and wasteful. His answer was instead that every individual should universalize his feelings of love, thus leading to the end of contention. At the same time, he had a strong utilitarian streak, arguing that ending ritual and ending strife would both free up productive resources, and suggesting pragmatically that any doctrine proven beneficial should be adopted. This combination of utilitarianism and a sincere love that comes from within sounds strikingly modern in some ways, but the underlying reason for the similarity is that both Mohism and modernity share a sincere mode of understanding and a critique of the ritual mode. The juxtaposition of Confucian ritualism to the Mohist principles of a community of love reminds us of one very central aspect of ritual, one that distinguishes it in no small measure from sincerity: the role of repetition. For Confucius, social peace would come through the formal workings of the ritual order, that is, through the constraints of ritual repetition. For the Mohists, peace would arise through an integrated wholeness arising from a sincere internal transformation of people. Both were concerned with social peace and order, but one saw it arising through the shared participation in an invariant and reiterated order, the other through the sincere, singular, and unique acts of each individual agent.

Repetition and Ritual: Beyond the Political

Repetition is thus one of the arenas where we can feel the continual dynamics and tensions between ritual and sincere orientations and where they are in fact symbolized. Repetition as both memory and re-creation continually reestablishes the tension between ritual and sincerity by cycling between the reaffirmation and abrogation of what is repeated. The very act of repetition itself, through its infinite reproduction, erases what was already marked in the timelessness of repetition itself.

Repeat something enough times and it loses all specificity, all sense of quiddity. This loss of the object's boundaries or frames in continually repeated action (as in the *ilinx*-like activities of twirling on a swing, jumping on a trampoline, or dervish dancing) is a well-known aspect of play, as we discussed in the previous chapter. Freud studied a very different aspect of repetition in his essay *Beyond the Pleasure Principle*.[29] There he notes the individual proclivity to repeat experiences, even unpleasant ones—an action that seems blatantly to contradict the workings of the pleasure principle, the desire to reduce undue excitement and negative affect.

Freud is especially taken by the compulsion to repeat unpleasant and unsatisfying events. Eventually, he relates this compulsion to a desire to return to past states, even to that of inorganic matter—what Freud terms the "death instinct."[30] Like the pleasure principle, the nirvana principle as posited by Freud consists of a tendency to regulate "excitations in the mental apparatus, in modifying them as to quantity, quality or rhythm."[31] The individual compulsion to repeat, according to Freud, connects to this tendency, making it relevant to any attempt to understand the way ritual and sincerity interact in our approach to the world.

The element of pastness that we noted earlier relates closely to the dynamics of repetition. Repetition circumscribes the future in and by the past. It limits an otherwise infinite and uncontrolled set of all possible future events within the frame of a known, specific, particular, and felt (past) experience. Repetition creates by constraining. It creates community and union by replicating precisely delineated actions, words, and gestures. By doing so, it also re-creates. The act of re-creation opens repetition to the future, to what is not so circumscribed—to what is beyond the ritualized and formalized modes of apperception. It opens repetition to change. Repetition embraces both past and future, ritual and sincerity, the mediated and the unmediated.

The control of the world that repetition affords must itself be constantly renewed. This need is built in to the very nature of control. If it is true, as Freud claims, that repetition affords us a mastery of the world and that "mastery of an object coincides with the object's destruction," then we see the dynamic of repetition laid bare.[32] To be continually mastered, the object must continually reappear, and repeat its appearance in the face of the destruction that its very mastery brings about. Mastering the present means continually repeating what was destroyed in the mastery—otherwise we have only a void. The dynamic of presence and absence thus mirrors that of control and its denouement. Each moment replays the tension between a re-created past and a unique future. We see this exactly in ritual, when we realize that its continual re-creation over time is not only about the past but about the future as well.

Such processes, in life as in text, connect to the circumscription of the individual will, the circumscription of desire and of unstructured representation. Participation in repetitive activity does certainly circumscribe the will; in many ways that is the very point of it. Repetition places the individual actor in a very particular relation to a body of practices (or even modes of speech and address), a way of being, which imposes obligations. Perhaps this continual circumscription of the will, the positioning of the individual as the "slave of

God" (to adopt the Muslim locution), the binding of the heart (or head or arm, as in the Jewish laying on of phylacteries) is what creates a strong awareness of the boundaries between the past and the future, the ego and the world. Here we can see the role of repetition in expressing the different levels of symbolic meaning discussed earlier as it both makes distinctions between entities (creating boundaries) and abrogates those very distinctions in a new unity.

Return and iteration are of course connected. Iteration means returning to actions over and over again. The past is made present. It stamps a shape onto the formlessness and chaos of existence. On one level change cannot be denied, nor can the dangers of the unknown that accompany it. On another level, though, constant repetition can mitigate the effects of time, denying the ontological character of the new in favor of what is beyond time. This is what ritual accomplishes through its continual repetition within time. In Jewish ritual, every Passover re-creates the Exodus from Egypt, every Sabbath recalls the creation of the world, every wedding, the creation of man, every death, the glory of God. In Christianity every mass is as much a recollection of the Passion of Christ as a look toward an eschatological future. In Islam every Muharram reenacts the defeat and death of Hussein at Karbala.

Kierkegaard expressed this point well when he noted that "in modern philosophy . . . *repetition* is a crucial expression of what 'recollection' was to the Greeks. Just as they taught that all knowing is recollecting, modern philosophy will teach that all is like a repetition. . . . Repetition and recollection are the same movement, except in opposite directions, for what is recollected has been, is repeated backwards, whereas genuine repetition is recollected forward."[33] Perhaps indeed one of the critical differences in the rituals of different civilizations is in the respective weights of repetition and recollection, respectively. Confucian rituals are heavily freighted on the side of recollection, the Christian Eucharist with repetition. The differential emphasis may be significant for how the tensions between ritual and sincerity are articulated and resolved in different civilizations.

"Form comes first," as Suzanne Langer reminded us, and it is the formal characteristics of ritual that initiate the "presencing" of all objects in the world.[34] This is an important insight for students of ritual. The phylacteries of the Jew, the ablutions of the Muslim, and the funeral rite of the Confucian are formalized behavior in repetitive and distinct patterns. Ritual is the ornament of life.

It would be good to remember this. Those movements that search for an integrated wholeness have largely abandoned this understanding of ritual. Rather than understanding ritual in terms of form, of ornament, of a reiterated pattern of actions and speech that mediates the eternal ambiguity of existence, they seek for something much more permanent, pure, and singular: sincerity.

Sincerity, Fundamentalism, and Modernity

Although aspects of the sincere mode have characterized human action in all societies at all times, the modernist or Enlightenment project has particularly privileged them. In part this grows from the very Cartesian orientations of modern science, which seeks to build certitude by linking the categories of the world to those of the human mind itself. Importantly, this project is not only framed scientifically, but, as Eric Voegelin has made clear in his numerous and influential writings, the political concomitants of this project have come to characterize what he termed the "gnostic" nature of modernity. He means by this the reframing of the soteriological project of Axial or transcendent traditions in terms of immanent, human processes that take place within history and within the orders of society. In Voegelin's terms: "Gnostic speculation overcame the uncertainty of faith by receding from transcendence and endowing man and his intramundane range of action with the meaning of eschatological fulfillment."[35] He saw nineteenth-century nationalisms and twentieth-century communism, fascism, and Nazism as various forms of such gnostic approaches to political order. Empire, on the other hand, is free from this modernist orientation because it claims no cosmic role to the organization of the whole political community.

Many of the movements we call "fundamentalist"—whether Christian, Jewish, Islamic, or Hindu—are gnostic in this sense. They take a religious, transcendent set of meanings and coordinates and infuse them with nineteenth-century nationalist immanent ideologies to produce a gnostic version of their respective religious traditions. Such movements are quite common in the Middle East, where they characterize both the extreme-right wing of the Israeli settler movement (such figures as R. Ginzburg the Kabbalist) as well as Hamas and Islamic Jihad.[36] They are also prevalent in the Balkans, where their ideologies led to the horrific slaughter of the 1992–95 Balkan wars.

Voegelin relates gnosticism in this sense to the immanent nature of Christianity and shows how "gnosticism was an accompaniment of Christianity from its very beginnings; its traces are to be found in St. Paul and St. John." He most clearly identifies it, however, with the modernist program of sixteenth-century Puritanism.[37] That is, he sees the sources of modern gnosticism in the very social movement that we identified so strongly with the sincere models of understanding. There is nothing surprising in this, for both sincerity and gnosticism rest on the internal, humanly defined core of experience, on the perception of the world as arising out of self-generated categories of order, rather than as a created, external, and heteronomous—essentially, transcendent—reality. In this sense gnosticism infuses both the nationalist political programs of modernity and Cartesian science, which, we are claiming, bears a strong "elective affinity" with the sincere mode of intersubjective understanding.

The impulse to sincerity thus helps us conceptualize what are today termed as fundamentalist movements—but which we believe can much more helpfully be conceived of as forms of sincere action. These movements strive for an integrative wholeness, an overcoming of dissonances (cognitive and other) that a more ritualized mode of behavior would perhaps find ways of accommodating. Ritual, in its iterated movement between different orders of being, accepts the existence of rupture and contradiction much more than does the sincere mode, which seeks to bring different orders of existence into a unitary framework. We have every reason to fear that this type of gnostic or modern politicized religion (or religious politics) is spreading. It increasingly defines issues of identity and meaning, and thus also of social conflict focused on issues of identity and meaning: a truly global ideology, if you will.

Our explanation of this rests on some well-known perspectives in anthropology and in semiotics. It draws significantly on the posthumously published work of Roy Rappaport.[38] We note first that we can distinguish three patterns of ordering or establishing systems of meaning, symbolic as well as social, ideal as well as material. The first, "lower order meaning," is grounded in distinctions between entities—precisely those very distinctions around which the division of labor and social order are organized. It requires the kind of boundary creation that we have been discussing. We see it in simple indicatives like "the cat is on the mat," where distinction (cats and mats, in this case) conveys meaning. This is how much of the economic realm is ordered, where the value difference between entities becomes the logic of exchange.

The second order of meaning, "middle-level meaning," is characterized by analogies or similarities between such distinguished objects. Much of what is generally understood as symbolic meaning resides on this level. Allegory and metaphor are the residents of this level: "My love is like a red, red rose." Here, boundaries are somewhat blurred. They exist but are neither absolute, as in lower level meaning, nor eradicated, as in the following.

The final, "higher order of meaning" is a unity, grounded in the radical identification of self and others and the dissolution of boundaries. We see it most clearly in religious statements such as "shema yisrael adoshem elokeinu, adoshem echad" (Hear O Israel the Lord Our God, the Lord is One). This erasure of all boundaries, of course, brings along problems and dangers of such eradication that we have discussed.

These three sets of meanings characterize not only signs and symbols—as pointed out a hundred years ago by the American philosopher Charles Peirce—but also social order. This was Rappaport's point: social order consists of both distinction and reaggregation, differentiation and reintegration. Thus, the realms of distinction and differentiation underpin the very division of labor that allows our species life and that enables economic exchange in a market. The orders of social aggregation and unity work at what we termed the middle level of meaning. We see them in the workings of social empathy and trust. We can draw analogies in social affect (his pain is my pain) just as we do in language (my love is like a red, red rose). This ability thus serves as the basis of empathy and generalized trust in society. Beyond this lies the ultimate (highest) level of unity, which is sought in religious rituals and the gathering together in houses of worship across the world. The life of human beings in society thus continually vacillates between orders of differentiation and distinction and orders of reaggregation and unity. Such reaggregation is that metaphysical unity, the "thing in itself," that—as we have seen—Ernst Cassirer identified as being beyond all distinctions and hence beyond all cognition.

Now while there is perhaps nothing terribly new in this insight, we can take a further step and connect it with Niklas Luhmann's theories of structural and system differentiation.[39] This suggests that as social differentiation and the processes of social and economic distinction progress (according to liberal/secular and scientific methodological criteria, which are today's logic of globalization), people increasingly feel the need to reintegrate them at a higher order meaning. This cannot happen solely within the terms of differentiation and distinction—being economic in nature, they can only deal with differentiation itself. We thus see a greater and greater push to reintegrate, but using symbolic orders that no longer define the terms of distinction and disaggregation. The result is some of the most dangerous forms of religious sentimentality that we witness in today's world.

In the religiously ordered universe—whether contemporary Qom in Iran or Bnei Brak in Israel, in the worlds of antiquity or medieval Europe—the orders of distinction and those of reaggregation were one, or at least shared the same logic. The most important social categories and taxonomies in those contexts encompassed both the orders of reintegration (what we now call the religious world) and those of differentiation (the organization of the division of labor). What we would call the language of religion was shared, or at least not sharply differentiated from that of the social division of labor. Laws against usury, or women in the contemporary workplace, or the organization of family law or of charity are cases in point. This was to a great extent the whole thrust of Islamic modernization in places like Pakistan, for example, or in the organization of Islamic banks.[40]

In the taxonomies, exchanges, and differentiations of most of the modern world, however, this is no longer the case. The relevant units of social organization (that is, those of distinction) come from liberal/individualist utilitarian economic theory of one sort or another. The language of reaggregation, on the other hand, is usually that of religion divorced from worldly affairs, a privatized religion. We should recognize that the promotion of modern "secularism" has in fact always occurred in conjunction with the growth of "religion" as a category, because these are the two remnants from the splitting apart of worlds where religion and daily life were intertwined.

Various forms of militant religious fundamentalism—from radical Islamicism to Hindu nationalism to the commitments of the radical religious Right in Israel—attempt to overcome this distinction by reimposing religious categories on the organization of the social order. Ridding the Land of Israel of Muslims, or the Dar-al-Islam of infidels, murdering doctors who perform abortions, or attacking religious monuments in India (or, for that matter, advocating a constitutional amendment that would ban gay marriage) all attempt to overcome the chasm between the religious terms of meaning, transcendence, and unity, on the one hand, and the simple fact that the taxonomic orders of the world do not, on the whole, recognize these orders of meaning. This has created the contradictory and often debilitating character of certain forms of religion in the contemporary world. The teaching of Hindu astronomy in India and the movements to reintroduce animal sacrifice among certain Jews in Israel today (seemingly more purely cognitive but having a political element) are similar examples of the same dynamic. So, for that matter, is the growth of Christian banking in the United States among evangelical communities, where banker and client join hands and pray together in search of a good mortgage.[41]

As we see, not all such attempts are violent, nor do all involve imposing the religious orders of reaggregation on the social world of distinction and differentiation. Some movements in fact seek the opposite, to reinterpret the world of religious meanings in terms of the secular categories of individual difference and distinction. New Age religions do this to a great extent, by stressing individual fulfillment and expression. Followers of Rabbi Zalman Shacter Shlomi's Jewish renewal group in Boulder, Colorado, redefined the Jewish dietary laws of kashruth to mean that free-range chickens were kosher. They used modern, secular categories of meaning (happy chickens and yuppie values) to infuse religious terms of meaning.

In some cases this trend penetrates even more traditionally organized religious communities and practices. Some of the new forms of radical right-wing religious Zionism in contemporary Israel evince a religiosity that stresses individual fulfillment and autonomy. They take over modern liberal and secular ideas of the autonomous and expressive self that are totally at odds with their own explicitly traditional understandings of the person as a subordinate entity under external injunctions.[42] This is a very interesting development, especially because it shows that many of these groups are attempting to integrate the orders of distinction and reaggregation in both directions. On the one hand, they seek to transform the social and political orders of the world in a religious direction (through their exclusivist religio-nationalist policies). This aspect of their movement imposes the logic or taxonomies of religious unity on the realm of economic and social differentiation. On the other hand, through articulating a religious vision that stresses modernist terms of individual meaning and fulfillment, they are also attempting, if unconsciously, to reframe the terms of reaggregation in the direction of the secular orders of differentiation. Ultimately this implies the positing of autonomous, distinct individual selves, each, in Bernard de Mandeville's terms, "a little world in himself." A very similar logic is also at work in Hamas, Islamic Jihad, and many other such movements in the Islamic world.

With this we arrive at a much better understanding of what is behind "fundamentalist" movements. We can now understand them in relation to their sister phenomenon of New Age religiosity and the various types of spiritualism and spiritual practice common today. All are trying to overcome the chasm between the terms of differentiation and those of reaggregation, but they go about it in very different ways. The so-called fundamentalist movements are uniquely interesting in their dual movement: they impose a religious logic of reaggregation on the orders of worldly distinction (bans on gay marriage, say). At the same time, they subtly incorporate the logic of differentiation and distinction (individual expression, for example) into their religious calculus. This is what we meant earlier when we referred to dangerous forms of religious sentimentality.

To appreciate this, compare these movements with the influence of feminism on the organization of religious meaning and ritual action (as women become priests and deacons). This is a more unidirectional movement, in the terms posited earlier. Here, by imposing the taxonomies of worldly order—in this case, gender equality rooted in liberal rules about the equality of citizens before the law—on the world of religious ritual, the work of ritual can more easily reaggregate the divisions of the world. This works because we must treat all sellers and buyers equally in the world of market exchange—of first-level meaning. We expect that we can best manage to reaggregate these distinct, differentiated units when the logic of equality is also at work in the liturgical orders of reintegration—with women priests, say—than where such equality does not apply. This certainly seems to be the case in Jewish communities, where in all non-Orthodox synagogues, women not only read the Torah, but 2,000-year-old prayers have been rewritten in politically correct terms.

Whatever the effects of this move on the nature of traditional practice, its social effects are much less deleterious for all involved than the violent attempts to bring worldly meanings in line with religious ones. While some people may not like women administering the Lord's Supper or laying phylacteries, or gay Anglican bishops and lesbian Methodist ministers, or 2,000-year-old dietary restrictions being reinterpreted to require free-range chickens, there can be little doubt that these are expressions of creativity. They are certainly more creative than the blowing up of mosques, pizza parlors, discos, and abortion clinics.

Note that the present situation is not only unlike the medieval world where a common set of meanings that we now call religious framed the orders both of differentiation and of aggregation. It is also unlike the high secular modernism of the late nineteenth and early twentieth centuries, where a liberal-individualist or socialist (or later fascist) framework posited a more or less unitary set of meanings that organized both economic and social differentiation and its reintegration in the symbols of unity and self-referential meaning. Liberalism, socialism, communism, and fascism all construct the principles of differentiation, of the division of labor, at the same time as they create the principles of reaggregation, unity, and solidarity. They do this through very different principles, of course, but that is not our concern at the moment. The taxonomies of forced collectivization are the same as those of the May Day parade in Moscow. The reality may not be pretty, but it is not dissonant, and that is the point we are making.

Currently, most people experience a divorce between the orders of distinction and differentiation and those of reaggregation and reintegration. The former are secular, individualist, and universal, while the latter are religious, collectivist, and particularistic. This situation can be compared to what Gregory Bateson once termed the "double bind," which he famously related to the etiology of schizophrenia—a diagnosis that may not be far from defining our present state of affairs.[43] The point is that both New Age religiosity and so-called fundamentalist movements attempt to overcome this contradictory situation, though in very different ways.

Clearly, we are using the concepts of ritual and sincerity very much as Weberian "ideal types," which never exist in their pure form in the empirical

world of human action and interaction. As we saw with the case of the gay
bishop in the Anglican communion or when viewing the actions of those
"Calvinists with phylacteries" in the Judean hills, empirical events tend to
produce mixed responses. Indeed, just as Jewish extremists mix sincere tropes
with ritualist behavior, so too do Muslim suicide bombers attempt to ritualize
the very height of sincerity (the act of suicide) to make it appear as a ritual act.
This is what distinguishes these acts of political murder from those Europe-
ans and North Americans are more familiar with from the nineteenth and
early twentieth centuries. In those cases Sorelian violence was not ritualized
but maintained its unique and singular status as a sincere act—indeed, this is
what legitimized it. For example, the Russian Decembrists/Narodnikii saw
their own death as the legitimizing device for the political assassination they
were undertaking. The unmediated sincerity in those cases, we would claim,
is very different from sincerity masked as ritual. Riding roughshod over these
distinctions, we fail to appreciate some of the most crucial forms of political
action operative in today's world.

Conclusion

Both sincerity and ritual are perennial aspects of the human condition. All
human civilizations oscillate between them and combine them in various
ways. Wang Yangming was no less sincere than Cotton Mather, the later
prophets no less than Jonathan Edwards. While both models are ideal types,
neither can exist purely on its own terms. Neither can constitute a perduring
social order on its own. Each must be continually mediated by the other.

Sincerity taken to its final point would take one totally outside of social
order. The model of total sincerity is the anchorite (or de Sade's fictional
characters, in a reversal of the theme). The "true" self ends up in the no-self.
The self disappears when emptied of its social characteristics—age, gender,
status, roles, and all the distinctions of social convention. This of course is the
self that we can see in social moments that Victor Turner understood as
communitas and Max Weber spoke of as "pure charisma."

Human life, however, takes place within society. Even those who leave
society—such as beggar monks, anchorites, and saints (or sadists, we may
add)—depend on the society they have rejected. Within the orders of life, one
must always at some point step back from the extremes of the otherworldly
abyss and reengage with the world. As soon as one does so, however, sincerity
becomes mediated by ritualized forms of behavior and appropriation.[44] Once

clothes are admitted, dress codes follow; once food is admitted, food restrictions (kashruth, halal, Lent, etc.) follow as well. These are the ritual markers of a subjunctively shared universe. One cannot enter the division of labor without also engaging in all the ritualized aspects of human interaction that both distinguish and unite those involved.

The ritual side has its own constraints. The very necessities of social life restrain the extremes of sincerity, while the very facts of historical/temporal change limit any attempt to organize life solely according to ritual. Time, and so change, is built in to our existence in the world. Temples are burned down, sacrifices rendered useless, priests slaughtered, and new modes of understanding emerge.[45] All of this challenges the efficacy, indeed the very possibility, of ritual. Ritual must then be rethought, and it thus becomes mediated by the reflective processes of sincere reasoning. Change results, invariance is mediated, and actors encode these changes even as they think them through. Recall Franz Kafka's wonderful parable of the leopards in the Temple: "Leopards break into the temple and drink to the dregs of what is in the sacrificial pitchers; this is repeated over and over again; finally it can be calculated in advance, and it becomes part of the ceremony."[46]

This process disturbs the formal order and repositions the frames of the world. It breeches existing limits, tears down constraints, and unpacks clichés to let new meanings emerge. The very openness of the future thus carries the potential to question existing categories and the boundaries through which we construct them. Existing forms are constantly contested, and the open-ended nature of this challenge makes the integration of ritual and sincerity an endless project. As we argued in the previous chapter, some past referent and some future orientation are always part of any culture and every human order.

The impulse to inject the meanings and attributes of sincerity into ritual is beset with danger. It tries to short-circuit the endless play of ritual and sincerity and conflate the one with the other. Reformulating ritual in terms of sincerity works to the detriment of both. We must, rather, learn to appreciate, or perhaps to appreciate anew, both modes of understanding and to refrain from the impulse to wholeness, to the totality that seems to characterize so much of contemporary attitudes to both ritual and sincerity.

Our aim here is not so much to advocate for ritual as opposed to sincerity, but to develop a new appreciation of ritual freed from contemporary frames of sincerity. Such an appreciation rests to a great extent on ritual's formal qualities, rather than its substantive content. Ritual's repeated, performative, and antidiscursive nature, we have argued, provides a critical way of dealing with, rather than overcoming, the eternal contradiction and ambiguity of human existence. We are not, however, advocating an unchanging ritual—ritual historically undergoes change, often responsive to changed historical and social circumstances. Indeed, ritual traditions typically include mechanisms for effecting change in ritual practice. But we are urging that contemporary attempts to make ritual more discursive and more responsive to modern sensibilities must take into account the very features that make ritual a unique resource in the human encounter with the world.

5

Movements of Ritual and Sincerity

At the end of the previous chapter we explored a number of arenas that show the tensions between ritual and sincerity. We noted with special interest how many contemporary political movements, especially those identified as "fundamentalist," show a unique blending of ritual and sincere forms of behavior and orientation. Both extreme right-wing Jewish settlers in the occupied territories as well as Hamas and Islamic Jihad exemplify this fusion of traditional ritualist orientations with modernist themes of individual expression around the trope of sincerity. This fusion of orientations is not limited to the Jewish or Islamic world but occurs in many contemporary Hindu movements, as well as in such Christian movements as Opus Dei or the use of the Eastern Orthodox rite within any number of nationalist groups and movements in the Balkans, Greece, and Russia.

This should not surprise us because, as we indicated throughout, the trope of sincerity is quite modernist. It is not only modernist, of course, not just the invention of the Enlightenment. We can see this from Jesus' admonition to the apostles (Mark 7:14–15), where he places sincere expression above following ritual dietary laws: "Nothing that enters one from outside can defile that person; but the things that come out from within are what defile." Other examples, can—as we observed—be found across different civilizations, where many reform movements do indeed invoke a sincere orientation. We already noted the Christian break with Judaism, the Buddhist break with Hinduism, the Protestant revolution, and so on. Reform movements seem to have an "elective affinity" (to use a Weberian term) with sincerity.

Reform is the key link between the pervasiveness of the sincere trope and modern consciousness and politics. Modern civilizations are, to a great extent, civilizations of permanent reform. The language of reform permeates the mechanisms for incorporation of protest, for periphery impingement on the centers of material and symbolic power, and for the very force of revolution as fact and as myth, from the late eighteenth century and the French Revolution through the mid-nineteenth-century national revolutions in Europe, the anticolonial struggles of the twentieth century, the feminist "revolution" of the 1970s, up to the revolutions in 1989 in Eastern Europe and beyond.[1] The reader may add her own examples, but all illustrate the strong connection of ongoing reform to the mentalities of contemporary life.

There were, of course, movements of reform before the emergence of the modern world, and a sincere orientation is not exclusive to our contemporary world. Both reform movements and sincere orientations were always part of our social baggage. What we are arguing, however, is that the world we currently inhabit has an overwhelming tendency to understand reality (shared, social reality as well as individual reality) in terms taken from the sincere side of the spectrum rather than from the ritual one. The prototypical source of this reading, in terms of both individual sincerity and, for that matter, political reform, is Jean-Jacques Rousseau.[2] For him, sincerity and truth were practically interchangeable. Moreover, and with Rousseau in mind, we may well wonder if this emphasis on the sincere, and our tendency to view it as a sort of panacea to all ills ("if only others were sincere ...") may not in fact be somewhat dangerous.

Dangerous or not, we have been habituated to view reform as intimately tied to sincerity, at least since the period of the Reformation and the Counter-Reformation. This was Voegelin's point, as we discussed in the previous chapter. He wrote about the particular "gnostic" nature of the modern world, which made transcendent processes appear as immanent ones and understood the possibility of human praxis as contributing to the realization of a very this-worldly *eschaton*. Infamously, as Aron argued, these orientations gave birth in our times to the enormously powerful "secular religions" of the twentieth century: Nazism, fascism, and communism (or, perhaps better, Leninism rather than all forms of communism).[3] The firmly held conviction of the leaders, followers, and elites of these movements—that they *knew* the course of history, the telos of existence, that they possessed both the practical and the theoretical knowledge necessary to realize the *Endzeit*—led to the worldwide horrors of what were, at their outset, reform movements par excellence.[4]

In many ways—and Voegelin's work on this is seminal—this orientation, while going back in some forms at least as far as the Manicheans, achieved a power and persuasiveness in the Reformation beyond any of its previous forms. Martin Luther's "Hier stehe ich und kann nicht anders!" (Here I stand, I cannot do otherwise) and the revolution that followed—a revolution that rent Christian Europe asunder—was (and is) a powerful indicator of the strength of individual conscience as a force of reform and revolution. This force continued in the Puritan revolutions of the seventeenth century in England, the Sea Beggars in Holland, the Huguenots in France, the "errand into the wilderness" of the founders of Puritan New England, and so on. As we all know and as libraries of scholarship attest, it was one of the major forces in forming the modern world.[5]

It is still with us: in the orientations of some forms of contemporary religious Zionism, in the desiderata of ethno-nationalism in the Balkans, among large groups of evangelical Protestants in the United States (committed to enacting their interpretation of God's word on the whole polity), among suicide bombers in Palestine whose last recorded words frame their act not only in the name of God (*bisminallah*) but also in their own name and that of their family— all evincing precisely that form of cosmic hubris that Voegelin attributed to modern gnosticism.

It is with us in more benign forms as well, whether in the form of New Age spirituality or in the increasing openness of traditional religious structures to individual expression (women putting on phylacteries, gay bishops, etc.). This emphasis on individual conscience and its capacity to "trump" all other arguments in fact seems to be a defining feature of much of what has passed for radical (i.e., revolutionary) politics in the United States since the 1960s. From Jerry Rubin's Yippies to today's "spiritual activists," there is a pervasive stress on what each and every individual feels and experiences as providing the ultimate standard of legitimacy, action, and definition of collective goals.

A recent meeting at the Garrison Institute in New York of more than 100 individuals, self-defined as "spiritual activists" and representing more than thirty organizations, was a fine example of such orientations. All participants were radical in their politics; many were engaged in fascinating projects of reform (teaching yoga in prisons, helping gang members become useful to their community, organizing janitors in New York City, providing legal services in poor neighborhoods). Yet, on the level of symbolic articulation they were nothing if not reminiscent of Congregational Puritans in the 1640s participating in the test of relation—giving evidence to saving grace. They phrased all claims in the public sphere in terms of the self—"me," "mine," "I feel," "I want." They never adduced any other standard to justify a claim or statement.

The individual, and individual wants, desires, feelings—the compass of the heart—became the touchstone of everything said.

This had profound consequences. With nothing beyond personal feelings to anchor statements in the public realm it became terribly important in this meeting to have everyone "feel" the same—or else the group threatened to fly apart. There was nothing to hold it together beyond shared feelings. Consequently, the group either denied differences in feelings or launched a huge mechanism to get everyone to "feel" the same. Some considered such mechanisms to be coercive and totalistic. Both spiritual activists and Leninist apparatchiks deny any constitutive differences between people. For both, the group has to be "whole," "one"—and indeed the stress on oneness was overwhelming and continual at this meeting. For a group of spiritual activists committed to diversity and giving voice to all sorts of marginalized voices, this was a very ironic unintended consequence, greatly inimical to the value orientations of most people there.

Symbolic markers to perpetuate this idea of oneness pervaded the meeting, with much "honoring" of shared histories, "naming" of metaphorical shared ancestors, and so on. No real ancestors or real histories could of course actually be invoked, because those differentiate. There was a persistent hope that this effort at an imagined unity was itself the stuff of a shared culture. In fact, rather than a shared culture, there was a continual stress on the intentional symbolic recognition of various isolated elements. Cultures do not need such intentional design; they allow the continual oscillation between sameness and difference to flow without constantly being marked and reflected upon.

We suggest that there is thus a line, a thread of reform, connecting the sincerity of the nonseparating Congregational Puritan of the early seventeenth century through the nineteenth century and to the "spiritual activists" of the early twenty-first century.[6] The line runs through American history—and indeed through most of modern culture and society. Parts were delineated by Trilling, other parts by Voegelin.

Yet, and this is critical to our whole argument, this is only one thread. While modern experience predisposes us to see and understand reform movements in terms of sincerity—and indeed while these have been most salient in the past 200 years—they are not the only calculus of reform. There are, and have been throughout history, reform movements that were not oriented in this direction but took their bearings from much more ritualized understandings of people's existence in the world. These are not simply those gradual evolutions of sincere movements as they take on ritual trappings—expressed architecturally in the cathedralesque Methodist "chapels" of ex-Methodist institutions like Duke University or Boston University. Reform movements promoting dynamic and rapid change can also grow from the concern for ritual.

Among the earliest such movements on record, according to J. C. Heesterman, was the very institutionalization of the axial vision in Vedic India.[7] According to Heesterman, Vedic rituals, no less than Buddhism, represent that fundamental movement of social, political, and ethical reform that Karl Jaspers termed the Axial Age.[8] This was the period between 500 BCE and AD 600 that saw the development of a basic tension between the transcendent and mundane orders that differed greatly from the mutual embeddedness of those orders in so-called pagan religions.[9] Heesterman makes a strong case that Vedic rituals constituted a rational order of ultimate truth that not only outlawed conflict and violence but also permitted questioning the very principles of kingship.

The reforms of King Josiah of the kingdom of Judah in the seventh century BCE offer a similar case. In the period from about 640 to 621 BCE, King Josiah (with the approval of the prophet Jeremiah) undertook a vast program of social and religious reformation that is also known as the Deuteronomic reform.[10] This is when the book of Deuteronomy (the second law) was composed and a full-fledged theology with a well-articulated doctrinal core put in place. This is not just a case of institutionalization of charisma, of the sort that we have known well since Weber, where personal charisma evolves into the charisma of office or kinship. It was a legal and ritual reform from the first.

There are many other examples as well. The famous rectification of names (*zhengming*) movement in the time of Confucius was also part of a broad-based attempt to create a ritualizing reform. The rectification was not the move of sincerity—to make the names properly reflect the true nature of the thing. Instead, the goal of the movement was to make the nature of the thing correspond to its name. That is, kings should "king"; they should act in the way that true kings are supposed to act (*as if* they were kings).[11] By the same token, fathers should "father," and wives should "wife." Kings, fathers, and wives should stop acting from their true self and align themselves with their proper roles.

Even modern movements of reform have not all been sincere in nature. The famous "sacramental renaissance" of the last third of the seventeenth century in New England—which arose in response to the oft bemoaned "declension" and falling away of church membership of midcentury, was a movement of ritualization.[12] In the very teeth of sincerity, ritual raised its head not as a form of institutionalization but as a vehicle of reform.

The Oxford movement in England in the middle of the nineteenth century was similar, much more elite in character, and less wide in its popular appeal and effect, but nevertheless a reform that defined itself in terms of ritual and practice rather than sincerity and *innerlichkeit*. Political considerations aside, the Tractarians' writings, those of J. H. Newman (who later converted to Catholicism), Keble, Pusey, Church, and others, were all part of a movement toward ritualism and tradition.

In the Jewish world, too, we can look to the establishment of the modern Yeshiva movement in Lithuania at the turn of the nineteenth century as an example. The establishment of the Volozhin Yeshiva near Vilna by Rav Hayyim, disciple of the great Gaon of Vilna, in 1803, marked the revival of an institution devoted to ritualized learning and a reasoned approach to tradition. Yeshivot—centers of learning and study—had been a fixture of Judaism since the time of the Exile. Yet in early modern Europe they had entered a period of relative decline with the growth of Hasidism (which was an enthusiastic religious movement) and, by the mid–nineteenth century, by the growth of Reform currents in Judaism. Both Hasidism and Reform were to a great extent modernist movements—privileging individual experience and expression. For the Hasidim this took place within the independently constituted world of Jewish tradition, while the Reform movement had a severely attenuated connection to that world. By contrast, the great Yeshiva in Volozin represented an attempt at a social reformation—but along very different lines than the more "sincere" inner-oriented movements of either Hasidut or Reform. Prayer provides a simple, illustrative example here. For Hasidim (adherents to the Hasidic movement), prayer was an obligation that could be fulfilled "when the spirit listeth," as it were, and not only at its properly proscribed times. This was an attitude firmly rejected by R. Hayyim, his teacher R. Elijah (the Gaon of Vilna), and the Yeshiva movement in general, which demanded strict adherence to the prescribed times of morning, noon, and evening prayer. The traditional, ritual prescriptions were to govern the foremost religious injunction of prayer, not the spiritual state of the inner man.[13]

A very different assessment of the proper place of reasoning in religion was the movement of reform sponsored by Muhammad 'Abduh of Egypt in the second half of the nineteenth century. Concerned with the decline of Islamic society and the slavish imitation of Western mores, he advocated a set of principles and practices predicated on a reasoned approach to religious dictates and traditions. The offshoots of his efforts would influence both secularists and Salafists (hence modernists in every way). 'Abduh responded to the perceived "decay" of his society with an appreciation of the importance of law, education, and institutional reform aimed at bringing Islam into the modern world.[14]

While there are some parallels here with the founders of the modern Yeshiva movement, there are also many differences. For while R. Elijah, the

Gaon of Vilna, was credited by many to have been a proto-*maskil*, or early instantiater of the Jewish Enlightenment through his emphasis on the role of reason and reasoning in the strictly traditional world of Torah study and practice, he hardly can be understood as rejecting traditional learning and ways of being. In contrast, 'Abduh (like his teacher, al-Afghani) reassessed tradition in the rather sincere terms of modernist rationality similar in some ways to the Reform Judaism of the nineteenth century—one of the poles against which the modern Yeshiva movement defined itself. Other more traditional responses to the forces of the modern world can of course be found in Islam, such as the devotees of Shaikh Ahmad al-Alawi throughout North Africa and beyond.[15]

Social reform movements can thus lean to either the sincere or the ritualist pole of action and orientation. There is and has always been a tension between the two. We believe there always will be. Such tension seems to be built in to the ambiguous nature of our existence. Proper attention to each, in its place, will help us live with and in this ambiguity, we hope, rather than try vainly to erase it.

We have so far focused on the political and social dimensions of this tension. In this chapter we want to suggest a wider purchase. We believe our categories and analysis go beyond the purely political or the social narrowly defined. To explore these possibilities further, we present here three cases where the tensions between ritual and sincerity that we analyzed in the previous chapter extend beyond the sociopolitical. We shall look briefly at literature, architecture, and music in the hope of broadening our appreciation of the categories and their relevance. These ideas are more suggestive than definitive, but they illustrate both the extent of the categories of analysis and some of the dynamics of the relation between ritual and sincere attitudes in particular contexts.

Ritual, Sincerity, and *The Merchant of Venice*

Within much of the mainstream of the West Asian civilizations (our own), the tension between ritual and sincerity contributed to the defining boundaries of our theological, political, social, and communal identities. It has informed our vision of both perfect order and the overcoming of all order. Law and the strictures of law have often been identified with ritual prescriptions and obligations, while love—as absolute value—has been understood as obviating ritualistic modes of behavior by the sincerity of belief and the inward turning of the heart to God. Posed in these terms, it is not difficult to understand how, in our civilization, the juxtaposition of ritual to sincerity, as law to love, came to be understood as the juxtaposition of the Jew to the Christian. This has been a continual trope of European civilization for two millennia and continues, if no longer in high Christian art, then in the simple storybooks read to children. We recall a schoolbook that one of the authors' fifth-grade children read, in a Jewish school no less. *The Bronze Bow* contrasted "the proud Pharisees" trailing their phylacteries with the followers of Jesus' message of love.[16] No one even recognized the cultural messages encoded in the story—so deep are they embedded within our taken-for-granted categories.

Stereotypes of course are no more than caricatures—as the juxtaposition of Jewish ritual law to the idea of Christian love has been throughout the ages—albeit with horrible consequences for the well-being of Jews in Christian Europe. As caricatures they can of course be ridiculed (and so perhaps they should), but they should nevertheless be studied as part of the attempt to understand the nuanced ways each pole has developed within particular cultures. Love as a category exists and plays a critical role in Judaism no less than law does in Christianity. All scholars of religion know this, however immaterial it may be to regnant cultural perceptions. A recent, posthumous book by Jacques Ellul, *Islam et jude-christainisme* (with a foreword by the prominent philosopher Alain Besançon) exemplifies the continued use of these horrific stereotypes, with Islam replacing Judaism as the religion of law, devoid of all love.[17] It is just one example of how, today, the very dangerous boundary that once was understood as running between Jew and Christian is now seen as running between Western (Christian or, sometimes, Judeo-Christian) civilization and Islam. The consequences of this contemporary apotheosis of imagined boundaries may well be no less horrific than its earlier incarnation.

We wish to claim that Shakespeare's play *The Merchant of Venice* was one of the most significant attempts to puncture these caricatures of law and love. There, Shakespeare manages to send up the ideas of both law and love—and, with them, the opposition between ritual and sincerity that they entail. He undercuts them as absolute opposites, as well as the cultural identification of law with Jews and love with Christians. He shows the hypocrisy of such an attitude as well as that caused by any claim to construct society solely on the basis of love. In its very questioning of the absolutization of this prime boundary marker of our civilizational enterprise, the play presents a major critique of the type of totalizing tendencies discussed in the previous chapter.

The Jew, the representative of the law and so of necessity was left outside and beyond this community. As we all know, the absolutizing of this difference—indeed, the cultural, legal, and social separation of the carriers of the idea of love and law, sincerity and ritual—led to horrible consequences for

Jewish history certainly, but for Christian civilization as well. Because both are caught in the selfsame contradictory injunctions (as are all human societies), the difference is one of valence, not the absolute difference that has so often been projected unto the historical and cultural canvas. The current situation of the Muslims in Europe makes this a pressing political no less than theoretical matter.

The Merchant and the Jew

The Merchant of Venice interests us because Shakespeare seems well aware of the ambivalence attendant on either law or love (what we are identifying as ritual or sincerity) as a "pure" form of social behavior.[18] Indeed, two undercurrents of the play's very structure are (1) how Shylock's strict legality, his insistence on the letter of the law brings him to forfeit everything; and (2) the hypocrisy that characterizes all the major Christian characters (with the possible exception of Portia, though this is debatable), whose statements on grace and forgiveness (and whose sincerity) are continually undermined by their actions.

Shylock's very scrupulosity results in his loss of fortune, position, status, indeed his very identity; it is the mechanism of the play's comic structure. Indeed, until the nineteenth century and the portrayal of Shylock by the actor Edmund Keane, the play was performed as a comedy. It was Keane and following him such actors as Edwin Booth and Henry Irving who drew out the humanity of Shylock's predicament. As Irving himself declared: "I look on Shylock as the type of a persecuted race; almost the only gentleman in the play and the most ill-used. . . . He feels and acts as one of a noble and long oppressed nation. In point of all intelligence and culture he is far above the Christians with whom he comes in contact, and the fact that as a Jew he is deemed far below them in the social scale is gall and wormwood to his proud and sensitive spirit."[19]

In fact and as Martin Yaffe, Richard Weisberg, Stanley Cavell, and other (interestingly, Jewish) commentators have pointed out, the play is not at all unfriendly to Jews.[20] The easy, popular assimilation of Shylock to anti-Semitic stereotypes was a hallmark of an all too popular political correctness *avant la lettre*. (And like political correctness today, it was a sign of people's marked difficulty in dealing with ambiguous situations and characters. Ironically, one of us studied *The Merchant of Venice* in a yeshiva in New York in the 1940s, though it was not taught in the New York public schools in those days because it was seen as an anti-Semitic text.)

It is not only the familiar soliloquy of "Hath not a Jew eyes" that evinces Shylock's humanity, though we should recall those famous lines and what follows as well:

> Hath not a Jew eyes? Hath not a Jew hands, organs, dimensions, senses, affections, passions? Fed with the same food, hurt with the same weapons, subject to the same diseases, healed by the same means, warmed and cooled by the same winter and summer as a Christian is? If you prick us do we not bleed? If you tickle us, do we not laugh? If you poison us, do we not die? And if you wrong us, shall we not revenge? If we are like you in the rest, we will resemble you in that. If a Jew wrong a Christian, what is his humility? Revenge. If a Christian wrong a Jew, what should his sufferance be by Christian example? Why, revenge! The villainy you teach me, I will execute; and it shall go hard but I will better the instruction. (3.1.60–75)

Note that Shylock not only claims a shared, general humanity with its common capabilities and sentiments; he also claims no more than his rights within the prevailing mores of the majoritarian Christian culture.

Shylock's fundamental humanness recurs throughout the play and not only in this scene—as does the overwhelmingly Christian refusal to entertain that shared human status and to admit Shylock into that realm of generalized Eros and *universal love* claimed by the Christian characters. Recall Shylock's pain at Jessica's betrayal and her flight with Launcelot and subsequent conversion. Recall, too, Shylock's desire for Antonio's friendship and Antonio's constant humiliating words to Shylock

> SHY   Signior Antonio, many a time and oft
> You have rated me
> About my moneys and my usances:
> Still have I borne it with a patient shrug;
> For sufferance is the badge of all our tribe.
> You call me a misbeliever, cut-throat dog,
> And spit upon my Jewish gabardine,
> And all for use of that which is mine own.
> Well then, it now appears you need my help:
> Go to, then; you come to me, and you say
> "Shylock, we would have moneys:" you say so;
> And foot me as you spurn a stranger cur
> Over your threshold: moneys is your suit.
> What should I say to you? Should I not say

"Hath a dog money: is it possible
A cur can lend three thousand ducats?" or
Shall I bend low and in a bondsman's key
With bated breath and whispering humbleness,
Say this—
"Fair sir, you spit on me on Wednesday last;
You spurned me such a day; another time
You call'd me dog; and for these courtesies
I'll lend you thus much moneys"?

ANT   I am as like to call thee so again,
To spit on thee again, to spurn thee too.
If thou wilth lend this money, lend it not
As to thy friends; for when did friendship take
A breed for barren metal of his friend?
But lend it rather to thine enemy;
Who, if he break, thou mayest with better face
Exact the penalty.

SHY   Why, look you, how you storm!
I would be friends with you, and have your love,
Forget the shames that you have stain'd me with,
Supply your present wants, and take no doit
Of usance for my moneys, and you'll hear me:
This is kind I offer. (1.3.96–136)

Antonio's continual hatred of Shylock, refusal of offers of friendship, and exclusion of Shylock from the terms of a common humanity provide the clear background for Shylock's desire for revenge quoted earlier. Recall that the "Hath not a Jew eyes" speech begins with Shylock's recognition that a pound of Antonio's flesh is good only "To bait fish withal: if it feed nothing else, it will feed my revenge" (3.1.54). The continual mockery to which Shylock is subject prompts this revenge. Rejected from any participation in the community of love, he has no recourse but to the mediated relations of the law.

Shylock's legalisms are continually juxtaposed to Christian "kindness." Yet the play shows this very "kindness" to contain no small measure of hypocrisy. "The Hebrew will turn Christian: He growes kind," declares Antonio (1.3.178). But where is that kindness? In the aid given to Jessica as she runs away from her father and steals his property? In the rejection of Shylock's request for recognition by Antonio? In Launcelot's leaving Shylock's household? In the failure of both Antonio and Bassiano to keep their heartfelt promises to their betrothed (in the matter of the rings)? In Portia's demand of

Shylock to go down and beg his life from the duke? In the final stripping of all Shylock's property, leaving him with his bare life?

As much as the Christian characters are presented, on one level, as *articulating messages* of charity, mercy, kindness, and otherworldly grace, they are shown on the level of *their actions* to betray—even to their beloved—these very sentiments and ideals. In contrast, Shylock, the Jewish usurer, who demands a pound of flesh in payment for his loan, remains one of the most human and sympathetic characters in the play.

As noted earlier, the one possible exception to this characterization is Portia, whose very identification with mercy and forgiveness—when testing Bassiano in the matter of the rings, or to some extent with Shylock in attempting to extend forgiveness to him as well in her requests to Antonio and Bassiano—puts her somewhat beyond the framework of motives and passions to which all the other characters are subject. Portia, as Sir Israel Gollancz pointed out, is "actually mercy personified"—an image that he shows is rooted in medieval Jewish literature and the commentary on Psalms 85:10–14: "Mercy and truth are met together; Righteousness and peace have kissed each other." The identification of Portia with Mercy is drawn from the Hebrew allegory on the four daughters of God (derived from Mercy, Truth, Righteousness, and Peace), according to Gollancz.[21] Still, her triumphal demands that Shylock beg for his life somewhat undercut this image of gentle Portia.

Indeed, Belmont itself is an almost otherworldly and heavenly realm (in juxtaposition to mercantile and worldly Venice). Even here, however, the world of Christian fellowship falls well below its ideal female representative. The plot's whole engine turns after all on Bassiano's loan of Shylock's ducats to woo Portia. But Portia is uninterested in wealth, has rejected wealthy suitors, and in fact found favor in Bassiano on his first visit without borrowed wealth. The theme of the three caskets also represents a rejection of wealth and the standards of worldly success as measures of Portia's rightful suitor. Bassiano himself comes to Portia very much bereft of the knowledge of grace and the otherworldly directives of love, thinking it can be won by gold and fancy dress. The juxtaposition of Portia is thus not only with the all-too-human (and very self-reflective) Jew, but even more to the oblivious other Christians. Their hypocrisy is opaque to themselves, though it is transparently clear to the observer, among other ways through Shylock's own asides along the order of "This be Christian kindness."

The matter of love and law, of legal obligations and the mercy of forgiveness, goes to the heart of the play's tension and its characters' portrayal. It appears perhaps most clearly through the images of usury and the gift. Usury, represented by Shylock the Jew, is the icon of law, with all its dual meanings—that is to say, it is both the law of the Jews, represented by the Jews, but also the law of necessity, that of the division of labor upon which civilization itself turns. Recognition of this is made clear in the appeal of Shylock to the Duke:

SHY   If you deny it, let the danger light
Upon your charter and your city's freedom. (4.1.38–39)

And again in the very recognition by Antonio that without the law and respect for the law Venice cannot thrive and prosper:

ANT   The Duke cannot deny the course of law:
For the commodity that strangers have
With us in Venice, if it be denied,
Will much impeach the justice of his state;
Since that the trade and profit of the city
Consisteth of all nations. (3.4.25–30)

The Jew Shylock represents the law of necessity, Freud's civilizing necessity. His demands for justice are legitimized by the very sine qua non of ordered human existence (represented by the laws and charters of the city of Venice).

These demands juxtapose against the gift, as icon of love, grace, and merciful forgiveness beyond the province of the law. Antonio himself is almost Christlike in his sacrifice, offering himself up on the altar of mercantile necessity. In fact, his self-sacrifice, especially in terms of the cutting of his heart, calls to mind the medieval image of the pelican, as icon for Jesus, plucking its breast to feed its young.[22] One scholar, Ronald Sharp, has in fact made a list of all the gifts given in *The Merchant of Venice*. These include:

> 1. The many gifts that Antonio gives to Bassiano prior to the action of the play. 2. The money Antonio borrows from Shylock for Bassiano. 3. The gifts Bassiano bring to Portia. 4. The estate Portia's father wills to her. 5. The money Jessica gives to Lorenzo, a dowry stolen from Shylock. 6. The ring Shylock's wife gives to him. 7. The ring Portia gives to Bassiano. 8. The money and property that Shylock is forced to give to Jessica and Lorenzo. 9. The ring Bassiano gives to the judge. 10. The ring Nerrisa gives to Gratiano. 11. The ring Gratiano gives back to the clerk.[23]

Even the inscription on the lead casket left by Portia's father reads, "Who chooseth me must give and hazard all he hath." Hence the gift—whose most important instantiation may well be Portia herself—contrasts strongly against the law of the marketplace and indeed of the City itself. The city glories in its splendor, like Pisanello's representation of the city in his *St. George and the Princess*, but cannot totally divest itself from the thieves hanging in the background.

In the structure of the play, Law:Love :: Necessity:Mercy :: Usury:Gift :: Jew:Christian :: Shylock:Antonio/Portia (both in essence lovers of Bassiano). Except—and most critically—the whole construct begins to unravel with the embodiment in the last two pairings of Shylock the Jew and Antonio the Christian.[24] As discussed previously, Shylock himself is rejected, humiliated, and scorned by Antonio, whose friendship he seeks. Except for Portia, the Christian characters themselves show just how unchristian are their actions. They cannot be trusted, even to keep their promises to their wives. They aid in the theft of Shylock's jewels via Jessica. Despite their most beautiful words and noble sentiments, Shylock—in asides—continually shows what their actions really reveal—mendacity, rapaciousness, vengeance, and hypocrisy. The Christians' attitude toward Shylock hardly approaches the idea of loving one's enemies; indeed, it does not meet the most elementary standards of trustworthiness (a theme also developed in Christopher Marlowe's plays).[25]

It is the very unraveling of the dichotomies of love and law, grace and necessity that is so instructive in the play. Shakespeare is teaching us that these categories cannot be experienced (and we stress experienced, rather than simply thought or theorized) as absolute contradictions. In the real world of men and women motives are mixed. "Which [indeed] is the merchant here and which the Jew" (4.1.171)? That would seem the epigraph of the play as a whole. It is of course the opening line in Portia's entry into the trial scene, which is the most revealing area to view the moral complexity of the plot and its characters.

The trial scene begins with Shylock's refusal of money in lieu of Antonio's bond (earlier Portia was willing to offer 36,000 ducats instead of the 3,000 owed). In his explanation he makes two things quite clear: first, for the duke, failure to enforce the contract would threaten the city's well-being, and second, his refusal of the sum and demand for enforcing the contract is motivated by nothing other than his "humor." He will not seek to explain why, other than "a certain loathing I bear Antonio." In the exchange that follows, Antonio points out:

> You may as well go stand upon the beach
> And bid the main flood bate his usual height;
> You may as well use question with the wolf
> Why he hath made the ewe bleat for the lamb,
> You may as well forbid the mountain pines

To wag their high tops, and to make no noise
When they are fretten with the gusts of heaven;
You may we well do anything most hard
As seek to soften that—than which what's harder?—
His Jewish heart. (4.1.70–80)

Here again, the Jew is distanced from the world of mercy, grace, and forgiveness—from love. To which Shylock replies:

What judgment shall I dread, doing no wrong?
You have among you many a purchased slave,
Which, like your asses and your dogs and mules,
You use in abject and in slavish parts,
Because you bought them: shall I say to you,
Let them be free, marry them to your heirs?
Why sweat they under burdens? Let their beds
Be made as soft as yours, and let their palates
Be season'd with such viands. (4.1.90–98)

Shylock, in invoking the Christian keeping of slaves, turns the situation on its head.[26] First he shows the duplicity of those who identify themselves with love and mercy, which does not prevent them from keeping slaves as property; then as he exclaims "fie upon your law" if they do not keep the law—their own law of the bonded creditor—when it ceases to suit their interests. Property is property, he is saying, whether of the slave or the creditor's bond. He implies that law in Christian societies is only mediated by grace when one's very material interests are at stake (and thus not, as in the case of one's slaves, when one's comfort must be sacrificed in having the slave's bed as soft as the master's).

In his insistence on being paid Antonio's flesh and the keeping of the agreement, Shylock is of course not motivated by material interests. "To feed fish" is all the flesh is worth and, as we know from Jessica, he would refuse any compensation. In an interesting way, then, Shylock is not at all about material interests. He is iconic of law, but not of material wants and desires (that seems the province of Bassiano and the Merchant himself, Antonio). His desire for revenge stems instead from his hurt and his anger at Antonio, rooted in the other's cruel treatment of him throughout the play. His "lodged hate" of Antonio is no mere argument drawn from the necessity of contract law. Rather, hate itself is the mirror of love. It is love rejected, friendship despised. It refers to the world of sentiment, empathy, and sympathy—not to the world of exchange, barter, and the rule of the division of labor.

Following the entrance of Nerissa, Portia appears in the trial scene with her famous "The quality of mercy is not strained" speech (4.1.180). Mercy, she points out, "is an attribute of God himself" and "that in the course of justice, none of us would see salvation, we do pray for mercy. And that same prayer doth teach us all to render mercy." To which of course Shylock responds, "I crave the Law." While we will not analyze Portia's famous soliloquy in depth, we would like to draw attention to two aspects of the brief lines just quoted. First, her appeal to the godlike qualities of mercy echoes the Jewish, biblical description of God's attributes: "Eternal, Merciful, Gracious, Long-suffering, Abounding in Kindness and Truth, Preserving Clemency unto the thousandth generation, Forgiving iniquity, transgression and sin." The Jewish God is a god of mercy and forgiveness, and the Jews have always recognized that salvation could not be found "in the course of justice alone." Portia can thus be seen not as juxtaposing a Christian trope to the Jewish Shylock but rather reminding him of his own sources and appealing to him through these.[27] The old law, the law of the Old Testament that Shylock quotes to justify usury, is also the law of mercy and forgiveness. Moreover, as the famous nineteenth-century critic and essayist William Hazlitt pointed out, "The appeal to the Jew's mercy [given their treatment of him throughout], as if there were any common principle of right and wrong between them, is the rankest hypocrisy, or the blindest prejudice."[28]

After reminding Shylock of his own sources of moral authority, Portia makes a critically important claim to empathy: that our own need to appeal to God's mercy (rather than to rely simply on his justice) should teach us to render mercy to our fellow humans "to mitigate the justice" that is Shylock's due. We therefore need to extrapolate from our own situation to that of our fellow humans and, on this basis, be merciful. We need to feel empathy and sympathy and on that basis be merciful to another. Yet it is precisely empathy and sympathy and fellow feeling that Antonio has consistently denied to Shylock. Cast beyond the boundaries of a common humanity, of a shared empathy, excluded by the "narcissism of the small difference" from the universality of love, Shylock has no recourse but the demand for the law. The law, of course, regulated relations between strangers, those not included in the intimate circle of love and family affection. And "stranger" he was to remain: his conversion to Christianity on pain of death is hardly an example of mercy, no more indeed than Portia's "Down then and beg mercy of the Duke." Recall, too, how Portia's speech, which ends with these lines, begins by threatening Shylock with the laws of Venice, enacted "against an alien that by direct or indirect attempts seek the life of any citizen" (4.1.348). Shylock remains forever the alien and the stranger.

Shylock's status notwithstanding, his demand, in its very scrupulous legality, leads to his undoing and loss of all. The law, when demanded too rigorously, too obsessively, is turned on its head and becomes self-defeating. In our terms, pure ritual, when pursued too scrupulously, too steadfastly, and too sincerely, leads to our undoing. Shylock's refusal to be merciful is met with Antonio's refusal to show mercy to him. Antonio's response to Portia's request that he show mercy is to divest Shylock of all his provisions (half in the fine, half to put in a trust to go to Launcelot on his death) and to forcibly convert him. Shylock's legalistic precision is met with Antonio's own. The law is turned into a vehicle of revenge. Love is nowhere to be seen except, again, in the person of Portia, who forgives her husband's breach of his own vows. Portia, the woman, is the final unsullied dispenser of grace—though not to the Jew—and it is not coincidental that she, rather than any of the male characters, overcomes the dialectic of law and love, necessity and mercy. Her defeat of Shylock and triumph is, after all, through the law (trial), even as it provides the medium through which she acclaims the qualities of mercy.

In today's world we have witnessed the horrors of too grand an apotheosis of the principle of love and sincerity, as indeed we continue to witness the horrors of too narrow an understanding of law and of ritual. If our own work in the study of ritual and sincerity is to mean anything, it must be oriented toward the near-impossible task of rethinking the past centuries, of bringing together what the social world all too easily tears asunder, and of overcoming the worst forms of civilizational narcissism.

Many decades ago, when Adam Seligman was a child in the Yeshiva of Flatbush in New York, the front of his classroom had a sign saying "derech eretz kadma la'torah" (ethical behavior precedes the Torah). A simplistic reading would see that as putting love before law, sincerity before ritual. We now know that no such simplistic reading is possible. As young students, however, the Yeshiva youths just treated it as one more homily taught to children, and thus not to be taken too seriously. After all, Seligman and his classmates had a good measure of what was serious, and they were never tested in "ethical behavior." He had failed enough examinations in Talmud (Jewish law) to know the consequences of inadequacy in a serious realm, and so to know the definition of seriousness, and this definitely was not included. In many ways it still is not. Perhaps we have all to learn from the Confucians who, in the concept of *li*, unite the ethical and the legal, the rite with the duty, the mores of tradition with the "reasonable conventions of society."[29] To do so, however, we must overcome those dichotomies that, to such a great and tragic extent, define who we still are.

Ritual, Sincerity, and Ornament

In our analysis of ritual and sincerity, we emphasized the importance of repetition in ritual, as indeed, in human life. We can follow this thread into the realm of the visual arts and find yet another fascinating case of the tension between ritual and sincerity, here contrasted as the tension between ornamental art (which is always repetitive) and representational art. Moreover, as we shall see, this problem of repetition and singularity connects as well to earlier struggles over icons and iconoclasm, and to the terms of modernist architecture in our own time.

Repetition is central to the very nature of ornament. In fact, it has been argued that the fundamental ornamental components of our architecture—derived from the Grecian orders—are all, in essence, tropes (that is, similes, or metaphors, associative devices) for Greek sacrificial rites. Greek architectural ornaments (and hence, in essence, our own) reproduce (i.e., repeat) the elements of Greek sacrifice; from the dentils on the ceiling, to the cavetti (bonds) at the base, inclusive of garlands (on bulls and emblatures alike), flutes and the hornlike Corinthian capitals, and so forth.[30]

In this way (as in some others noted in the previous chapter), ornament repeats, and through this repetition, imposes order on the cosmos—which, in fact, some scholars identify with the root meaning of the word.[31] Indeed, as the basis of rhythm, the patterning of repetition has been identified by William McNeil as the most fundamental and earliest way that order was imposed on the chaos of existence (see figures 5-1 and 5-2).[32] In this context, then, the contrast to representational art is telling. For representational art tends toward the unique, the singular. While an artist may make countless studies for a figure or portrait or still life, these are works in progress toward the realization of a unique, representational figure. Representation is of the unique, the one.

Within much of Christian art, this representation of the one was very much part of a philosophy of becoming. It had pedagogical value, where art told a story whose aim was to bring people into the church (or, in Counter-Reformation art, to return them to the fold). Representation was thus art in the service of self-transformation. Even ornament in Romanesque design, for example, told a story—its very asymmetry was there to remind us of the perfection of God alone. Baroque ornament is even more singular in its reduced orders of iteration, its slide into the singular and nonrepeatable (see figure 5-3).

Compare this with the ornamental, an-iconic art of Islam or Judaism (figures 5-4 and 5-5). Here there are no singular, nonrepeated elements. Instead we see the continual, infinite play of iteration, of a formal order that

FIGURE 5-1. Entablature, library at Appolinia, Albania (photograph by Adam Seligman).

FIGURE 5-2. Townhouse detail, Lower East Side, New York City (photograph by Adam Seligman).

FIGURE 5-3. Trevi Fountain, Rome. Note the subtle differences in the figures on either side of the escutcheon (photograph by Manfred Leiter, with permission).

FIGURE 5-4. House ornament in Hatay, Turkey (photograph by Adam Seligman).

FIGURE 5-5. Alhambra, Spain (photograph by Howard Davis/Artifice Images, with permission).

begins beyond the "frame" of the particular object before us and ends in an infinite beyond. Such ornamental and rhythmic art tells no story of transformation, no singular and unique representational message. It has no point or axis of meaning and history but rather shows that endless, formal play of presence and absence that we noted earlier. What we see is not a story of becoming, in fact, not a story at all (narrative, after all, always tells of uniquely articulated moments in a progressive story of change and transformation). Marking presence and absence rather than transformation, the iteration of ornament (as of all ritual) shows the infinite play of being rather than becoming.

Not surprisingly, this ornamental attitude contrasts with that of the Gothic style in architecture, which is all movement, all transformation. "Gothic space is unbridled activity. It does not receive the beholder with soft gestures, but carries him violently along, acting as a mystical compulsion to which the burdened soul deems it a delight unresistingly to yield."[33] The "restlessness" and the "need for activity" that the Gothic manifests is in a sense the absolute opposite of the ornamentalism that finds repose in iteration, and solace in abstract form (see figure 5-6). The abstraction of the Gothic is one of construction, of achievement, of attaining spirit, of denying matter. It is, in short, a move of striving and, ultimately, of becoming.

This allows some thought-provoking speculation as to the connection between different architectural and artistic styles and their corresponding social philosophies—somewhat along the lines opened by Erwin Panofsky in his classic study *Gothic Architecture and Scholasticism*.[34] One is thus tempted to draw a connection between the eschewal of ornament and what we would call a culture of sincerity. Antiritualist and sincere attitudes deny the value to the *as if*, to the play of illusion, and seek to root interaction in some attestation to the sincerity of the interlocutors. These, however, can only be encoded in arbitrary signs, which lack an inherent indexical connection to the signified. These signs thus become the basis of a new architectural code.

An excellent illustration of this attitude can be found in modern architecture, which denies all validity to the ornament. The ornament is an artifact that blurs boundaries, that reaches out from the entity and engages the space outside of it. It plays with the world around it and in so doing integrates the artifact into the world. In contrast, we can find a quintessential modernist rejection of ornament (and in essence of play) in Otto Wagner's saying, "Nothing that is not practical can be beautiful."[35] When ornament exists in modern architecture (and it always does, even if only as a trace), it is generated out of the structure itself, if not out of function and utility. Frank Gehry's work is a most excellent example of structure itself serving as the basis of something

FIGURE 5-6. Side aisle, Gothic cathedral of St. Etienne, Bourges (photograph by Q. T. Luong, with permission).

FIGURE 5-7. Southwest entrance, Peter B. Lewis Building, Case Western Reserve University (by permission of the university).

like ornament, where the roofline—one of the boundaries so typically ornamented in earlier architecture—plays with the border between building and sky through the moving form itself (see figure 5-7).

Viewed as a peroration on boundaries, much twentieth-century architecture draws on the same sensibilities as much of modern thought, including its politics. That is, it imagines each of us as autonomous individuals related through the pursuit of our interests alone. This is a total reconfiguration of the meaning of social boundaries along the lines of utility functions rather than constituted entities. Boundaries and the distinctions they enshrine become purely instrumental or functional—aspects of utility. Boundaries as such are devalued, becoming but predicates of some other utility-bearing value. They are no longer a place of significance, no longer a place where a plural and multivocal truth can be apprehended. Rather than being broadened, they are to be narrowed and firmly delimited.

In modernism, value to a great extent follows function. This is as true in architecture and design as it is in politics (see, for instance, the Hancock Tower in figure 5-8). Here, the ultimate reference of value is the distribution of mass and space and other aspects of tectonics, that is—in the broadest sense—of utility. Utility presents value as an external object—value for use, value for something external to the object, value for what is other (or, in the economic realm, what is valuable for another economic actor). This is a very different idea of beauty from the boundary as a zone of complex interplay, in which ornament presents value as inherent to a set of noninstrumental cri-

FIGURE 5-8. John Hancock Tower, Boston (photograph by Gorchev & Gorchev, with permission).

teria, and value inheres to an object as itself. For all their differences, this is common to architectures as disparate as Doric temples and Gothic cathedrals (see figures 5-6 and 5-9).

It may well be, as Worringer has noted, that Greek architecture achieves its message "through the stone" while the Gothic cathedral attained its significance "in spite of the stone."[36] That is, the relation of the signifier to the

FIGURE 5-9. Doric ruins of Tempio de Cerere, Campania, Italy (photograph by Q. T. Luong, with permission).

signified in each case reflects different conceptions of the role of the material. The Greek architect imbued stone with sensuous qualities. The Gothic architect sought to dematerialize the stone itself, to soar beyond it. Neither case, however, expressed a pure utility of form.

In much premodern architecture and design, function was not a value in itself. Function existed in reference to symbol and to transcendent, socially shared values, though of course the symbol and value systems were very different. Ornament formed an intimate part of this process, with its rhythmic mediation of the boundaries of space and time. Hence, when ornament inhered to structure, it was not simply a reflection of the tectonic function of structure, but established a relation with transcendent values (see figures 5-5, 5-6, and 5-9 to 5-11).

Though these examples of course represent very different forms of religious architecture, different accounts of creation, and very different notions of God or gods, they share certain similarities. In all, the space is not constructed solely in accordance with a set of utility principles extrinsic to their being. Rather, in some sense all partake of symbol systems to which they point and in which their value lies (or lay) to their communities.

This conception changed radically, at least in western Europe, during the Protestant Reformation of the sixteenth century. Luther was crucial in reor-

FIGURE 5-10. Bukkoji Pure Land temple, Tendou, Japan (photograph by Christal Whelan, with permission).

ienting the purpose of all church art from substance to function. In his conception—let alone that of the Calvinists and other radical iconoclasts—a substantive church art was but idolatry. Catholic signs and Catholic rituals were meaningless and contentless gestures that were an abomination to the pure spirituality of Protestant faith. The rejection of works (*sole fide*) implied as well the rejection of *poesis*, of human making, as substantively connected to the ultimate value of salvation. In the sixteenth century, Calvinists took this position to the extreme, not only doing away with all images, altars, and statuary but going so far as to whitewash the walls of the churches, thus doing away with any trace of previous imagery.

The position of radical iconoclasts, whether Calvinists in the sixteenth century, the Taliban in Afghanistan, or the iconoclasts in the eighth-century Byzantine Church, was that the image or icon was indeed a repetition of the divine—a representation in material terms of what was unique and un-circumscribable. They thus attributed to the icon a character and meaning that the iconodules were at pains to refute. For these, the icon was in fact just an "image," a "typos" or a "shadow" of its referent.[37] In fact, icons represent a marked departure from the type of representationalism that characterized much of Christian art and which we noted earlier. Conceived of in terms of

Christian revelation, of the Image as well as of the Word, the icon was not understood as consubstantial with the original, as sharing the same nature with it. Rather, as explicated by Leonid Ouspensky, icon and entity were essentially different, while yet maintaining "a certain participation of the one in the other."[38] In fact, according to Ouspensky, the icon moves between unity and difference, oneness and separation, and, for the believer "the possibility of being at the same time identical and different is quite evident—hypostatically different, yet in nature identical (the Holy Trinity), and hypostatically identical, yet in nature different (the holy icons)."[39] This situation strongly recalls our earlier discussions of the subjunctive and of the splitting of the ego—the potential to be "both-and" rather than "either-or." It was the iconoclastic (and very sincere) position that reduced the icon to one meaning, to one reading, and hence to a form of idolatry.

For the iconodule, however, the image did not re-create a prototype, but just reflected it on a lower level. The nature of this typos was explained by John of Damascus, the famous defender of images in the Byzantine Church: "In a certain way, the first is an image of the second, Melchisedek [an image] of Christ, just as one might say that a sketch of a picture is a shadow of the picture in colors; therefore the law is called a shadow, grace truth, and reality what is to come. So the law and Melchisedek are preparatory sketches of the picture in colors, and grace and truth are that picture in colors, while reality belongs to the age to come, just at the Old [Testament] is a type of a type, and the New [Testament] a type of reality."[40] In line with this logic of representation: "If the image of the emperor is the emperor, and the image of Christ is Christ, and the image of a saint is a saint, then the power is not divided nor the glory shared, but the glory of the image becomes that of the one depicted in the image."[41] The iconoclasts (who, interestingly, carry a certain similarity across the ages and across at least the monotheistic religions) found this position difficult to accept. Rather, they attributed to the image maker a belief in the divinity of the image and so its status as an idol.

In rabbinic thought, the locus classicus of the Jewish position toward idol making may be the following story recounted in the Babylonian Talmud, tractate *Avodah Zarah*, the section dealing with idolatrous practices and the proper relations between Israelites and idol worshipers:

> Proclos, son of a philosopher, put a question to Rabbi Gamaliel in Acco when the latter was bathing in the bath of Aphrodite. He said to him, "it is written in your Torah, and there shall cleave nought of the devoted thing to thine hand; why are you bathing in the bath of Aphrodite?" He replied to him, "We may not answer [questions re-

lating to Torah] in a bath." When he came out he said to him, "I did not come into her domain, she has come into mine. Nobody says, the bath was made as an adornment for Aphrodite; but he says, Aphrodite was made as an adornment for the bath. Another reason is, if you were given a large sum of money, you would not enter the presence of a statue reverenced by you while you were nude or had experienced seminal emission, nor would you urinate before it. But this [statue of Aphrodite] stands by a sewer and all people urinate before it. [In the Torah] it is only stated, their gods—i.e., what is treated as Deity is prohibited, what is not treated as Deity is permitted."[42]

Raban Gamaliel's reply offers insight into the monotheist understanding of pagan worship, as idolatry. He observes that different statues of Aphrodite may well mean different things in different contexts. Some statues are purely decorative, such as, he argues, the case at hand; but other statues in which an aura of sanctity inheres are meant to be worshiped. It would seem that the context in which the statue is situated defines its nature. In one context it is nothing but a decoration (and hence there is no injunction against Jewish presence in their midst). In another context—such as at a pagan cultic site—they clearly take on their characteristics as sacred objects, and the injunctions of Jewish law take effect to proscribe numerous forms of (Jewish) behavior in their presence. What makes an idol is the requisite attitude toward the image. A similar attitude, within the Christian tradition, could be used both to defend images and to attack them, by imputing to all images and all image makers a veneration of the image (another claim that John of Damascus defended against in his treatises).

In many ways, this radical iconoclastic position is the less interesting for our concerns because it rejects the visual, representational world completely. This was the position of the radicals among the Protestant reformers, men such as Karlstadt and Zwingli.[43] Indeed, among many of the sixteenth-century Protestant reformers church imagery was replaced with the written word—quotes from the New Testament and the Hebrew Bible, sometimes in the original Hebrew.[44] Luther's own position was more complex and ultimately more decisive in structuring our approach to the world of visual representation—Luther did not reject the image outright. What he did reject was the idea of the image (or altar, or votive, or icon) as value in itself. The image could, rather, be preserved if its function was made absolutely clear—its use-value as a tool for religious instruction. To quote Joseph Leo Koerner, the foremost authority on the role of the visual images in the period of the Protestant Reformation: "Didacticism required that the image become less

rather than more: less visually seductive, less emotionally charged, less se-
mantically rich. Deemed useless save as school pictures, images were built
to signal the fact of their impotence. Expressing their mundaneness through
willfully crude visible forms, and valuable only for what they meant rather
than for how they looked, they emptied out any residual expectation of
magical efficacy, any lingering faith in the participation of the likeness with
what the likeness represents."[45] Church art became, in these Lutheran
churches, naught but "theological tracts."[46] Moreover, to ensure this purity of
the didactic and pedagogical role of the visual, to guard against the very power
that inheres to the image, Lutheran iconography de-emphasizes form to such
an extent that, according to one contemporary scholar, the image qua image
(i.e., devoid of its "content") is totally meaningless.[47] Imagery became characterized by "formal blandness and semantic transparency," just like a page of
text. Contrast this with what we said earlier on the role of noise in ritual, that
is, on the nondiscursive aspects of ritual as opposed to the very critical role of
semantic transparency and discursive apprehension within more sincere forms
of religious expression. With the great thinkers of the Protestant Reformation, sincerity achieved its greatest apotheosis (at least in Western religious
thought).[48] In fact, with the Reformation, form began its separation from
content—a separation that would lead to nineteenth-century Romantic ideas
of art for art's sake, that is, an ideology of pure form, and the manifestos of
Novalis and Teicke. Art then emerges as a modern category "when religious
images, rejected, were remade into objects of disinterested satisfaction."[49]

The effects of this separation of form from content and the orientation of
content to the purely utilitarian goal of pedagogy to the detriment of all formal
criteria played itself out in many different ways. It certainly boded ill for
ornament, which has little or no pedagogical content. The utilitarian focus on
value as extrinsic to the object led, in architecture, to a rejection of all ornament as value in itself. The examples are many. Adolf Loos wrote a famous
tract titled *Ornament and Crime* where he proudly claimed, "We have van-
quished decoration and broken through into an ornamentless world."[50] The
most critical exponent of this attitude in architecture was of course Le Cor-
busier, who postulated:

> We must have the courage to view the rectilinear cities of America
> with admiration. If the aesthete has not so far done so, the moral-
> ist, on the contrary, may well find more food for reflection than
> at first sight appears.
>
> The winding road is the Pack-Donkey's Way. The straight road is
> man's way.

The winding road is the result of happy-go-lucky heedlessness of looseness, lack of concentration and animality.

The straight road is a reaction, an action, a positive deed, the result of self-mastery.

It is sane and noble.[51]

We would add that this is also a rejection of ornament as pure form, and of its production as an attempt to escape from function. Rather, it enshrines function itself.

We present here two styles of mosques, currently struggling for mastery of the landscape in Bosnia following the destruction of more than 1,200 mosques during the 1992–1995 war. Figure 5-11 shows the Sulejmanija Mosque in Travnik, which is in a traditional Bosnian style. Figure 5-12 is the new King Fahd Mosque in Sarajevo, designed and funded by Saudi Arabia. The Saudi building, that which we most clearly identify with a "fundamentalist" religious orientation, is also the most modern and sincere—it is devoid of ornament and so also least playful. This is an irony that bears further thought.

As a form of what Eric Voegelin termed "modern gnosticism," the Wahabbism championed by the Saudis rejected (and continues to reject) traditional religious practices and representations in search of an authentic, original religious experience—a pure, that is, sincere religious expression that cuts

FIGURE 5-11. Sulejmanija mosque, Travnik, Bosnia (photograph courtesy of ISSRPL Archive).

FIGURE 5-12. King Fahd mosque, Sarajevo, Bosnia, 2005 (photograph by Eldar Sarajlic, with permission).

through the historicity of all real, lived traditional religious practice. In fact, it rejects tradition in favor of a putative original, founding moment, of which it claims unique understanding. This is the core of what today is so often termed "fundamentalism." It equates truth, which is nonindividual and supraindividual, with its interpretation, which is invariably personal and conditional. This is where the basic contradiction between fundamentalism and true tradition lies. There is no tradition that permits the individual or group, solely on the basis of its own assertion, to proclaim its own knowledge to be infallible and absolute.[52] Yet the newly designed mosques that the Saudi version of Islam is exporting throughout the world represent precisely this modern, sincere religious understanding. Modernist in their design, in their rejection of ornament, in their use of function itself as ornament, they represent that particular marriage of sincerity and ritual, of tradition and modernity that is becoming so dangerous in today's world.

The term "fundamentalism" is thus perhaps misplaced—unless we wish to push it back 400 years. For, as analyzed earlier, a dynamic very similar to contemporary Wahabbism can be found in the Protestant Reformation rejection of tradition and tradition's tools of meaning. The rejection of the image or, at best, its replacement with one almost devoid of form that we saw in sixteenth-century Europe matches the contemporary reduction of the rich symbolic polyvocality of Islamic ornament to the relatively limited semantic field of the written, textual word. The dynamics are strikingly similar, even if most would recoil from the comparison. This correspondence of sensibilities reflects similar orientations to tradition, and to traditional ritual—it especially rejects those ornamental forms in which ritualistic meaning was expressed and woven into the orders of the world, in the name of a putative sincerity of pure intention of the inner self. In this move, the rhythm of the ornament's play on the boundary is devalued in the name of a pure, sincere truth or meaning that, as we have seen, destroys the very idea of boundary-work in the name of a differentiated existence that separates form from content and value from the world.

The "engine" of modern gnosticism that Voegelin himself identifies with Protestantism and its rejection of "serious play" may well be the maintenance of a philosophy of becoming together with the rejection of all representation.[53] That divinization of the individual (or, in later forms of nationalism and communism, of the nation, ethnic group, or class) as an agent of history's telos— secret sharer in the knowledge (gnosis) of history's meaning and hence actor and agent in its realization—is itself the play of representation, no longer externalized in the iconic representation of sacred art but driven inward, where the "true" acts of becoming and transformation (in the soteriological orders) take place. The Protestant rejection of the church's sacred arts of representation is matched here in the Wahabbist rejection of the sacred Islamic art of ornament with all its esoteric meanings (and esotericism is, needless to add, the bane of all sincere movements of transparency). In their iconoclasm, both strive to "leave nothing in the church where of any memory will be," as expressed by one sixteenth-century Calvinist.[54] Memories, traditions, and all past orientations are replaced with the promise of an eschatological future, that utopian message we explored previously, that seeks to dissolve all categories, overcome all boundaries, and posit a pure vision of absolute, transhistorical truths. Arrogating the essentially transcendent to the immanent realm of history is perhaps the inherent dynamic of a world devoid of ornament, the price of which we know full well.

Common to all iconoclast positions is a horror of pure formality. Though expressed in rejection of the image, iconoclastic positions are in fact repelled by the formal elements that inhere to representation, rather than to its purely substantive content. They perceive this abstraction of the form as a threat. An image can be countenanced only when it can be denuded of its formal characteristics and articulated as pure content, and hence manipulated into a functionally substantive narrative or pedagogic. While extremes of this position appear in socialist realism or in Nazi kitsch, the impulse is also present in Luther's attitudes toward church images (to use as a pedagogical tool), as well as in the Wahabbite acceptance of television while rejecting visually representative art. In television the formal qualities of the image are reduced to a minimum.

This attitude can also be found close to home in myriad examples. A recent exhibit (December 2004) at the Whitney Museum in New York, showing the work of Romain Bearden, is a case in point. The explanatory tapes given to the visitors, with disquisitions on the paintings by H. L. Gates Jr. and other luminaries, were fascinating in their reduction of art to ideology. The formal qualities of the collages were, to a great extent, ignored in favor of their ideological or sociological purchase. Like Luther and the church images, the formal qualities were ignored (if not erased) in search of their pedagogical and ideological purposes. The single-minded drive for explanation and ideological reduction replaced the play of form and content that is the great magic of all art. We should perhaps in this context recall that one of the prime charges of the iconoclasts against the iconophiles in the eighth-century debates was that in rendering an image of Christ they were reducing his hypostatic union as man and God to one substance alone. While clearly this has been understood in the scholarly literature as a continuation of the fourth- and fifth-century Christological debates, it also betrays a marked difficulty to abide with the ambiguity that would mark such representation. Navigating Monophysite, Nestorian, and Paulicist heresies was difficult enough, without having to deal with the visible image of Christ's hypostatic essence. Sincere belief at the time would seem to have required leaving this unrepresented, the better to steer clear of the slippery slope of heresy. Indeed, while icons were interpreted as idolatry under Leo III (the first iconoclast emperor), they were understood as heretical under his son Constantine V.[55]

To return to our earlier nomenclature, what these examples show, despite their deep differences in time, culture, and focus, is the rejection of the *as if*, the subjunctive universe of form. They reject the unique universe that the subjunctive evokes through its particular engagement with the world, marking presence and absence in its iterated and repeated patterns. The *as if* is replaced with a world assumed to be *as is*, a claim to substantive content that can then be manipulated in terms of whatever grand narrative the culture advocates.

Wilhelm Worringer noted a very similar tension in the world of artistic production 100 years ago—between "abstraction" and "empathy." What he termed "empathy" concerned ego's ability to "enjoy a sensuous object diverse [from itself]." A product of our apperception of the "sensuously given," its crux lies in "inner motivation, inner life and inner self-activation."[56] In contrast to this internally generated as is, Worringer defines the movement of abstraction as the "powerful urge . . . to wrest the object of the external world out of its natural context, out of the unending flux of being, to purify it of all its dependence on life, i.e. of everything about it that was arbitrary, to render it necessary and irrefragable, to approximate it to its *absolute* value."[57] He identifies this urge most strongly with two-dimensional ornamental design, which, by replacing the mimetic qualities of the spatial dimension, seeks to take "the individual thing of the external world out of its arbitrariness and seeming fortuitousness, of eternalizing it by approximation to abstract forms and, in this manner, of finding a point of tranquility and a refuge from appearances."[58]

For Worringer "the primary artistic impulse has nothing to do with the rendering of nature. It seeks after pure abstraction as the only possibility of repose within the confusion and obscurity of the world-picture, and creates out of itself, with instinctive necessity, geometric abstraction."[59] He thus identifies ornament, which he sees as the purest expression of this urge, with the creation of a subjunctive and formalized "as if" out of the perennially fractured world of nature, just as ritual does out of the world of humanity and gods.

On Music

Music is not ritual, but it has very close links in two ways: music's formal features greatly resemble those we have identified for ritual, and music is a part of many ritual performances. Here we will mostly address the first of these issues, much as we have already done for architecture and ornament, to see how thinking about ritual and sincerity might help our understanding of music. Of all the arts, music comes closest to pure form. Like ritual, it is highly repetitive and relatively nondiscursive (completely so in the case of instrumental music). Both exist only in the performance—there are ritual manuals and musical scores, but neither is the same as the ritual or music itself. Both are social in Rappaport's sense that they are not entirely encoded by the performers themselves.[60] And neither is primarily about expressing truth values. We can sensibly ask whether some kinds of paintings or novels seem "true" to life, even though they may depict quite imaginary scenes, but the question loses all sense for the purer formalities of music.

Perhaps most crucially, however, both music and ritual work at the intersection between an idealized perfection of form and the messy demands of the real world, between consonance and cacophony. As we will discuss, nearly anything we call music plays on that boundary to some extent. Just as we have seen throughout this book, though, this feature also makes music subject to competing pressures toward ritual and toward sincerity. In the more "ritual" mode, we see increased interest in form for its own sake, and in elaborations of repetition and ornament that combine permanence and temporality, just as we have seen in architecture. Sincere reactions combat those trends and also tend to push words back to the forefront. Only with words does music begin to lose its purely formal character and to be pedagogical instead of merely performative. Let us start, though, with the simplest act of music—making a note—and gradually work our way back to arguments over sincerity.

Perfect Pitch in a Broken World

"Music is based on government," as Zhou Dunyi wrote almost a millennium ago.[61] Zhou was one of the founders of neo-Confucianism and thought a great deal about the tradition's long engagement with music. He explains how the ancient sage-kings fostered rituals and moral education, and how they created music:

> As it [music] enters the ear and affects the heart, everyone becomes calm and peaceful. Because of calmness, one's desires will be appeased, and because of harmony, one's impetuousness will disappear. Peace, calmness, and moderation—these are the height of virtue.... Later generations have neglected ceremonies.... Rulers have claimed that ancient music is not worth listening to and replaced it by or changed it into modern music, which is seductive, licentious, depressive, and complaining. It arouses desires and increases bitterness without end.... To hope for perfect government without restoring ancient and changing modern music is to be far off the mark.[62]

Zhou is harking back here to numerous classical works, but especially to the chapter on music in the *Book of Rites* (sometimes identified as the *Yue Ji*, the *Book of Music*), thought to have been written (or reconstructed) another millennium before Zhou's time. This chapter also relates the quality of music to the quality of rule: "If the endeavors of a ruler are trivial, his music will be made of feeble sounds and the thoughts of the people will be sad. If he is noble, kind and gentle in nature, his music will be varied and dignified with many changes and the people will be gratified and happy."[63]

The idea that music shaped people (rather than people shaping music, as we more often say today) was just as widespread in ancient Greece. Aristotle, for instance, wrote that "it is plain that music has the power of producing a certain effect on the moral character of the soul, and if it has the power to do this, it is clear that the young must be directed to music and must be educated in it."[64] Plato was rather more glum about the possibilities this entailed, and less pleased with the idea that music might serve as pure entertainment. That is why he proposed banning most modes of music from his ideal city-state in *The Republic*, leaving only the few he felt encouraged proper works of war and peace rather than lamentation, sloth, or even conviviality.

Crucially in both the Chinese and Greek contexts, the ability to govern through music stemmed from a knowledge of tones, proper pitches. As the *Book of Music* said, "Whoever does not understand the tones, cannot discuss melodies, and whoever is ignorant of melodies cannot know music. (Only) he who understands music will know the rules and secrets of ceremony."[65] China and Greece achieved an early understanding of the relationships between vibration and pitch. They knew, for example, that doubling the number of vibrations per second (by halving the length of a pipe or string) created a tone an octave higher, and that a ration of 3:2 created a fifth. They could also generate their full set of twelve tones by moving up by fifths (called the circle of fifths in Western music theory).[66]

In Greece this is most closely associated with the discoveries of the Pythagoreans, but philosophers in both ancient societies were struck by the mathematical beauty and elegance with which a few simple universals explained an enormously complex range of empirical experience. Here was indeed a way to put human life in tune with the fundamental orders of the universe. For China, more than for Greece, there was an added concern for getting the absolute pitch right. What exactly was the true base tone (the *huangzhong*, yellow bell) from which all the others derived? In the Chinese case, where these ideas became built into state ritual, this was a crucial political question, and each new dynasty usually determined a new base tone, and thus had to create entirely new sets of ritual musical instruments—primarily bells and chimes. Heads occasionally rolled in political battles over these issues.[67]

Beautiful as the mathematical cosmology may be, it has two problems that make perfect pitches and perfect intervals impossible in this broken world. The first is the obvious practical problem of playing perfectly in tune. This is especially obvious to anyone who plays an instrument capable of infinite pitch variations, but it also applies to fixed-pitch instruments like bells and chimes, which can change pitch as temperature changes, and which greatly complicate pitch through overtones. Worse still, the actual pitches of each scale tone differ depending on the starting note. In other words, changing keys means changing intonation—something not possible for fixed-pitch instruments like bells, chimes, and pianos.

The more fatal problem for perfection, however, is that the theory is wrong. If one really generates the scale by moving up the circle of fifths in exact ratios of 3:2, each interval will sound perfectly in tune to a trained ear, but the final note will not be in tune with the starting note. Violins, violas, and cellos normally tune their strings in these perfect fifths, but if a string quartet does this, starting from the cello's lowest string and ending with the violins' highest string, the violins' high notes will not be in tune with the cello's low notes.

Musicians have ways of adjusting, of course, from tuning the cello's bottom string very slightly high in the string quartet to finding systems of temperament that allow all notes to sound relatively in tune, as in a modern piano. The modern system of equal temperament was actually first discovered in China by Zhu Zaiyu, a Ming dynasty ritualist and mathematician, driven by the desire to get the pitches of the ritual instruments exactly right and thus to reverse a period of dynastic decline.[68] Every tone and every interval is thus a compromise between the ideals of perfection and the broken world. This is the work of music as ritual: not to achieve perfection but to recall it while living in an unperfectable world.

Repetition and Ornament

Music repeats at many levels of structure. At the broadest level, most musical pieces are played more than once. Chinese music, for instance, centers on a repertoire of basic melodies that can be used in many different contexts. Beijing operas have been performed over and over, for centuries in some cases, as have Western pieces of all kinds. No performance is exactly identical to the previous ones, and in the case of more improvised music, it may be quite different. As we have argued for ritual, however, that is the very nature of repetition, as opposed to what we have been calling simple reiteration.

Music typically also repeats internally—a song will cycle through chorus after chorus, a theme and variations play through the same idea over and over, a sonata has a set pattern of repetition, and so on. Phrases also repeat, again often as variants of an original. Think of the first few measures of Beethoven's Fifth Symphony or Coltrane's "A Love Supreme," in which a very short pattern of notes is introduced, repeated in a new key, and then elaborated. Repetition is never identity, but instead brings the variations of performance in an altered context. Baroque performers, for instance, liked echo effects where one phrase would be loud and its immediate repetition would be soft; they would also vary the amount of ornamentation from one repetition to the next. Repetition remains firmly within a predefined framework, while still allowing its own form of creativity.

Even the most fundamental musical repetition—the rhythmic pulse that underlies everything—is not a simple reiteration, as if we were chronometers. Rhythm coordinates; it allows cooperation across boundaries and imposes order on chaos, as we said about architectural ornament. That is why the various muscles of the heart beat in rhythm and work crews sing in rhythm. It connects musician to audience as well, perhaps even physiologically—the correlation between beat and heartbeat or phrase and breath has long been noted. This repetition is an organic thing, though, never mechanically perfect. As in intonation, we see an interplay between a perfected ideal of regularity and the compromises of living in an imperfect world.

More than with intonation, though, musicians will often manipulate rhythm on purpose, as when an orchestra slows during a final cadence or a jazz soloist plays always just behind the beat. These intentional departures from metronomic regularity work to raise and release tension in the performance. It is the equivalent of what Rappaport called the self-referential aspects of ritual, which communicate the momentary state of the people involved rather than the invariant, "canonical" content of the ritual.[69] This only works, however, if the formal structure (in this case the regular pulse) has been clearly established. There must be an interplay between the discipline of the formal order and the creative tension of how that order becomes realized in performance.

We can see much the same tension between the canon and self-reference in any of the improvised aspects of music, from the kinds of rhythmic manipulation we have mentioned to complete invention. Even a traditional jazz solo, which may sound utterly different from the melody that inspired it, must follow a formal structure by keeping the same beat, the same number of measures as the original tune, and the same underlying harmonic pattern. There need not even be a melody. The players may just decide to jam on the blues in the key of F, but everything they play still must follow a strict formal structure— choruses of exactly twelve bars based on a simple, repeated harmonic pattern, to take a simple example.

Baroque musicians also improvised extensively on given melodies. Figure 5-13 shows a violin sonata by Arcangelo Corelli. He originally published these in the late seventeenth century with the bottom line of each set of three representing the figured bass (as a guide for the keyboard accompaniment) and the middle line for the violin. The uppermost line was added only in a 1708 edition, as one example of how the violinist might actually play the part in real performance. Those who can read music will see that the worked-out example has its roots in Corelli's original version, but anyone can see that the structure also allowed (really required) an enormous amount of elaboration.[70]

FIGURE 5-13. A. Corelli, Violin Sonata V, Score, 1708 (reprinted in *Archivum Musicum: Collana di Testi Rari*, Florence: Studio per Edizioni Scelte, 1979).

Ornament provides an important realm for self-referential improvisation in many forms of music around the world. Ornament toys with the structure of the piece, with its rhythm or harmony or both at once. A turn, for example, squeezes in the nearby scale tones just before the target note, thus extending the time we have to wait before hearing the note. A trill leaves the rhythm alone but plays with the harmony by oscillating between two notes, usually implying two different keys. Both forms play with boundaries, complicating them, making them longer in time and more complex in harmonic depth. Ornament, like play and like much of ritual, is about the ability to maintain and transcend boundaries simultaneously.

Harmonia Mundi

The word "harmony" comes from a Greek root that referred to joining together. As our brief references to early Greek and Chinese thinkers suggested, music was often subsumed into a kind of larger joining together to form a single, coherent, and consonant whole. The ideal of harmony has been with us ever since, often with no reference to music, but to invoke a kind of frictionless state of social order in which all the parts work together beautifully. Viewed more negatively, of course, the idea is just a typical apologetic for the inequalities of power and hierarchy. While much of the literature reduces ritual to the effort toward such a "harmony"—viewed positively by some and negatively by others—we have been trying to show instead that it has a much more complex and interesting relationship to the world.

Looking at the idea of harmony as musicians instead of as idealists or apologists brings in a suggestive richness that opens the concept up. While music theorists of earlier eras emphasized the consonance of certain intervals, especially the octave and the fifth, actual compositions made use of a far wider range of intervals and thus created possibilities for different degrees of dissonance. Scales of five or seven notes, common in many parts of the world, allow musicians to create and release tension through the use of dissonant intervals, even when writing just for a single voice. Just like the use of rhythm and ornament, harmonic tension is crucial to making music powerful for an audience.

This became considerably more complex and rich in the West as polyphonic music developed in the Middle Ages. By the time of Bach and other Baroque composers, music had become a kind of fractal "unfolding" (to use the term Arnold Schoenberg would later apply to this sort of harmony) of the harmonic possibilities of one or more basic themes, the way a kaleidoscope might reveal unsuspected and ever-changing patterns in a single set of colored glass bits. Ideas of musical harmony changed quite a bit after this, but its fundamental use to create and resolve tension never disappeared. This is thus neither the harmony of a utopia nor the music of the spheres. It is instead a world in which a simple melody or chord plays out its inner dialectic into a complex and elaborated universe filled with inner tensions and resolutions. Again like ritual in its social contexts, music is not a simple exercise in the "harmony" of unities and consonances ("symphonies," as the term was once used), whatever its theoreticians may have claimed.

Both ritual and music rely more on pure form than most other activities. Both work at the edge between perfection and reality. And neither is primarily about its utilitarian functions, although music can certainly accomplish things like coordinating work gangs as ritual also has social functions. Both are performative—they exist in the doing rather than in the saying. Yet, as the *Book of Music* pointed out so long ago, they are not performative in exactly the same way:

> To unite and harmonize is the objective of music; variance and discernment are the objectives of ceremony. (People experience) mutual endearment (which arises) from harmony. From discernment comes mutual esteem. If music predominates, an unstable union can be observed; if ceremony predominates, a leaning toward dissociation can be noted. The purpose of music and ceremony is to harmonize the feelings of the people and to create balanced propriety to their outward expressions. . . . Music comes from within and ceremony comes from without.[71]

This claim that music unites and ritual divides, that music is internal and ritual is external, stems from the idea (shared by the Greeks) that music works directly on people's emotional state. Because this is a direct process, it works the same way for everyone. It creates us as emotional beings and leaves all of us in the same state. Ritual, however, creates distinctions—a claim still echoed by anthropologists today. Both music and ritual create worlds, but music shapes our inner emotional lives in ways that make us resemble each other, while ritual shapes the social and natural universe in ways that clarify our differences.

Music and Sincerity

Uniting or dividing, this is a performative view of the world, in which formalized action through music and ritual shapes us as social and emotional selves. It is very different from the general standpoint of sincerity, in which our external actions should properly grow out of our internal states. Music, as much as ritual, poses problems for the sincere attitude because it relies so greatly on form and convention and it so resists discursive interpretation. The only real exception is music that adds words.

That is why we can see periodic attacks on certain kinds of music for as long as we have historical records. Typically, critics attack the musicians of their day for playing too enthusiastically with form—making the rhythms more complex, adding multiple voices, letting the harmonies get too dissonant, and generally playing with the boundaries of the form rather than trying to emulate perfection. In a closely related way, they also attack purely instrumental music, or music in which the harmonic complexity or the sheer quantity of ornament makes the words impossible to understand. Recall Zhou Dunyi's complaint (cited at the beginning of the section) that modern (i.e., eleventh-century) music was seductive and licentious, and thus spread popular discontent. A millennium earlier, Mozi (the sincere anti-Confucian whom we mentioned in the previous chapter) had condemned all music as a waste of resources and time.

In the West, after Plato's attack on improper musical modes, we see this most clearly in the church's long and anxious relationship to music. The early church fathers, like Confucianists, recognized the potential of music to unite and harmonize their flock, when used appropriately as a way of making the words live for people. Yet they also recognized the potential threat and seduction of pure music, none more clearly than Augustine, who wrote at a time (early fifth century) when psalm singing was just becoming widespread. Augustine loved music, as in this passage on the *jubilus*, the long and highly ornamented extension of the final syllable of the word "Alleluia": "It is a certain sound of joy without words, the expression of a mind poured forth in joy. A man rejoicing in his own exultation, after certain words which cannot be understood, bursteth forth into sounds of exultation without words."[72] At the same time, however, he was deeply suspicious of this power. As he wrote in his *Confessions*,

> I fluctuate between peril of pleasure, and approved wholesomeness; inclined the rather . . . to approve of the usage of singing in the church; that so by the delight of the ears, the weaker mind may rise to the feeling of devotion. Yet when it befalls me to be more moved with the voice than the words sung, I confess to have sinned penally, and then had rather not hear music. See now my state; weep with me, and weep for me, ye, who so regulate your feelings within, as that good action ensues.[73]

The Church struggled with this dilemma ever afterward, as in Pope John XXII's bull of 1323, complaining about new musical techniques in which performers "hinder the melody with hockets, they deprave it with discants, and sometimes they pad out the music with upper parts made out of secular songs. . . . The consequence of all this is that devotion, the true aim of all worship, is neglected, and wantonness, which ought to be eschewed, increases."[74]

As we have seen for ritual and architecture, the Reformation provided a powerful push toward a more sincere music. Both Calvin and Zwingli allowed only unison psalms, to be sung by the whole congregation in church. Much the same feeling swept through England, as in this injunction of 1552 at York Minster: "We will and command that there be none other note sung or used in the said church at any service there to be had, saving square note plain [i.e., unaccompanied hymns], so that every syllable may be plainly and distinctly pronounced."[75] Even the organ was banned in this attempt to reduce music to a pedagogical lesson through the truth content of the words. The Counter-Reformation responded through imitation, by placing its own limits on music. This argument between form and content, complex musical structure and simple words, was as old as the church, although the Protestant movement brought an especially powerful shift. None of this was permanent, though, as musicians (and probably their audiences) allowed music to drift back toward its joy in complex rhythms, elaborate ornaments, and sophisticated harmonies. The cycle had turned again by the time of J. S. Bach, a century later, who worked in Protestant Germany but hardly in the manner of Calvin or Zwingli.[76] Bach himself had been castigated by his church employers in 1706 for "having hitherto made many curious variations to the chorale, and mingled many strange tones in it."[77]

The eighteenth century brought further developments in the formal aspects of music, especially Rameau's theorization of harmony early in the century. Yet it also brought another powerful push toward sincerity and away from formalism. We already see an inkling of the Romanticism that would soon come in C. P. E. Bach's quip that "we must play from the soul, not like trained birds."[78] The loudest voice, though, was Rousseau, who wrote the entries on music in the *Encyclopedia*, and who had contributed an inflammatory pamphlet to the raging argument in France about the worth of the new Italian comic opera, which was less formally structured and more open to melodic freedom. In general, he argued for a great simplification of harmony in favor of moving melodies, less form and more content. He also favored other aspects of music that promoted content over form: the use of words (he was much less enthusiastic about that other new Italian invention, the symphony) and the use of passages that imitated identifiable objects or events so that music might become iconic, like painting.[79]

Many of these ideas continued to be elaborated through the nineteenth century. This was the moment when the West became convinced that music had to come from the depths of the self, rather than shaping the self from outside as in the Platonic understanding that had dominated for so long. Gluck wrote that the music should not distract from the words in opera, and Berlioz began a fad for "program music" with the program notes for his *Symphonie fantastique* (1830). These notes described in great detail the visual and emotional melodrama of love gained and lost, conjuring up scenes from pastoral peace to opium-induced visions of his own execution. Giving music a substantive content through imitation was hardly a new idea, but it became widely popular among his fellow Romantics.

Toward the end of the century, Richard Wagner seemed to bring many of these trends to a head. He championed program music and, like Rousseau, saw opera as the ultimate form of music because it had words. It was Wagner who foresaw the death of the entire formal harmonic structure of Western music, especially in the haunting, irresolvable chords of his overture to *Tristan and Isolde*—a work with no identifiable key. All of this is consistent with the powerful emphasis on sincerity among the Romantics. All of it weakens the formal aspects of music and attempts in every way possible to substitute the identifiable content of the composer's soul through words or programmatic imitation.

The entire formal order of music—its ritual structure, we might say—was dethroned by the beginning of the twentieth century. Composers as different as Busoni and Ives suggested new kinds of intonation, like quarter tones or third tones to subdivide the twelve generated by the Pythagorean circle of fifths. Ornament continued the decline it had been experiencing for a long time, reaching new lows in the twentieth century, although not quite as radically as in architecture.

In harmony, the most famous innovation was Schoenberg's continuation of the Wagnerian revolution. Tonality was dead, as God for Nietzsche, and Schoenberg invented an entirely new system of rules. He kept the original twelve tones but insisted that all twelve be used (the "tone row") before any other musical development took place. This made it impossible to write in any key at all. The rules of this new harmony were as elaborate as the old ones, but they consciously turned their backs on tradition in favor of the new invention. Anton Webern, who was Schoenberg's most successful student, wrote in the 1930s, "Adherence to the row is strict, often burdensome—but it is *salvation!* The dissolution of tonality wasn't our fault—and we did not create the new law ourselves; it forced itself overwhelmingly upon us. The commitment is so powerful that one must consider very carefully before finally entering into it.... Trust your inspiration! There is no alternative."[80] This is a voice as sincere as any Calvinist, and not very different in tone.

Popular music, of course, went in rather different directions. It picked up some new harmonic ideas from eastern Europe and Africa (especially in the blues and its descendants), but it retained the twelve basic tones and the descendants of the Greek keys and modes. Many strands also continued elaborate traditions of ornamentation, especially jazz, rhythm and blues, and gospel musics. Rhythm remained clear and usually relatively simple. After all, as long as people danced, they needed rhythm. As with ritual repetitions, rhythm creates society.

Sincerity in popular music came instead primarily from lyrics, the same arena through which sincerity and form had been played out in the church for almost two millennia. The really sincere singers let the words outweigh any other musical considerations. Rock musicians tend to stick to simple and traditional harmonic structures instead of tone rows, but they could express just as much yearning for salvation, for letting loose their internal truths and inspirations, as Anton Webern.

For the most sincere, just as for the most sincere Puritan preachers that we discussed in the previous chapter, words alone can never suffice. Words are conventions, and thus never adequate to express the full truth. Punk rockers—an extreme of this kind of thing—would thus physically abuse themselves and their equipment on stage; the flow of blood showed a sincerity that words never could.[81] For hard-core fans, even a hint of commercial success was anathema. Real sincerity meant being true only to the self and rejecting even the semblance of accepting social norms by catering to a market. Genuine sincerity cannot be expressed, but insists on the attempt.

G. G. Allin, one of the best known, had announced a date when he would commit suicide on stage, although his death from heroin came first.[82] When all words are false, when even cutting yourself with broken shards on stage could simply be pandering to the market, suicide is the ultimate rejection of convention and evidence of sincerity. It is not a coincidence that heroin has been a favorite drug of abuse in twentieth-century popular music. This is not just hedonism, since heroin reduces life to just one internal inspiration, for which all external rules can be broken. Unlike hedonism, there is nothing social about this. Sociality requires rules and rituals, as we have been arguing. As with suicide, this is the self reduced to a single truth. Punk rock deaths by suicide or heroin include Johnny Thunders, Sid Vicious, Darby Crash, Ian Curtis, G. G. Allin, Kurt Cobain—and a host of others, both within and beyond the punk movement.[83]

We are far from the twelve-tone experiments of Schoenberg or Webern here, but they share a rejection of convention and tradition and an attempt to find fresh means of self-expression. These are very different forms of sincerity, as varied as the more convention-accepting forms of twentieth-century music. Perhaps because the consumption and production of music works so very differently from something like architecture, we have seen an extremely wide variety of musical possibilities. Some revel in pure form, like the harmonic sophistication of bebop. Some radically simplify form down to just a few chords and a simple beat to highlight sincere self-expression through lyrics. And some just toss all conventions away in favor of sound "as is," like John Cage's "4'33"", which is scored for an unplayed piano, and the only sound is whatever the world produces at the moment.

Such purely sincere moments in music have been short-lived and relatively unpopular because music is almost an impossibility without some formal aspects. Contemporary life, especially since the nineteenth and twentieth centuries, brought a powerful push toward sincerity in music as in all else. Nevertheless, sincerity never triumphs completely, in music as in the rest of life. The dialectic between sincerity and ritual continues. Music remains at the same border between self and society, inspiration and discipline that the Chinese *Book of Music*, Plato, and St. Augustine had identified so long ago, the same border where ritual and ornament play their changes.

Afterword

A basic distinction between tradition and modernity pervades both the scholarly community and commonsensical readings of world history. Such understandings typically include the claim that traditional societies are governed by ritual—that is, by largely unquestioned external norms, customs, and forms of authority that regulate individual lives. In contrast, modern societies are seen as valuing individual autonomy, such that norms, customs, and authority are accepted only through the conscious choice of the rational individual. Fundamentalist movements, according to this same line of reasoning, represent a rejection of the modern world and an attempt to return to a traditional world of ritual.

One of our arguments in this book is that almost every aspect of this framework is wrong. It is based upon a misunderstanding of ritual, a misunderstanding of earlier societies, a misunderstanding of our current situation, and a misunderstanding of movements like fundamentalism. It also leads to a potentially dangerous normative goal—namely, that what we and indeed all societies need is just more individual autonomy.

Our opening attempt to rethink these misunderstandings came through a rereading of ritual and ritual theory. Much modern ritual theory rests on understandings of ritual and religion that began to take their current form with the radical Protestant rejection of Roman ritual during the Reformation of the sixteenth century, and that further developed during the Enlightenment. The most pervasive aspect of this is to read ritual as an authoritarian, unquestionable, irrational set of constraints on the individual. The academic analogue of such an approach has been a certain reductionism in the study of ritual, such as can be found in the functionalist theories of figures like Radcliffe-Brown. Even the reaction against such a reading of ritual, like the interpretive approach that grew out of Geertz's work, derives from a post-Protestant and post-Enlightenment framework of the meaning-making individual. Ritual, under such an understanding, seems less authoritarian, but only by positing a belief framework underneath it. Ritual in this reading appears as no more than an outward enactment of inner states of belief.

In contrast, we have begun our study with a rethinking of ritual itself. We have been aided greatly in this process by taking discussions of ritual in non-Protestant traditions as seriously as we take anthropological discussions of ritual. We show, for example, how early Chinese and Judaic writers provide ways of thinking about ritual that differ distinctly from both Protestant and most modern social scientific understandings, and that should themselves be taken seriously as theory. These views provide a reading of ritual as a subjunctive, as the construction of an "as if" world. While many social scientific theories imbue ritual with a coherent worldview, these texts on ritual assume a world that is fragmented and broken. The subjunctive world of ritual resides in inherent tension with such a broken world, and such a subjunctive world is at least implicitly understood to be limited and temporary. Ritual, then, involves the endless work of building, refining, and rebuilding webs of relationships in an otherwise fragmented world. The work of ritual ceaselessly builds a world that, for brief moments, creates pockets of order, pockets of joy, pockets of inspiration. There is indeed autonomy in such a work, but it is an autonomy that recognizes the limited and fragmented world in which we always act.

Once ritual is viewed in this way, we not only can begin to understand it in a different way than much current theory would imply, but we come to realize that ritual is something that is happening to some extent all the time, in the most seemingly common, mundane aspects of our lives. Indeed, the ability, really the necessity, of humans to reside simultaneously in multiple worlds, ceaselessly playing upon the boundaries between them, may be universal. It is certainly pervasive in our everyday lives. We therefore explored how ritual in fact shares much with play. We also explored, with the help of psychoanalysis, how the ability to split the ego is a constant and universal feature of the human mind. And we analyzed how such a vision of ritual opens up new avenues for reading literature and art. Ritual allows us to face the unavoidable ambiguities and ambivalences of our existence.

Within such a frame, it becomes clear that the opposite of ritual is not the frequently proclaimed virtue of individual autonomy. It is rather sincerity—the belief that truth resides within the authentic self, that it is coherent, and that incoherence and fragmentation are therefore themselves signs of insincerity. And just as ritual is a pervasive aspect of human behavior, rather than a "traditional" form of authority, so is sincerity a pervasive aspect of human behavior as well. We have argued that both of these are universal, and to some extent both are always at play in our everyday lives. In human history, sincerity claims tend to gain particular allegiance and strength when a given ritual order is perceived to be too restrictive. The Protestant revolt against the Roman Catholic Church is just one of many such instances throughout human history.

What we usually call the "modern" period, therefore, should instead be understood in part as a period in which sincerity claims have been given a rare institutional and cultural emphasis. As a consequence, ritual has come to be seen from the perspective of sincerity claims, and has come to be relegated in our minds to a supposedly "traditional" order that the modern period has heroically superseded. Indeed, so pervasive have these sincerity claims become that even revolts against this so-called modern era are done in the name of finding ever-more-authentic forms of sincerity. Among these revolts are punk rock and, more important, fundamentalist movements. One of the many implications of our argument, then, is that fundamentalist movements—with their totalizing claims of authentic belief—should be understood as prototypical sincerity movements, not as a return to some kind of "traditional" ritual order.

The ethical implications of these arguments are numerous. We need to rethink our history, taking it out of the tradition/modernity distinction in which it is so often and mistakenly read, and we need to rethink our normative claims accordingly. Our argument is not that we should reject sincerity and turn fully to ritual—such a move is impossible, and as misguided as current attempts to totalize sincerity claims at the expense of ritual. Our argument is rather that we need to restore the balance between ritual and sincerity by once again taking seriously the claims of ritual. Among other things, taking ritual theorists from other traditions seriously helps teach us the tremendous dangers of trying to build a totally coherent world of authentic, individual truth-claims. It helps teach us instead to recognize the fragmented and discontinuous nature of the world, the endless work entailed in building and refining our multiple and often conflicting relationships within that world, and the ultimately tragic fate of that work. And it helps teach us the powers of ethical action based upon such a tragic vision. To accept that the world is fragmented and discontinuous also means that the work of building and refining relationships is a process that will never end. Ritual, at least in its relationship to the rest of experience, is never totally coherent and never complete. Ritual is work, endless work. But it is among the most important things that we humans do.

Notes

PREFACE

    1. Heisenberg, *Physics and Beyond: Encounters and Conversations*, vii.

INTRODUCTION

    1. Freedlander, Hirsch, and Seltzer, *Emerging Worship and Music Trends in UAHC Congregations.*

    2. On the return to Jewish orthodoxy, see Danzger, *Returning to Tradition: The Contemporary Revival of Orthodox Judaism.*

    3. Browning, *A Fundamental Practical Theology: Descriptive and Strategic Proposals*; and Volf and Bass, *Practicing Theology: Beliefs and Practices in Christian Life.*

    4. Weller, "Divided Market Culture in China"; Tu, "The Search for Roots in Industrial East Asia: The Case for Revival."

    5. Durkheim, *Elementary Forms of Religious Life.*

    6. The best overviews of this literature continue to be Catherine Bell's two classic books: *Ritual Theory, Ritual Practice*, and *Ritual: Perspectives and Dimensions.*

    7. The primary exceptions have come from a line of anthropological thinking with roots in Durkheim on the ways society and ritual mutually shape each other, in Malinowski on the power of ritual words to act in the world, and in Douglas on rituals and boundaries.

    8. Bell, *Ritual*, 168.

    9. Humphrey and Laidlaw, *The Archetypal Actions of Ritual: A Theory of Ritual Illustrated by the Jain Rite of Worship*, 88.

10. Other authors who take loosely related views, most of whom we discuss later in the text, include Douglas, *Purity and Danger: An Analysis of Concepts of Pollution and Taboo*; Tambiah, *Culture, Thought and Social Action: An Anthropological Perspective*; Bloch, *From Blessing to Violence: History and Ideology in the Circumcision Ritual of the Merina of Madagascar*; Asad, *Genealogies of Religion: Discipline and Reasons of Power in Christianity and Islam*; and Rappaport, *Ritual and Religion in the Making of Humanity*.

11. We use the concept of "frame" in the manner first suggested by Gregory Bateson, as the organizing, intersubjectively constituted principle that orders experience, as worked out in his "Theory of Play and Fantasy," 177–93. This is similar to the notion of "primary frames" that Erving Goffman later developed, for example, in "Primary Framework," in his book *Frame Analysis: An Essay on the Organization of Experience*, 1–39.

12. Goody, "Against 'Ritual': Loosely Structured Thoughts on a Loosely Defined Topic," 27; Skorupski, *Symbol and Theory: A Philosophical Study of Theories of Religion in Social Anthropology*.

13. For various sides on this debate, see Grey, "Hands and Hocus-Pocus: The Manual Acts in the Eucharistic Prayer"; and Guardini, "Playfulness of the Liturgy." We are grateful to Daniel Lennox, whose term paper made us aware of these issues.

14. Winslow, *Meetinghouse Hill, 1630–1783*, 52, 56.

15. Moore and Myerhoff, *Secular Ritual*, 3–4.

16. Smith, *To Take Place: Toward Theory in Ritual*, 109.

17. Ibid., 110.

18. Smith, "The Bare Facts of Ritual," 53–65.

19. For Goffman, see his *Interaction Ritual: Essays on Face-to-Face Behavior* and *The Presentation of Self in Everyday Life*.

20. Robert Bellah's recent article "The History of Habit" argues similarly that habits in all their forms—including but not limited to ritual—are central to the creation of community, and that their increasingly poor reputation over the twentieth century constitutes a social problem.

21. Banerjee, "Going Church to Church to Find a Faith That Fits," A18.

22. Quoted in Radosh, "The Good Book Business," 59.

23. Peyre, *Literature and Sincerity*.

24. Fischer, "Self-Expression and Democracy in Radical Religious Zionist Ideology."

25. Rappaport, *Ritual and Religion in the Making of Humanity*, 24.

26. Dubner and Levitt, "Why Vote?"

27. Birnbaum, *Daily Prayer Book: Ha-Siddur Ha-Shalem*, 24.

28. Ibid.

29. Ibid., 136.

30. Ibid., 138.

31. Quoted in Shurkin, "Decolonization and the Renewal of French Judaism: Reflections on the Contemporary Jewish Scene."

CHAPTER I

1. *Xunzi*, Wangzhi, 9/39/1–2, 5.7a.

2. Ibid., 9/39/3–6, 5.7a–7b.

3. *Xunzi*, Xing'e, 23/114/9–11, 17.2b–3a.

4. *Liji*, Biao Ji, 151.33.27.

5. Quoted in Schofer, *The Making of a Sage: A Study in Rabbinic Ethics*, 134.

6. Radcliffe-Brown, "Religion and Society," 158.

7. Ibid., 160.

8. Geertz, *The Interpretation of Cultures*.

9. Asad, "Anthropological Conceptions of Religion: Reflections on Geertz."

10. This appears in both the Babylonian Talmud Tractate 10b and in later medieval texts such as *Hoshen Mishpat*, 1b.

11. Schutz, *On Phenomenology and Social Relations*.

12. Peirce, *Philosophical Writings of Peirce*, 98–119.

13. Langer, *Feeling and Form: A Theory of Art*.

14. Deacon, *The Symbolic Species: The Co-evolution of Language and the Brain*.

15. Burkett, *Structure and History in Greek Mythology and Ritual*, 51.

16. Hall, *Inventing the Barbarian: Greek Self-Definition through Tragedy*.

17. Durkheim, *The Elementary Forms of Religious Life*.

18. Needless to add, shared empathy also invokes the limits of empathy and of those beyond the boundaries of empathy—who are often recalled at the same moment of ritual enactment (as in Jewish Passover and Christian Easter).

19. Chan, *A Source Book in Chinese Philosophy*, 25.

20. Maimonides, *Mishne Torah*, Hilchot Tephila, 4.

21. In terms of mid-twentieth-century social theory, we are talking about a very different type of fit between incumbent and role. This is potentially important because most theories of modernization and democracy posit the sincere type as a basis for democratic, liberal societies. But there are certainly critical counterfactual cases. Ancient Greece and Renaissance Italy had democracies without this type of self-role relationship.

22. We refer here to Winnicott's psychoanalytic work on transitional objects, *Playing and Reality*, to which we will return in the following chapter. The mother's participation in the transitional object is in the form of her willingness to leave it in undefined space, free of origins or belonging (to world of mother or infant). Her recognition of its unique place in the infant's mental universe is critical to its success.

23. Alexiou, *After Antiquity: Greek Language, Myth and Metaphor*, 349.

24. Ibid., 318.

25. Smith, *Imagining Religion: From Babylon to Jonestown*, 65.

26. Ibid., 63.

27. Ibid.

28. Watson, "Of Flesh and Bones: The Management of Death Pollution in Cantonese Society," 155–86. Portions of this paragraph appeared earlier in Puett, "Bones," 1014–15.

29. Orsi, *Between Heaven and Earth: The Religious Worlds People Make and the Scholars Who Study Them*, 144.

30. Ibid., 170.

31. Ibid., 169.

32. Ibid., 186.

33. Ibid., 145.

34. Ibid., 170.

35. Smith, *Imagining Religion*, 61–64.

36. The "Nature Emerges from the Decree" (*Xing Zi Ming Chu*) is an excavated text from the Guodian tomb. For a discussion of the Guodian find itself, see Hubeisheng Jingmenshi Bowuguan, "Jingmen Guodian Yi Hao Chumu." Some of the most helpful analyses of the text are Guodian Chu Jian Zhuanhao, *Daojia Wenhua Yanjiu*, vol. 17; "Guodian Chujian Yanjiu," *Zhonguo Zhexue*, vol. 20; Wuhan Daxue Zhongguo Wenhua Yanjiuyuan, *Guodian Chu Jian Guoji Xueshu Yantaohui Lunwen Ji*; Allan and Williams, *The Guodian Laozi: Proceedings of the International Conference, Dartmouth College, May 1998*; Ding, *Guodian Chumu Zhujian Sixiang Yanjiu*; and Guo, *Guodian Zhujian yu Xian Qin Xueshu Sixiang*. Portions of this section, as well as the briefer discussion of the text in the conclusion of this chapter, appeared earlier in Puett, "Innovation as Ritualization: The Fractured Cosmology of Early China." For a fuller discussion of the text, see Puett, "The Ethics of Responding Properly: The Notion of *Qing* in Early Chinese Thought."

37. Xing Zi Ming Chu, strip 1, p. 179.

38. Ibid., strips 2–3, p. 179.

39. Ibid., strip 3, p. 179.

40. For a fuller discussion of the text's view of dispositions, see Puett, "The Ethics of Responding Properly."

41. Xing Zi Ming Chu, strips 15–16, 179.

42. Ibid., strips 16–18, 179.

43. Schofer, *The Making of a Sage*, 168.

44. See Soloveitchik, *Halakhic Man*, 128–37.

45. Puett, *To Become a God: Cosmology, Sacrifice, and Self-Divinization in Early China*.

46. Schofer, *The Making of a Sage*, 118.

47. The "talmid chacham" means both teacher and student: both the wise student and student of the wise. In a sense its own linguistic ambiguity expresses the self-same attitude toward creativity and tradition as is expressed in the statement (the wise master of course being the representative of the tradition within which the student learns and is acculturated).

48. In certain religions the study of religious texts, not only core texts such as the Bible or the Koran, but also the interpretative literature of tradition is, itself, a soteriological act of great significance. This is especially true in Judaism (and to a lesser extent in Islam), where text study in and for itself is granted the highest religious valuation. Halbertal, *People of the Book: Canon, Meaning and Authority*; and Halivni, *Peshat and Derash: Plain and Applied Meanings in Rabbinic Exegesis*.

49. Douglas, *Purity and Danger.*

50. Klawans, "Pure Violence: Sacrifice and Defilement in Ancient Israel."

51. Ostrer, Leviticus 13:13 and its Mishanic parallel.

52. Ibid., 25.

53. Modell, "The Transitional Object as the Creative Act," 188–92.

54. Ibid., 190.

55. Ibid., 191.

56. See Winnicott's chapter "Transitional Objects and Transitional Phenomena," in *Playing and Reality*, 1–30.

57. Worringer, *Abstraction and Empathy: A Contribution to the Psychology of Style*, 127.

58. On this general subject, see Klawans, *Impurity and Sin in Ancient Israel.* See also the literature review by Klawans in his "Ritual Purity, Moral Purity, and Sacrifice in Jacob Milgrom's *Leviticus*."

59. See Winnicott's chapter "The Place Where We Live," in *Playing and Reality*, 122–29.

60. On issues of purity and impurity, see by Klawans, *Impurity and Sin in Ancient Israel*; "The Impurity of Immorality in Ancient Judaism"; and "Notions of Gentile Impurity in Ancient Judaism." See also Buchler, *Studies in Sin and Atonement in the Rabbinic Literature of the First Century*; and Neusner, *The Idea of Purity in Ancient Israel.*

61. Klawans, "The Impurity of Immorality in Ancient Judaism"; and "Pure Violence."

CHAPTER 2

1. We are not attempting a comprehensive review of psychological aspects of, or psychological theories of, ritual, but rather highlighting capacities for tolerating, indeed cultivating, ambiguity. Nor are we exploring ritual with the tools and terminology of Gestalt psychology. There is an increasing body of literature examining ritual from perspectives of cognitive psychology, and some works attempting to formulate verifiable hypotheses about ritual behavior. See McCauley and Lawson, *Bringing Ritual to Mind: Psychological Foundations of Cultural Forms.*

2. See Levin, *The Flight from Ambiguity*; Mills, "Sociological Ambivalence and Social Order: The Constructive Uses of Normative Dissonance"; Zielyk, "On Ambiguity and Ambivalence"; Heilman, "Inner and Outer Identities: Sociological Ambivalence among Orthodox Jews"; Seeman, "Role Conflict and Ambivalence in Leadership"; and Frenkel-Brunswik, "Intolerance of Ambiguity as an Emotional and Perceptual Personality Variable."

3. See Merton, *Sociological Ambivalence and Other Essays*; Homans, *Social Behavior: Its Elementary Forms*; Coser, "The Complexity of Roles as Seedbed of Individual Autonomy"; and Coser, "Role Distance, Sociological Ambivalence, and Transitional Status Systems."

4. Merton, "The Role Set: Problems in Sociological Theory"; Merton, *Social Theory and Social Structure: Toward the Codification of Theory and Research*; and Coser, *In Defence of Modernity: Role Complexity and Individual Autonomy.*

5. Goode, "A Theory of Role Strain."

6. Merton, "Social Structure and Anomie."

7. For a fuller discussion of this problem, see Seligman, *The Problem of Trust*, 14–43.

8. Goffman, *The Presentation of Self in Everyday Life*; and Goffman, *Asylums: Essays on the Social Situation of Mental Patients and Other Inmates*.

9. By contrast, according to Gluckman, the greater the multiplicity of undifferentiated and overlapping roles, the more ritual is needed to separate them. See Gluckman, "Les rites de passage."

10. Seligman, *The Problem of Trust*, 37–39.

11. Goffman, *Interaction Ritual*.

12. For the purposes of this discussion, we use "private ritual" to refer to behaviors that are both idiosyncratic to the individual and that take place more or less in private (though another person might be used in some form as part of the ritual); "personal ritual" to describe a shared ritual developed by two or just a few people, such as a parent-child bedtime ritual; and "public ritual" to describe rituals practiced and performed by a group, done more or less in public, and agreed upon as important for all.

13. See Bruner and Lucariello, "Monologue as Narrative Recreation of the World," for discussion of how the child might not go to sleep right away, but continue the "ritual" in the form of a monologue, recounting various parts of the recent interchange and/or other parts of his day. Interestingly, they found that the child's language in these monologues is more complex and richer than in his ordinary interactive speech.

14. Erikson, "Ontogeny of Ritualization," 605.

15. Ibid.

16. Winnicott, *Playing and Reality*.

17. Modell, "The Self and the Solace of Ritual."

18. Francis Baudry, personal communication; Bruner and Lucariello, "Monologue as Narrative Recreation of the World"; Buchsbaum and Emde, "Play Narratives in 36-Month-Old Children: Early Moral Development and Family Relationships"; Emde, Kubicek, and Oppenheim, "Imaginative Reality Observed during Early Language Development."

19. This is explored in Freud, *The Psychopathology of Everyday Life*.

20. Halpert, "On Lying and the Lie of a Toddler."

21. There might be some gender predilections for these two broad categories of lie—male being the bolstering of the person's own ego, and female the protection of the other. There is certainly considerable overlap as well. See Wadsworth, "Experiences of Lying in Adolescence: Defense against Vulnerability."

22. Rappaport, *Ritual and Religion in the Making of Humanity*, e.g. 12–15, comes down very hard on lying and deception as diseases. In contrast, psychoanalytic and developmental perspectives suggest the variety of meanings, many adaptive, of lying. One definition of psychoanalysis, possibly originating with the psychoanalyst Heinz Hartmann, is "the systematic study of self-deception." Hartmann, *Essays on Ego Psychology: Selected Problems in Psychoanalytic Theory*, 335.

On daydreaming, see the classic works of Jerome L. Singer: *Daydreaming: An Introduction to the Experimental Study of Inner Experience*; *The Inner World of Daydreaming*; and *Daydreaming and Fantasy*.

23. Varon, on the occasion of the publication of his autobiography (*Professions of a Lucky Jew*), personal communication.

24. Freud, *Beyond the Pleasure Principle*.

25. See Waldinger, Toth, and Gerber, "Maltreatment and Internal Representations of Relationships: Core Relationship Themes in the Narratives of Abused and Neglected Preschoolers."

26. Intriguing, however, for our discussion of ritual is that Freud posits a basic need for repetition as a part of the psyche's attempt not just at mastery but at establishing a kind of Nirvana, a state promulgated by Thanatos, the death instinct. He sees repetition as leading to a quiescence, ultimately a death. The repetition of "beyond the pleasure principle" is not the work of Eros but the work of Thanatos. In repetition within the pleasure principle, it would seem that Eros is the unifier and the force that blurs boundaries (as in his contrast of Eros and Necessity in *Civilization and Its Discontents*). To our knowledge, no one has made an attempt to examine rituals from the perspective of those that are dominated by Eros, i.e., rituals reaffirming differentiation, and those dominated by Thanatos, i.e., rituals aiming to reaffirm nondifferentiation, to blur and undo boundaries.

27. For some examples of both the traumatized play and the astonishing resilience of children, see Eisen, *Children and Play in the Holocaust: Games among the Shadows*; and a movie made in just postwar Poland, about a Jewish orphanage, called (in Yiddish) *Unserer Kinder* (Our Children) (Brandeis Jewish Film Archives); or Cambodian children in the Khmer Rouge killing fields, playing soccer with skulls.

28. Freud, "Splitting of the Ego in the Process of Defence."

29. Freud, "Fetishism"; and Freud, "Splitting of the Ego in the Process of Defence." See the essays in the Standard Edition by the editors prefacing each of these Freud papers for a historical overview of the development of disavowal and splitting.

30. Reports of clinical cases used here are drawn in part from the clinical and teaching experiences of one of the authors as a psychoanalyst and in part from published case reports. Details are changed and the narratives partly fictionalized for reasons of confidentiality. There is always a tension in reporting cases between presenting material as accurately as possible and safeguarding the confidentiality of the patient and the therapist. These reports err on the side of protecting confidentiality.

31. "Are motives causes of behavior?" is a much debated question in psychoanalysis and psychiatry. One of the better discussions is Sherwood, *The Logic of Explanation in Psychoanalysis*. Certainly for obsessive-compulsive syndromes there have been important discoveries about biological causes and propensities and considerable therapeutic benefit from pharmacological treatment. The psychodynamic picture, however, remains valid, but not as a total explanation of the entity.

32. Goldberg, *The Problem of Perversion: The View from Self Psychology*, 67.

33. Ibid., 68.

34. Ibid., 66.

35. Modell, *Imagination and the Meaningful Brain.*

36. On the role of psychoanalysis in converting "ghosts" into ancestors, see Loewald, "On the Therapeutic Action of Psychoanalysis."

37. Apprey, "Dreams of Urgent/Voluntary Errands, and Transgenerational Haunting in Transsexualism."

38. For a discussion of lying in two abused adolescents, see Wilkinson and Hough, "Lie as Narrative Truth in Abused Adopted Adolescents." On imposters, see Greenacre, "The Imposter." On pseudologia phantasica, see Fenichel, *The Psychoanalytic Theory of Neurosis,* 528–30.

39. Gorgias, the fifth-century (BCE) Sophist, in Freeman, *Ancilla to the Pre-Socratic Philosophers: A Complete Translation of the Fragments in Diels, Fragmente der Vorsokratiker,* p. 138, fragment 23.

40. While lies and deceits are an expected part of the social fabric of the world depicted in these texts, there is, along with some admiration for skill at lying, also condemnation of such practices. The wise person learns how to lie, when not to lie, and how to recognize the lies of others. In these texts, oaths, and the deities that enforce oaths, are the stabilizers of the uncertainty introduced by lying.

41. See Detienne and Vernant, *Cunning Intelligence in Greek Culture and Society.*

42. Later rabbinic and Christian commentators, clearly uncomfortable, go through elaborate gymnastics trying to reconcile the behavior of these biblical texts with later standards of morality.

43. Mead, Macgregor, and Bateson, *Growth and Culture: A Photographic Study of Balinese Childhood.*

44. This is the same as the phenomenon identified by Marcel Mauss in his *Sociology and Psychology as Body Techniques,* 97.

45. Directed by Jean Renoir, 1951.

46. Apparently, books like Sacher-Masoch's *Venus in Furs* ("the bible of masochism") and the pseudonymous [Reage] *Story of O* invite correspondence to the authors from people offering themselves as participants in the ritualized perverse behavior described in the books.

47. See Crapanzano, "Rites of Return: Circumcision in Morocco," on the description of the circumcision ritual he studied in Morocco.

48. See Gilbert Herdt's account of the changes in Sambia (Highland New Guinea) male initiation rituals with the banning by Australia of warfare and head hunting—how the painful bleeding of the young boys has shifted and become modified. Herdt, *Guardians of the Flutes: Idioms of Masculinity.* See also Kenneth Read's example of how a ritual contest between men and women may become too literal—when tensions in the group rise to a point where the ritual does not contain the group conflict. The women moved from mock stoning of the men to serious pelting and assault, leading the men to flee in panic. Read, *The High Valley,* 171ff.

49. Lee and DeVore, *Kalahari Hunter-Gatherers: Studies of the !Kung San and Their Neighbors.*

CHAPTER 3

1. Radcliffe-Brown, "On Joking Relationships"; Douglas, "Jokes"; Gluckman and Gluckman, "On Drama, and Games and Athletic Contests"; and Turner, *Chihamba, the White Spirit.*

2. Piaget, *Play, Dreams and Imitation in Childhood.*

3. Huizinga, *Homo Ludens: A Study of the Play-Element in Culture,* 5, 25.

4. Ibid., 8–11.

5. Ibid., 9.

6. Ibid., 10.

7. Douglas, *Purity and Danger;* and Bloch, "The Past and the Present in the Present."

8. See especially Gadamer, "The Relevance of the Beautiful: Art as Play, Symbol, and Festival." See also Grondin, "Play, Festival, and Ritual in Gadamer: On the Theme of the Immemorial in His Later Works."

9. Sutton-Smith, *The Ambiguity of Play,* 29.

10. On Rangda and Barong, see Geertz, "Religion as a Cultural System," 114.

11. *Carnival and Lent* is sometimes seen as the Lutheran Carnival poking fun at the Catholic Lent, although it quite clearly refers more broadly to issues of abandon and control.

12. Delevoy, *Bruegel: Historical and Critical Study,* 58.

13. Caillois, *Man, Play, and Games.*

14. Ibid., 19.

15. Ibid., 23.

16. This was made famous in a well-known film, Kildea and Leach, *Trobriand Cricket: An Ingenious Response to Colonialism.*

17. A similar transformation occurred when the Pawnee hand game was incorporated into the Ghost Dance movement. See Lesser, *The Pawnee Ghost Dance Hand Game: A Study of Cultural Change.*

18. Bloch, "Symbols, Song, Dance and Features of Articulation."

19. Bloch, "The Past and the Present in the Present."

20. Jay, *Throughout Your Generations Forever: Sacrifice, Religion, and Paternity,* 94–111.

21. Basu, "Profit, Loss, and Fate: The Entrepreneurial Ethic and the Practice of Gambling in an Overseas Chinese Community."

22. Barbara Ward discussed much of this in a classic article. Ward, "Not Merely Players: Drama, Act and Ritual in Traditional China."

23. Turner, *Dramas, Fields, and Metaphors: Symbolic Action in Human Society,* 243.

24. Dodds, *The Greeks and the Irrational,* 72–73.

25. Kendall, *Shamans, Housewives, and Other Restless Spirits: Women in Korean Ritual Life;* and Boddy, *Wombs and Alien Spirits: Women, Men, and the Zar Cult in Northern Sudan.*

26. Hamberg, *The Visions of Hung-Siu-Tshuen and the Origin of the Kwang-si Insurrection,* 45.

27. For a much more detailed analysis, see Weller, *Resistance, Chaos and Control in China: Taiping Rebels, Taiwanese Ghosts and Tiananmen*, 16–110.

28. Heidegger, *Poetry, Language, Thought*, 154.

29. See Seligman, *Modest Claims: Dialogues and Essays on Tolerance and Tradition*.

30. Milner, "Aspects of Symbolism and Comprehension of the Not-Self," 182.

31. Ibid., 189.

32. Jones, "Theory of Symbolism."

33. Needham, "Percussion and Transition."

34. Geertz, *Negara: The Theatre State in Nineteenth-Century Bali*.

35. Bateson, "A Theory of Play and Fantasy."

36. We have also been strongly influenced here by the much earlier work of Alfred Schutz, especially on the *epoché*, the suspension of disbelief that allows one to enter an "as if" world. See Schutz, "Transcendences and Multiple Realities." More generally, see Schutz, *Reflections on the Problem of Relevance*.

37. Solomon, "The Sounds of Silence."

38. Bloch, "Symbols, Song, Dance and Features of Articulation."

39. Douglas, "Jokes," 158.

40. Coser, "Laughter among Colleagues: A Study of the Social Functions of Humor among the Staff of a Mental Hospital," 83.

41. In the Talmud and later rabbinic writings this problem is recognized and dealt with through the concept of "ein la'davar sof," i.e., there is no end to the matter. Hence an arbitrary line is drawn beyond which no further accommodation is made, given the recognition of infinite regress that inheres to the case.

42. Worsley, *The Trumpet Shall Sound: A Study of "Cargo" Cults in Melanesia*, 60–61.

43. Weller, *Resistance, Chaos and Control in China*, 83.

44. Eco, "The Frames of Comic 'Freedom,'" 2.

45. Ibid., 8.

46. For a broad summary of these cross-references, see Bloomer, *The Nature of Ornament: Rhythm and Metamorphosis in Architecture*, 67–83. Bloomer's own design of the ornaments on the Harold Washington Library Center in Chicago is a fine example of this.

47. Radcliffe-Brown, "On Joking Relationships."

48. Douglas, "Jokes," 161.

49. Drewal, *Yoruba Ritual: Performers, Play, Agency*, 99–102.

50. Ibid., 101.

51. There are some important exceptions, for instance, Handelman, "Postlude: Framing, Braiding, and Killing Play."

52. Srinivas, "Tradition in Transition: Globalisation, Priests, and Ritual Innovation in Neighbourhood Temples in Bangalore."

53. Lakoff and Johnson, *Metaphors We Live By*.

54. Alford, *The Psychoanalytic Theory of Greek Tragedy*.

55. Pitkin, *The Attack of the Blob: Hannah Arendt's Concept of the Social*.

56. Bakhtin, *Rabelais and His World*, 236.

57. Herodotus, *The History*, 78–81.

58. Ladurie, *Carnival in Romans*.

CHAPTER 4

1. Trilling, *Sincerity and Authenticity*, 3, 5.

2. Cohen, *God's Caress: The Psychology of Puritan Religious Experience*.

3. Kant, *Foundations of the Metaphysics of Morals*.

4. This quotation forms the beginning of the critique of Kant by Nagel and Williams in their seminal article on moral luck in Nagel, *Moral Questions*, 24.

5. Ibid., 25.

6. Falling in love and remaining in love are two separate states. See Kernberg, "Barriers to Falling and Remaining in Love."

7. Sartre, *Iron in the Soul*.

8. Pascal, *Pensées*, section I, no. 11.

9. Donald, *Origins of the Modern Mind: Three Stages in the Evolution of Culture and Cognition*.

10. Even in the process of dedifferentiation, the texts record very precise measurements of dates and dimensions of the ark(s)—another example of the ongoing tension between the doing and undoing of order and boundaries.

11. Freud, *Civilization and Its Discontents*.

12. Durkheim, *The Elementary Forms of Religious Life*; Weber, *Economy and Society*, vol. 2; and Turner, *The Ritual Process: Structure and Anti-Structure*.

13. Barfield, *Poetic Diction: A Study in Meaning*, 87–88.

14. Cassirer, *The Philosophy of Symbolic Forms*, vol. 1, *Language*, 76.

15. Laozi, *Dao De Jing: The Book of the Way*.

16. Buber, *Pathways in Utopia*.

17. Tillich, "Critique and Justification of Utopia," 296.

18. Braunthal, *Salvation and the Perfect Society*; and Nuita, "Traditional Utopias in Japan and the West." Utopia, of course, is Thomas More's coinage (in his work given the etymology of "no place," but also "good place" as if spelled "eu-topia." The earlier Greek characterization of "utopian" schemes is Aristotle's *kat' euchen*, "what you pray for," emphasizing the wish-fulfilling aspect. Clay and Purvis, *Four Island Utopias*, 2.

19. Mannheim, *Ideology and Utopia*, 192, 193.

20. Davis, *Utopia and the Ideal Society: A Study of English Utopian Writing 1516–1700*, 369.

21. *Funk & Wagnalls Standard Desk Dictionary*.

22. We are grateful to Shlomo Fischer for this insight.

23. Chittick, *Sufism: A Short Introduction*, 12.

24. It also puts Max Weber's discussion of the Protestant's fundamental tension with the world in a different light. Any movement based on sincerity—and Protestantism is only one of many in history—creates an irresolvable tension for adherents because their idealized wholeness can never be fully expressed in the world.

25. Schutz, *Reflections on the Problem of Relevance*, 4.

26. Deacon, *The Symbolic Species*; and Rappaport, *Ritual and Religion in the Making of Humanity*.

27. Bourdieu, *Outline of a Theory of Practice*; and Schutz, *Reflections on the Problem of Relevance*, 4.

28. Maimonides, *Mishne Torah*, Hilchot Tephila, Siman, dalet.

29. Freud, *Beyond the Pleasure Principle*. In the mid–twentieth century there were various attempts to bring psychoanalytic categories to bear on social scientific problems, and Talcott Parsons was, as is well known, deeply involved in these efforts. His warning that there is no simple correspondence between personality types and social structure must be heeded with utmost seriousness. Still, this does not imply that categories of analysis developed in the study of one field of inquiry cannot be found to be relevant in the other. This is the approach we adopt here—of a careful transposition of categories by way of illuminating certain phenomena connected to ritual action and the issue of boundaries. Parsons, "Psychoanalysis and the Social Structure." In addition to Parsons, see Hartmann, *Essays on Ego Psychology*, especially chapter 2, "Psychoanalysis and Sociology," and chapter 5, "The Application of Psychoanalytic Concepts to Social Science."

30. Freud, *Beyond the Pleasure Principle*, 56.

31. Hartman, *Essays on Ego Psychology*, 243.

32. Freud, *Beyond the Pleasure Principle*, 54.

33. Kierkegaard, *Fear and Trembling/Repetition*, 131.

34. Langer, *Philosophy in a New Key: A Study in the Symbolism of Reason, Rite, and Art*.

35. Voegelin, *The New Science of Politics: An Introduction*, 129.

36. On this orientation in the Israeli settlement movement, see Fischer, "Self-Expression and Democracy in Radical Religious Zionist Ideology."

37. Voegelin, *The New Science of Politics*, 125.

38. Rappaport, *Ritual and Religion in the Making of Humanity*.

39. Luhmann, *Essays on Self-Reference*; and *Risk: A Sociological Theory*.

40. See Kuran, *Islam and Mammon: The Economic Predicaments of Islamism*.

41. Shorto, "Faith at Work."

42. Fischer, "Self-Expression and Democracy in Radical Religious Zionist Ideology."

43. Bateson, "The Double Bind."

44. Ricoeur, *Oneself as Another*.

45. Within the practice of understanding of Jewish tradition, the allegorical method of Philo would be an example of this dynamic. See Wolfson, *Philo: Foundations of Religious Philosophy in Judaism, Christianity and Islam*, as well as his *Philosophy of the Church Fathers*.

46. Kafka, *Parables and Paradoxes*, 92.

CHAPTER 5

1. Eisenstadt, *Revolution and the Transformation of Societies: A Comparative Study of Civilizations*.

2. Peyre, *Literature and Sincerity*, 79–110.

3. Aron, *The Opium of the Intellectuals*; see Besançon, *The Rise of the Gulag: Intellectual Origins of Leninism*, 8.

4. Besançon, *The Rise of the Gulag*.

5. Walzer, *The Revolution of the Saints: A Study in the Origins of Radical Politics*; Eisenstadt, *The Protestant Ethic and Modernization: A Comparative View*; and Seligman, *Innerworldly Individualism: Charismatic Community and Its Institutionalization*.

6. Lewis, *The American Adam*.

7. Heesterman, *The Inner Conflict of Tradition: Essays in Indian Ritual, Kingship, and Society*, 95–107.

8. Jaspers, *The Origin and Goal of History*.

9. Swartz, "Wisdom, Revelation and Doubt: Perspectives on the First Millennium"; and Eisenstadt, *The Origins and Diversity of the Axial Age*.

10. Levy, *The Measure of Man: Incursions in Philosophical and Political Anthropology*, 152–69.

11. Confucius, *The Analects*, XII, 11.

12. Holifield, "The Renaissance of Sacramental Piety in Colonial New England."

13. Indeed, the whole issue of what was foremost, prayer or study (Talmud Torah), was, in fact, another issue of huge dispute between the Hasidim and the culture of the Yeshivot—again, the issue being personal expression versus binding the self to an already existing tradition of learning. On these and other issues, see Nadler, *The Faith of the Mithnagdim: Rabbinic Responses to Hasidic Rapture*; and Stampfer, *The Lithuanian Yeshiva*.

14. Hourani, *Arab Thought in the Liberal Age, 1798–1939*, 103–92; and Lapidus, *A History of Islamic Societies*, 620–23.

15. The groups that had formed around the late Martin Lings and Titus Burkhardt and the more contemporary works of David Grille and Leo Shaye are continuing examples, if minor, of this trend. See Lings, *A Moslem Saint of the Twentieth Century, Shaikh Ahmad al-Alawi*.

16. Speare, *The Bronze Bow*.

17. Ellul, *Islam et Jude-Christianisme*.

18. An appreciation of but some of the dimensions connected to this dichotomy can be found in Cooper, "Shylock's Humanity."

19. Quoted in Lelyveld, *Shylock on the Stage*, 82–83.

20. Yaffe, *Shylock and the Jewish Question*; and Cavell, *The Claim of Reason*. Other Jewish commentators sharing this view have been Shapiro, *Shakespeare and the Jews*; Sinsheimer, *Shylock: The History of a Character*; and Weisberg, "Antonio's Legalistic Cruelty."

21. Gollancz, *Allegory and Mysticism in Shakespeare: A Medievalist on "The Merchant of Venice,"* 27, 39, 64.

22. See Keefe, "Isolation to Communion: A Reading of *The Merchant of Venice*," 216.

23. Sharp, "Gift Exchange and the Economies of Spirit in *The Merchant of Venice*," 261.

24. Weisberg, "Antonio's Legalistic Cruelty."

25. See Cartelli, "Shakespeare's Merchant, Marlowe's Jew: The Problem of Cultural Difference."

26. See Moody, "The Letter of the Law," 82.

27. On this see, Stritmatter, "'Old' and 'New' Law in *The Merchant of Venice*: A Note on the Source of Shylock's Morality in Deuteronomy 15."

28. Hazlitt, "The Merchant of Venice," 242.

29. Fingarette, *Confucius: The Secular as Sacred*, 6.

30. Hersey, *The Lost Meaning of Classical Architecture*, 11–45.

31. Bloomer, *The Nature of Ornament*, 15.

32. McNeill, *Keeping Together in Time: Dance and Drill in Human History*.

33. Worringer, *Form in Gothic*, 159.

34. Ibid.

35. Quoted in Pevsner, "Introduction," 4.

36. Worringer, *Form in Gothic*, 106.

37. Florovksy, "The Iconoclastic Controversy," 116. On this, see also Pelikan, *Imago Dei: The Byzantine Apology for Icons*; Barnard, *The Graeco-Roman and Oriental Background of the Iconoclastic Controversy*; Sahas, *Icon and Logos: Sources in Eighth-Century Iconoclasm: An Annotated Translation of the Sixth Session of the Seventh Ecumenical Council (Nicea, 787)*; and Gero, "Byzantine Iconoclasm and the Failure of a Medieval Reformation."

38. Ouspensky and Lossky, *The Meaning of Icons*, 34.

39. Ibid.

40. John of Damascus, "Treatise I on Divine Images," paragraph 53 pp. 48–49.

41. Ibid., paragraph 36.

42. Babylonian Talmud, Tractate Avodah Zarah 44b, Sonchino translation, pp. 220–21.

43. Michalski, *The Reformation and the Visual Arts: The Protestant Image Question in Western and Eastern Europe*.

44. Koerner, *The Reformation of the Image*, 42.

45. Ibid., 28.

46. Worringer, quoted in Koerner, *The Reformation of the Image*, 30.

47. Koepplin, in Koerner, *The Reformation of the Image*, 30.

48. Koerner, *The Reformation of the Image*, 36.

49. Ibid., 35.

50. Quoted in Loos, *Ornament and Crime: Selected Essays*, 28.

51. Quoted in Skolimowski, "Rationality in Architecture and in the Design Process," 163.

52. For explication of these views, see Mahmutcehajic, *Learning from Bosnia: Approaching Tradition*.

53. Voegelin, *Modernity without Restraint*.

54. Koerner, *The Reformation of the Image*, 58.

55. Sahas, *Icon and Logos*, 30.

56. Worringer, *Abstraction and Empathy*, 5.

57. Ibid., 17.

58. Ibid., 16.

59. Ibid., 44.

60. Rappaport, *Ritual and Religion in the Making of Humanity*, 24.

61. Chan, *A Source Book in Chinese Philosophy*, 473.

62. Ibid., 472–73.

63. Kaufmann, *Musical References in the Chinese Classics*, 38.

64. This is from *The Politics*, reprinted in Strunk, *Source Readings in Music History: Antiquity and the Middle Ages*, 19.

65. Kaufmann, *Musical References in the Chinese Classics*, 33.

66. Chao-Mei-Pa, *The Yellow Bell: A Brief Sketch of the History of Chinese Music*.

67. Lam, "Ritual and Musical Politics in the Court of Ming Shizhong."

68. Hart, "Quantifying Ritual: Political Cosmology, Courtly Music, and Precision Mathematics in Seventeenth-Century China." The calculation is enormously sophisticated and relies on being able to take a twelfth root.

69. Rappaport, *Ritual and Religion in the Making of Humanity*, 52.

70. We are grateful to Marty Davids for bringing this example to our attention.

71. Kaufmann, *Musical References in the Chinese Classics*, 34; parentheses in the original.

72. Weiss and Taruskin, *Music in the Western World: A History in Documents*, 30.

73. Augustine, ca. 400, *The Confessions*, 240.

74. Weiss and Taruskin, *Music in the Western World*, 30.

75. Ibid., 110.

76. Luther, as in some other aspects of doctrine, was considerably less radical about the reform of music.

77. Cited in Atalli, *Noise: The Political Economy of Music*, 18.

78. Weiss and Taruskin, *Music in the Western World*, 272.

79. See especially Rousseau, "Lettre sur la musique française." See also Strong, "Theatricality, Public Space, Music and Language in Rousseau." Denis Diderot made similar points in the constant mocking of Rameau's formalism throughout his *Rameau's Nephew*.

80. Weiss and Taruskin, *Music in the Western World*, 435.

81. This analysis depends heavily on an important manuscript paper by Popham, "No Future: Punk Rock and the Gnostic Allure of Authenticity."

82. Ibid., 22.

83. Ibid., 29.

References

Alexiou, Margaret. *After Antiquity: Greek Language, Myth and Metaphor.* Ithaca, NY: Cornell University Press, 2002.

Alford, C. Fred. *The Psychoanalytic Theory of Greek Tragedy.* New Haven, CT: Yale University Press, 1992.

Allan, Sarah, and Crispin Williams, eds. *The Guodian Laozi: Proceedings of the International Conference, Dartmouth College, May 1998.* Berkeley: Society for the Study of Early China and Institute of East Asian Studies, University of California, 2000. [Chinese]

Apprey, Maurice. "Dreams of Urgent/Voluntary Errands, and Transgenerational Haunting in Transsexualism." *Journal of Melanie Klein and Object Relations* 10, no. 2 (1996): 1–29.

Aron, Raymond. *The Opium of the Intellectuals.* New York: Norton, 1962.

Asad, Talal. "Anthropological Conceptions of Religion: Reflections on Geertz." *Man* 18 (1983): 237–59.

———. *Genealogies of Religion: Discipline and Reasons of Power in Christianity and Islam.* Baltimore: Johns Hopkins University Press, 1993.

Atalli, Jacques. *Noise: The Political Economy of Music.* Translated by Brian Massumi. Minneapolis: University of Minnesota Press, 1985 [1977].

Augustine. *The Confessions.* New York: Book League of America, 1936.

Bakhtin, Mikhail. *Rabelais and His World.* Translated by Helene Iswolsky. Bloomington: Indiana University Press, 1984.

Banerjee, Neela. "Going Church to Church to Find a Faith That Fits." *New York Times*, December 30, 2005, A18.

Barfield, Owen. *Poetic Diction: A Study in Meaning.* Middletown, CT: Wesleyan University Press, 1984.

Barnard, Leslie W. *The Graeco-Roman and Oriental Background of the Iconoclastic Controversy.* Leiden: Brill, 1974.

Basu, Ellen Oxfeld. "Profit, Loss, and Fate: The Entrepreneurial Ethic and the Practice of Gambling in an Overseas Chinese Community." *Modern China* 17, no. 2 (1991): 227–59.

Bateson, Gregory. "The Double Bind." In *Steps to an Ecology of Mind*, 271–78. New York: Ballantine, 1972.

———. *Steps to an Ecology of Mind*. Chicago: University of Chicago Press, 2000.

———. "A Theory of Play and Fantasy." In *Steps to an Ecology of Mind*, 177–93. New York: Ballantine, 1972.

Bell, Catherine. *Ritual: Perspectives and Dimensions*. New York: Oxford University Press, 1997.

———. *Ritual Theory, Ritual Practice*. New York: Oxford University Press, 1992.

Bellah, Robert N. "The History of Habit." In *The Robert Bellah Reader*, edited by Robert N. Bellah and Steven M. Tipton, 203–20. Durham, NC: Duke University Press, 2006.

Besançon, Alain. *The Rise of the Gulag: Intellectual Origins of Leninism*. Translated by Sarah Matthews. New York: Continuum, 1981.

"Biao Ji." In *Liji*, edited by Ancient Chinese Text Concordance Series Institute of Chinese Studies. Hong Kong: Commercial Press, 1996. [Chinese]

Birnbaum, Philip. *Daily Prayer Book: Ha-Siddur Ha-Shalem*. New York: Hebrew Publishing, 1949.

Bloch, Maurice. *From Blessing to Violence: History and Ideology in the Circumcision Ritual of the Merina of Madagascar*. Cambridge: Cambridge University Press, 1986.

———. "The Past and the Present in the Present." *Man*, n.s., no. 12 (1977): 278–92.

———. "Symbols, Song, Dance and Features of Articulation." *European Journal of Sociology* 15, no. 1 (1974): 55–81.

Bloomer, Kent. *The Nature of Ornament: Rhythm and Metamorphosis in Architecture*. New York: Norton, 2000.

Boddy, Janice. *Wombs and Alien Spirits: Women, Men, and the Zar Cult in Northern Sudan*. Madison: University of Wisconsin Press, 1989.

Bourdieu, Pierre. *Outline of a Theory of Practice*. Translated by Richard Nice. Cambridge: Cambridge University Press, 1977.

Braunthal, A. *Salvation and the Perfect Society*. Amherst: University of Massachusetts Press, 1979.

Browning, Don. *A Fundamental Practical Theology: Descriptive and Strategic Proposals*. Minneapolis, MN: Augsburg Fortress, 1996.

Bruner, Jerome, and Joan Lucariello. "Monologue as Narrative Recreation of the World " In *Narratives from the Crib*, edited by Katherine Nelson, 73–97. Cambridge, MA: Harvard University Press, 1989.

Buber, Martin. *Pathways in Utopia*. Tel Aviv: Am Oved, 1983. [Hebrew]

Buchler, Adolph. *Studies in Sin and Atonement in the Rabbinic Literature of the First Century*. New York: Ktav, 1967.

Buchsbaum, H. K., and R. N. Emde. "Play Narratives in 36-Month-Old Children: Early Moral Development and Family Relationships." *Psychoanalytic Study of the Child* 45 (1990): 129–56.

Burkett, Walter. *Structure and History in Greek Mythology and Ritual*. Berkeley: University of California Press, 1979.

Caillois, Roger. *Man, Play and Games*. Translated by Meyer Barash. Urbana: University of Illinois Press, 1961.

Cartelli, Thomas. "Shakespeare's Merchant, Marlowe's Jew: The Problem of Cultural Difference." *Shakespeare Studies* 20 (1988): 255–60.

Cassirer, Ernst. *The Philosophy of Symbolic Forms*. Vol. 1, *Language*. New Haven, CT: Yale University Press, 1965.

Cavell, Stanley. *The Claim of Reason*. Oxford: Oxford University Press, 1979.

Chan, Wing-Tsit, ed. *A Source Book in Chinese Philosophy*. Princeton, NJ: Princeton University Press, 1963.

Chao-Mei-Pa. *The Yellow Bell: A Brief Sketch of the History of Chinese Music*. Baldwin, MD: Barberry Hill, 1934.

Chittick, William C. *Sufism: A Short Introduction*. Oxford: Oneworld Publications, 2000.

Clay, Diskin, and Andrea Purvis. *Four Island Utopias*. Newburyport, MA: Focus, 1999.

Cohen, Charles. *God's Caress: The Psychology of Puritan Religious Experience*. Oxford: Oxford University Press, 1986.

Confucius. *The Analects*. Translated by D. C. Lau. New York: Penguin, 1998.

Cooper, John R. "Shylock's Humanity." *Shakespeare Quarterly* 21, no. 2 (1970): 117–24.

Coser, Rose. "The Complexity of Roles as Seedbed of Individual Autonomy." In *The Idea of Social Structure: Papers in Honor of Robert K. Merton*, edited by Lewis Coser, 237–64. New York: Harcourt Brace, 1975.

———. *In Defence of Modernity: Role Complexity and Individual Autonomy*. Stanford, CA: Stanford University Press, 1991.

———. "Laughter among Colleagues: A Study of the Social Functions of Humor among the Staff of a Mental Hospital." *Psychiatry* 23 (1960): 81–95.

———. "Role Distance, Sociological Ambivalence, and Transitional Status Systems." *American Journal of Sociology* 72 (1966): 173–87.

Crapanzano, Vincent. "Rites of Return: Circumcision in Morocco." *Psychoanalytic Study of Society* 9 (1981): 15–36.

Danzger, M. Herbert. *Returning to Tradition: The Contemporary Revival of Orthodox Judaism*. New Haven, CT: Yale University Press, 1989.

Davis, J. C. *Utopia and the Ideal Society: A Study of English Utopian Writing 1516–1700*. Cambridge: Cambridge University Press, 1983.

Deacon, Terrence W. *The Symbolic Species: The Co-evolution of Language and the Brain*. New York: Norton, 1997.

Delevoy, Robert L. *Bruegel: Historical and Critical Study*. Geneva: Skira, 1959.

Detienne, Marcel, and Jean-Pierre Vernant. *Cunning Intelligence in Greek Culture and Society*. Translated by Janet Lloyd. Chicago: University of Chicago Press, 1991.

Diderot, Denis. *Rameau's Nephew*. London: Penguin, 1966.

Ding, Sixin. *Guodian Chumu Zhujian Sixiang Yanjiu*. Beijing: Dongfang chuban she, 2000. [Chinese]

Dodds, E. R. *The Greeks and the Irrational*. Berkeley: University of California Press, 1951.

Donald, Merlin. *Origins of the Modern Mind: Three Stages in the Evolution of Culture and Cognition*. Cambridge, MA: Harvard University Press, 1991.

Douglas, Mary. "Jokes " In *Implicit Meanings: Selected Essays in Anthropology*, 146–64. London: Routledge, 1999 [1970].

———. *Purity and Danger: An Analysis of Concepts of Pollution and Taboo*. London: Routledge, 1986.

Drewal, Margaret Thompson. *Yoruba Ritual: Performers, Play, Agency*. Bloomington: Indiana University Press, 1992.

Dubner, Stephen J., and Steven D. Levitt. "Why Vote?" *New York Times Magazine*, November 6, 2005.

Durkheim, Émile. *The Elementary Forms of Religious Life*. Translated by Joseph Ward Swain. London: George Allen and Unwin, 1915.

Eco, Umberto. "The Frames of Comic 'Freedom.' " In *Carnival*, edited by Thomas A. Sebeok, 1–9. Berlin: Mouton, 1984.

Eisen, George. *Children and Play in the Holocaust: Games among the Shadows*. Amherst: University of Massachusetts Press, 1990.

Eisenstadt, S. N., ed. *The Origins and Diversity of the Axial Age*. Albany: State University of New York Press, 1986.

———. *The Protestant Ethic and Modernization: A Comparative View*. New York: Basic Books, 1968.

———. *Revolution and the Transformation of Societies: A Comparative Study of Civilizations*. New York: Free Press, 1978.

Ellul, Jacques. *Islam et Jude-Christianisme*. Paris: Presses Universitaries de France, 2004. [French]

Emde, R. N., L. Kubicek, and D. Oppenheim. "Imaginative Reality Observed during Early Language Development." *International Journal of Psycho-Analysis* 78 (1997): 115–34.

Erikson, Erik H. "Ontogeny of Ritualization." In *Psychoanalysis—a General Psychology: Essays in Honor of Heinz Hartmann*, edited by Rudolph M. Loewenstein, Lottie M. Newman, Max Schur, and Albert J. Solnit, 601–21. New York: International Universities Press, 1966.

Fenichel, Otto. *The Psychoanalytic Theory of Neurosis*. New York: Norton, 1966.

Fingarette, Herbert. *Confucius: The Secular as Sacred*. New York: Harper Torchbooks, 1972.

Fischer, Shlomo. "Self-Expression and Democracy in Radical Religious Zionist Ideology." Ph.D. diss., Hebrew University, 2007.

Florovksy, George. "The Iconoclastic Controversy." In *Christianity and Culture*, 101–20. Belmont, MA: Nordland, 1974.

Freedlander, Daniel, Robin Hirsch, and Sanford Seltzer. *Emerging Worship and Music Trends in UAHC Congregations*. New York: Union of American Hebrew Congregations, 1994.

Freeman, Kathleen. *Ancilla to the Pre-Socratic Philosophers: A Complete Translation of the Fragments in Diels, Fragmente der Vorsokratiker*. Cambridge, MA: Harvard University Press, 1952.

Frenkel-Brunswik, Else. "Intolerance of Ambiguity as an Emotional and Perceptual Personality Variable." *Journal of Personality* 18 (1949): 108–43.

Freud, Sigmund. *Beyond the Pleasure Principle*. New York: Norton, 1961 [1920].

———. *Civilization and Its Discontents*. New York: Norton, 1989.

———. "Fetishism." In *The Standard Edition of the Complete Psychological Works of Sigmund Freud*, edited by James Strachey and Anna Freud, vol. 21, 149–56. London: Hogarth Press, 1927.

———. *The Psychopathology of Everyday Life*. New York: Norton, 1971.

———. "Splitting of the Ego in the Process of Defence." In *The Standard Edition of the Complete Psychological Works of Sigmund Freud*, edited by James Strachey and Anna Freud, vol. 23, 271–78. London: Hogarth Press, 1938.

Funk & Wagnalls Standard Desk Dictionary. New York: Harper and Row, 1984.

Gadamer, Hans-Georg. "The Relevance of the Beautiful: Art as Play, Symbol, and Festival." In *The Relevance of the Beautiful and Other Essays*, 3–53. Cambridge: Cambridge University Press, 1977.

———. *Truth and Method*. Translated by Joel Weinsheimer and Donald Marshall. second revised ed. New York: Crossroads, 1989.

Geertz, Clifford. *The Interpretation of Cultures*. New York: Basic Books, 1973.

———. *Negara: The Theatre State in Nineteenth-Century Bali*. Princeton, NJ: Princeton University Press, 1980.

———. "Religion as a Cultural System." In *The Interpretation of Cultures*, 87–125. New York: Basic Books, 1973.

Gero, Stephen. "Byzantine Iconoclasm and the Failure of a Medieval Reformation." In *The Image and the Word: Confrontations in Judaism, Christianity and Islam*, edited by Joseph Gutmann, 49–62. Missoula, MT: Scholars Press, 1977.

Gluckman, Max. "Les rites de passage." In *The Ritual of Social Relations*, 34–35. Manchester: Manchester University Press, 1962.

Gluckman, Max, and Mary Gluckman. "On Drama, and Games and Athletic Contests." In *Secular Ritual*, edited by Sally Falk Moore and Barbara G. Myerhoff, 227–43. Amsterdam: Van Gorcum, 1977.

Goffman, Erving. *Asylums: Essays on the Social Situation of Mental Patients and Other Inmates*. New York: Anchor Books, 1961.

———. *Interaction Ritual: Essays on Face-to-Face Behavior*. New York: Anchor Books, 1967.

———. *The Presentation of Self in Everyday Life*. New York: Anchor Books, 1959.

———. "Primary Framework." In *Frame Analysis: An Essay on the Organization of Experience*, 1–39. Cambridge, MA: Harvard University Press, 1974.

Goldberg, Arnold. *The Problem of Perversion: The View from Self Psychology*. New Haven, CT: Yale University Press, 1995.

Gollancz, Israel. *Allegory and Mysticism in Shakespeare: A Medievalist on "The Merchant of Venice."* Folcroft, PA: Folcroft Press, 1931.

Goode, William. "A Theory of Role Strain." *American Sociological Review* 25, no. 4 (1960): 483–96.

Goody, Jack. "Against 'Ritual': Loosely Structured Thoughts on a Loosely Defined Topic." In *Secular Ritual*, edited by Sally F. Moore and Barbara G. Myerhoff, 22–35. Amsterdam: Van Gorcum, 1977.

Greenacre, Phyllis. "The Imposter." *Psychoanalytic Quarterly* 27, no. 3 (1958): 359–82.

Grey, Donald. "Hands and Hocus-Pocus: The Manual Acts in the Eucharistic Prayer." *Worship* 69 (1995): 306–13.

Grondin, Jean. "Play, Festival, and Ritual in Gadamer: On the Theme of the Immemorial in His Later Works." In *Language and Linguisticality in Gadamer's Hermeneutics*, edited by L. K. Schmidt, 43–50. Lanham, MD: Lexington, 2001.

Guardini, Romano. "Playfulness of the Liturgy." In *Primary Sources of Liturgical Theology*, edited by Dwight Vogel, 38–45. Collegeville, Minnesota: Liturgical Press, 2000.

Guo, Yi. *Guodian Zhujian Yu Xian Qin Xueshu Sixiang*. Shanghai: Shanghai Jiaoyu Chuban She, 2001. [Chinese]

"Guodian Chu Jian Zhuanhao." *Daojia Wenhua Yanjiu* 17 (1999). [Chinese]

"Guodian Chujian Yanjiu." *Zhongguo Zhexue* 20 (1999). [Chinese]

Halbertal, Moshe. *People of the Book: Canon, Meaning and Authority*. Cambridge, MA: Harvard University Press, 1997.

Halivni, David Weiss. *Peshat and Derash: Plain and Applied Meanings in Rabbinic Exegesis*. Oxford: Oxford University Press, 1991.

Hall, Edith. *Inventing the Barbarian: Greek Self-Definition through Tragedy*. Oxford: Clarendon Press, 1989.

Halpert, Eugene. "On Lying and the Lie of a Toddler." *Psychoanalytic Quarterly* 49 (2000): 659–76.

Hamberg, Theodore. *The Visions of Hung-Siu-Tshuen and the Origin of the Kwang-si Insurrection*. Hong Kong: China Mail, 1854.

Handelman, Don. "Postlude: Framing, Braiding, and Killing Play." *Focaal: European Journal of Anthropology* 37 (2001): 145–56.

Hart, Roger. 2002. Quantifying Ritual: Political Cosmology, Courtly Music, and Precision Mathematics in Seventeenth-Century China. http://uts.cc.utexas.edu/~rhart/papers/quantifying.html (accessed September 29, 2003).

Hartmann, Heinz. *Essays on Ego Psychology: Selected Problems in Psychoanalytic Theory*. New York: International Universities Press, 1964.

Hazlitt, William. "The Merchant of Venice." In *The Merchant of Venice, Critical Essays*, edited by Thomas Wheeler, 241–46. New York: Garland, 1991.

Heesterman, J. C. *The Inner Conflict of Tradition: Essays in Indian Ritual, Kingship, and Society*. Chicago: University of Chicago Press, 1985.

Heidegger, Martin. *Poetry, Language, Thought*. New York: Harper and Row, 1971.

Heilman, Samuel C. "Inner and Outer Identities: Sociological Ambivalence among Orthodox Jews." *Jewish Social Studies* 39, no. 3 (1979): 227–40.

Heisenberg, Werner. *Physics and Beyond: Encounters and Conversations*. Translated by A. J. Pomerans. New York: Harper and Row, 1971.

Herdt, Gilbert H. *Guardians of the Flutes: Idioms of Masculinity*. New York: McGraw-Hill, 1981.

Herodotus. *The History*. Translated by David Grene. Chicago: University of Chicago Press, 1987.

Hersey, George. *The Lost Meaning of Classical Architecture*. Cambridge, MA: MIT Press, 1988.

Holifield, E. Brooks. "The Renaissance of Sacramental Piety in Colonial New England." *William and Mary Quarterly* 29 (1972): 33–48.

Homas, George. *Social Behavior: Its Elementary Forms*. New York: Harcourt Brace, 1961.

Hourani, Albert. *Arabic Thought in the Liberal Age, 1798–1939*. Cambridge: Cambridge University Press, 1983.

Hubeisheng Jingmenshi Bowuguan. "Jingmen Guodian Yi Hao Chumu." *Wenwu* 7 (1997): 35–48. [Chinese]

Huizinga, Johan. *Homo Ludens: A Study of the Play-Element in Culture*. Boston: Beacon, 1950.

Humphrey, Caroline, and James Laidlaw. *The Archetypal Actions of Ritual: A Theory of Ritual Illustrated by the Jain Rite of Worship*. New York: Oxford University Press, 1994.

Jaspers, Karl. *The Origin and Goal of History*. New Haven, CT: Yale University Press, 1953.

Jay, Nancy. *Throughout Your Generations Forever: Sacrifice, Religion, and Paternity*. Chicago: University of Chicago Press, 1992.

John of Damascus. "Treatise I on Divine Images." In *Three Treatises on the Divine Images*. Crestwood, NY: St. Vladimir's Seminary Press, 2003.

Jones, Ernest. "Theory of Symbolism." In *Papers on Psycho-Analysis*. London: Maresfield Reprints, 1948 [1916].

Kafka, Franz. *Parables and Paradoxes*. New York: Schocken, 1961.

Kant, Immanuel. *Foundations of the Metaphysics of Morals*. Translated by Lewis White Beck. Upper Saddle River, NJ: Prentice-Hall, 1989.

Kaufmann, Walter. *Musical References in the Chinese Classics*. Detroit: Information Coordinators, 1976.

Keefe, Maryellen. "Isolation to Communion: A Reading of *The Merchant of Venice*." In *The Merchant of Venice: New Critical Essays*, edited by John W. Mahon and Ellen M. Mahon, 213–24. New York: Routledge, 2002.

Kendall, Laurel. *Shamans, Housewives, and Other Restless Spirits: Women in Korean Ritual Life*. Honolulu: University of Hawai'i Press, 1985.

Kernberg, Otto F. "Barriers to Falling and Remaining in Love." *Journal of the American Psychoanalytic Association* 22 (1974): 486–511.

Kierkegaard, Søren. *Fear and Trembling/Repetition*. Translated by Edna H. Hong and Howard V. Hong. Princeton, NJ: Princeton University Press, 1983.

Kildea, Gary, and Jerry Leach. *Trobriand Cricket: An Ingenious Response to Colonialism*. 53 min: University of California, Extension Media Center, 1976.

Klawans, Jonathan. *Impurity and Sin in Ancient Israel*. New York: Oxford University Press, 2004.

———. "The Impurity of Immorality in Ancient Judaism." *Journal of Jewish Studies* 48, no. 1 (1997): 1–16.

———. "Notions of Gentile Impurity in Ancient Judaism." *Association for Jewish Studies Review* 20, no. 2 (1995): 285–312.

———. "Pure Violence: Sacrifice and Defilement in Ancient Israel." *Harvard Theological Review* 94, no. 2 (2001): 133–55.

———. "Ritual Purity, Moral Purity, and Sacrifice in Jacob Milgrom's *Leviticus*." *Religious Studies Review* 29, no. 1 (2003): 19–28.

Koerner, Joseph Leo. *The Reformation of the Image*. Chicago: University of Chicago Press, 2004.

Kuran, Timur. *Islam and Mammon: The Economic Predicaments of Islamism*. Princeton, NJ: Princeton University Press, 2005.

Ladurie, Emmanuel Le Roy. *Carnival in Romans*. New York: G. Brazillier, 1979.

Lakoff, George, and Mark Johnson. *Metaphors We Live By*. Chicago: University of Chicago Press, 2003.

Lam, Joseph S. C. "Ritual and Musical Politics in the Court of Ming Shizhong." In *Harmony and Counterpoint: Ritual Music in Chinese Context*, edited by Evelyn S. Rawski and Rubie S. Watson Bell Yung, 35–53. Stanford, CA: Stanford University Press, 1996.

Langer, Suzanne. *Feeling and Form: A Theory of Art*. New York: Scribner's, 1953.

———. *Philosophy in a New Key: A Study in the Symbolism of Reason, Rite, and Art*. Cambridge, MA: Harvard University Press, 1957.

Laozi. *Dao De Jing: The Book of the Way*. Berkeley: University of California Press, 2001.

Lapidus, Ira M. *A History of Islamic Societies*. 2nd ed. Cambridge: Cambridge University Press, 2002.

Lee, Richard B., and Irven DeVore, eds. *Kalahari Hunter-Gatherers: Studies of the !Kung San and Their Neighbors*. Cambridge, MA: Harvard University Press, 1976.

Lelyveld, Toby. *Shylock on the Stage*. Cleveland, OH: Press of Western Reserve University, 1960.

Lesser, Alexander. *The Pawnee Ghost Dance Hand Game: A Study of Cultural Change*. New York: Columbia University Press, 1933.

Levin, Donald. *The Flight from Ambiguity*. Chicago: University of Chicago Press, 1985.

Levy, David J. *The Measure of Man: Incursions in Philosophical and Political Anthropology*. Columbia: University of Missouri Press, 1993.

Lewis, R. W. B. *The American Adam*. Chicago: University of Chicago Press, 1959.

Lings, Martin. *A Moslem Saint of the Twentieth Century, Shaikh Ahmad Al-Alawi*. London: George Allen and Unwin, 1961.

Loewald, Hans W. "On the Therapeutic Action of Psychoanalysis." *International Journal of Psycho-Analysis* 41 (1960): 16–33.

Loos, Adolf. *Ornament and Crime: Selected Essays*. Edited by Adolf Opel. Riverside, CA: Ariadne Press, 1998.

Luhmann, Niklas. *Essays on Self-Reference*. New York: Columbia University Press, 1990.

———. *Risk: A Sociological Theory*. Piscataway, NJ: Aldine Transaction, 2005.

Mahmutćehajić, Rusmir. *Learning from Bosnia: Approaching Tradition*. New York: Fordham University Press, 2005.

Maimonides. *Mishne Torah*. Brooklyn: Moznaim Publishing, 1989. [Hebrew]

Mannheim, Karl. *Ideology and Utopia: An Introduction to the Sociology of Knowledge*. San Diego, CA: Harvest Books, 1936.

Mauss, Marcel. *Sociology and Psychology as Body Techniques*. London: Routledge and Kegan Paul, 1979.

McCauley, Robert N., and E. Thomas Lawson. *Bringing Ritual to Mind: Psychological Foundations of Cultural Forms*. Cambridge: Cambridge University Press, 2002.

McNeill, William H. *Keeping Together in Time: Dance and Drill in Human History*. Cambridge, MA: Harvard University Press, 1997.

Mead, Margaret, Frances Cooke Macgregor, and Gregory Bateson. *Growth and Culture: A Photographic Study of Balinese Childhood*. New York: Putnam, 1951.

Merton, Robert K. "The Role Set: Problems in Sociological Theory." *British Journal of Sociology* 8 (1957): 106–20.

———. "Social Structure and Anomie." *American Sociological Review* 3 (1938): 672–82.

———. *Social Theory and Social Structure: Toward the Codification of Theory and Research*. Glencoe, IL: Free Press, 1957.

———. *Sociological Ambivalence and Other Essays*. New York: Free Press, 1976.

Michalski, Sergiusz. *The Reformation and the Visual Arts: The Protestant Image Question in Western and Eastern Europe*. London: Routledge, 1993.

Mills, Edgar W. "Sociological Ambivalence and Social Order: The Constructive Uses of Normative Dissonance." *Sociology and Social Research* 67, no. 3 (1983): 279–87.

Milner, Marion. "Aspects of Symbolism and Comprehension of the Not-Self." *International Journal of Psycho-analysis* 33 (1952): 181–95.

Modell, Arnold H. *Imagination and the Meaningful Brain*. Cambridge, MA: MIT Press, 2003.

———. "The Self and the Solace of Ritual." Paper presented at the Workshop on Ritual, Identity and Boundaries. Boston, 2003.

———. "The Transitional Object as the Creative Act." In *Psychoanalysis in a New Context*, 187–98. New York: International Universities Press, 1984.

Moody, A. D. "The Letter of the Law." In *The Merchant of Venice, Critical Essays*, edited by Thomas Wheeler, 79–102. New York: Garland, 1991.

Moore, Sally Falk, and Barbara G. Myerhoff, eds. *Secular Ritual*. Amsterdam: Van Gorcum, 1977.

Nadler, Allan. *The Faith of the Mithnagdim: Rabbinic Responses to Hasidic Rapture*. Baltimore: Johns Hopkins University Press, 1997.

Nagel, Thomas. *Moral Questions*. Cambridge: Cambridge University Press, 1979.

Needham, Rodney. "Percussion and Transition." *Man*, n.s. 3, no. 2 (1967): 606–14.

Neusner, Jacob. *The Idea of Purity in Ancient Israel*. Leiden: Brill, 1973.

Nuita, S. "Traditional Utopias in Japan and the West." In *Aware of Utopia*, edited by D. Plath, 11–32. Chicago: University of Illinois Press, 1971.

Orsi, Robert A. *Between Heaven and Earth: The Religious Worlds People Make and the Scholars Who Study Them*. Princeton, NJ: Princeton University Press, 2005.

———. *Thank You, Saint Jude: Women's Devotion. To the Patron Saint of Hopeless Causes*. New Haven, CT: Yale University Press, 1996.

Ostrer, Boris. "Leviticus 13:13 and Its Mishnaic Parallel." *Journal of Jewish Studies* 53, no. 1 (2002): 18–26.

Ouspensky, Leeonid, and Vladimir Lossky. *The Meaning of Icons*. Crestwood, NY: St. Vladimir's Seminary Press, 1982.

Parsons, Talcott. "Psychoanalysis and the Social Structure." *Psychoanalytic Quarterly* 19 (1950): 371–84.

Pascal, Blaise. *Pensées*. New York: Penguin Classics, 1995.

Peirce, C. S. *Philosophical Writings of Peirce*. Edited by Justus Buchler. New York: Dover, 1955.

Pelikan, Jaroslav. *Imago Dei: The Byzantine Apologia for Icons*. Princeton, NJ: Princeton University Press, 1990.

Pevsner, Nickolaus. "Introduction." In *The Anti-Rationalists and the Rationalists*, edited by J. M Richard, Nikolaus Pevsner, and Dennis Sharp, 1–8. Oxford: Architectural Press, 2000.

Peyre, Henri. *Literature and Sincerity*. New Haven, CT: Yale University Press, 1963.

Piaget, Jean. *Play, Dreams and Imitation in Childhood*. New York: Norton, 1962.

Pitkin, Hanna Fenichel. *The Attack of the Blob: Hannah Arendt's Concept of the Social*. Chicago: University of Chicago Press, 1998.

Popham, George. "No Future: Punk Rock and the Gnostic Allure of Authenticity." Unpublished paper, 2005.

Puett, Michael. "Bones." In *Encyclopedia of Religion*, edited by Lindsay Jones, 1014–15. New York: Macmillan Reference Books, 2005.

———. "The Ethics of Responding Properly: The Notion of *Qing* in Early Chinese Thought." In *Love and Emotions in Traditional Chinese Literature*, edited by Halvor Eifring, 37–68. Leiden: Brill, 2004.

———. "Innovation as Ritualization: The Fractured Cosmology of Early China." *Cardozo Law Review* 28, no. 1 (2006): 23–36.

———. *To Become a God: Cosmology, Sacrifice, and Self-Divinization in Early China*. Cambridge, MA: Harvard University Asia Center, 2002.

Radcliffe-Brown, A. R. "On Joking Relationships." In *Structure and Function in Primitive Society*, 90–104. New York: Free Press, 1952.

———. "Religion and Society." In *Structure and Function in Primitive Society*, 153–77. New York: Free Press, 1965.

Radosh, Daniel. "The Good Book Business." *New Yorker*, December 18, 2006.

Rappaport, Roy A. *Ritual and Religion in the Making of Humanity*. Cambridge: Cambridge University Press, 1999.

Read, Kenneth. *The High Valley*. New York: Scribener's, 1965.

Reage, Pauline. *Story of O*. New York: Ballantine, 1965.

Ricoeur, Paul. *Oneself as Another*. Translated by Kathleen Blamey. Chicago: University of Chicago Press, 1995.

Rousseau, Jean-Jacques. "Lettre sur la musique française." In *Source Readings in Music History: The Classic Era*, edited by Oliver Strunk, 62–80. New York: Norton, 1965 [1753].

Sacher-Masoch, Leopold von. *Venus in Furs*. Translated by Joachim Neugroschel. New York: Penguin, 2000.

Sahas, Daniel J. *Icon and Logos: Sources in Eighth-Century Iconoclasm: An Annotated Translation of the Sixth Session of the Seventh Ecumenical Council (Nicea, 787)*. Toronto: University of Toronto Press, 1986.

Sartre, Jean-Paul. *Iron in the Soul*. Harmondsworth: Penguin Classics, 1987.

Schofer, Jonathan Wyn. *The Making of a Sage: A Study in Rabbinic Ethics*. Madison: University of Wisconsin Press, 2005.

Schutz, Alfred. *On Phenomenology and Social Relations*. Chicago: University of Chicago Press, 1970.

———. *Reflections on the Problem of Relevance*. Edited by Richard M. Zaner. New Haven, CT: Yale University Press, 1970.

———. "Transcendences and Multiple Realities." In *On Phenomenology and Social Relations*, 242–62. Chicago: University of Chicago Press, 1970.

Seeman, Melvin. "Role Conflict and Ambivalence in Leadership." *American Sociological Review* 18, no. 4 (1953): 373–80.

Seligman, Adam B. *Innerworldly Individualism: Charismatic Community and Its Institutionalization*. New Brunswick, NJ: Transaction, 1994.

———. *Modest Claims: Dialogues and Essays on Tolerance and Tradition*. Notre Dame, IN: University of Notre Dame Press, 2004.

———. *The Problem of Trust*. Princeton, NJ: Princeton University Press, 1997.

Shakespeare, William. *The Merchant of Venice*. New York: Penguin, 1988.

Shapiro, James. *Shakespeare and the Jews*. New York: Columbia University Press, 1996.

Sharp, Ronald. "Gift Exchange and the Economies of Spirit in *The Merchant of Venice*." *Modern Philology* 83 (1986): 250–65.

Sherwood, Michael. *The Logic of Explanation in Psychoanalysis*. New York: Academic Press, 1969.

Shorto, Russell. "Faith at Work." *New York Times Magazine*, 31 October 2004.

Shurkin, M. "Decolonization and the Renewal of French Judaism: Reflections on the Contemporary Jewish Scene." *Jewish Social Studies* 6, no. 2 (2000): 156–76.

Singer, Jerome L. *Daydreaming: An Introduction to the Experimental Study of Inner Experience*. New York: Random House, 1966.

———. *Daydreaming and Fantasy*. London: Allen and Unwin, 1976.

———. *The Inner World of Daydreaming*. New York: Harper and Row, 1975.

Sinsheimer, Hermann. *Shylock: The History of a Character*. New York: B. Blom, 1947.

Skolimowski, Henryk. "Rationality in Architecture and in the Design Process." In *The Anti-Rationalists and the Rationalists*, edited by J. M Richard, Nikolaus Pevsner, and Dennis Sharp, 160–73. Oxford: Architectural Press, 2000.

Skorupski, John. *Symbol and Theory: A Philosophical Study of Theories of Religion in Social Anthropology*. Cambridge: Cambridge University Press, 1976.

Smith, Jonathan Z. "The Bare Facts of Ritual." In *Imagining Religion: From Babylon to Jonestown*, 53–65. Chicago: University of Chicago Press, 1982.

———. *Imagining Religion: From Babylon to Jonestown*. Chicago: University of Chicago Press, 1982.

————. *To Take Place: Toward Theory in Ritual.* Chicago: University of Chicago Press, 1987.

Solomon, Larry J. 1998. "The Sounds of Silence." *Arizona Daily Star.* http://www.azstarnet.com/~solo/4min33se.htm (accessed October 29, 2001).

Soloveitchik, Joseph B. *Halakhic Man.* Philadelphia: Jewish Publication Society, 1983.

Speare, Elizabeth George. *The Bronze Bow.* Boston: Houghton Mifflin, 1997.

Srinivas, Tulasi. "Tradition in Transition: Globalisation, Priests, and Ritual Innovation in Neighbourhood Temples in Bangalore." *Journal of Social and Economic Development* 6, no. 1 (2004): 57–75.

Stampfer, Shaul. *The Lithuanian Yeshiva.* Jerusalem: Zalman Shazar Center, 2005. [Hebrew]

Stritmatter, Roger. "'Old' and 'New' Law in *The Merchant of Venice*: A Note on the Source of Shylock's Morality in Deuteronomy 15." *Notes and Queries*, n.s., 47, no. 1 (2000): 70–72.

Strong, Tracy B. 1997. "Theatricality, Public Space, Music and Language in Rousseau." http://www.focusing.org/apm_papers/strong.html (accessed August 22, 2003).

Strunk, W. Oliver. *Source Readings in Music History: Antiquity and the Middle Ages.* New York: Norton, 1966.

Sutton-Smith, Brian. *The Ambiguity of Play.* Cambridge, MA: Harvard University Press, 1997.

Swartz, Benjamin, ed. "Wisdom, Revelation and Doubt: Perspectives on the First Millennium." *Daedalus*, Special issue (1975).

Tambiah, S. *Culture, Thought and Social Action: An Anthropological Perspective.* Cambridge, MA: Harvard University Press, 1985.

Tillich, Paul. "Critique and Justification of Utopia." In *Utopias and Utopian Thought*, edited by F. Manuel, 296–309. London: Souvenir Press, 1965.

Trilling, Lionel. *Sincerity and Authenticity.* Cambridge, MA: Harvard University Press, 1972.

Tu, Wei-Ming. "The Search for Roots in Industrial East Asia: The Case for Revival." In *Fundamentalisms Observed*, edited by Martin E. Marty and R. Scott Appleby, 740–81. Chicago: University of Chicago Press, 1991.

Turner, Victor. *Chihamba, the White Spirit.* Manchester: Manchester University Press, 1962.

————. *Dramas, Fields, and Metaphors: Symbolic Action in Human Society.* Ithaca, NY: Cornell University Press, 1974.

————. *The Ritual Process: Structure and Anti-Structure.* Hawthorne, NY: Aldine de Gruyter, 1995.

Varon, Benno Weiser. *Professions of a Lucky Jew.* New York: Cornwall Books, 1992.

Voegelin, Eric. *Modernity without Restraint.* Columbia: University of Missouri Press, 2000.

————. *The New Science of Politics: An Introduction.* Chicago: University of Chicago Press, 1987 [1952].

Volf, Miroslav, and Dorothy C. Bass, eds. *Practicing Theology: Beliefs and Practices in Christian Life*. Grand Rapids, MI: Eerdmans, 2002.

Wadsworth, Susan B. "Experiences of Lying in Adolescence: Defense against Vulnerability." Ph.D. diss., Harvard University, 1986.

Waldinger, Robert. J., Sheree L. Toth, and Andrew Gerber. "Maltreatment and Internal Representations of Relationships: Core Relationship Themes in the Narratives of Abused and Neglected Preschoolers." *Social Development* 10 (2001): 41–58.

Walzer, Michael. *The Revolution of the Saints: A Study in the Origins of Radical Politics*. Cambridge, MA: Harvard University Press, 1982.

"Wangzhi." In *Xunzi*, edited by Ancient Chinese Text Concordance Series Institute of Chinese Studies. Hong Kong: Commercial Press, 1996. [Chinese]

Ward, Barbara. "Not Merely Players: Drama, Act and Ritual in Traditional China." *Man* 14, no. 1 (1979): 18–39.

Watson, James. "Of Flesh and Bones: The Management of Death Pollution in Cantonese Society." In *Death and the Regeneration of Life*, edited by Maurice Bloch and Jonathan Parry, 155–86. Cambridge: Cambridge University Press, 1982.

Weber, Max. *Economy and Society*. Berkeley: University of California Press, 1975.

Weisberg, Richard. "Antonio's Legalistic Cruelty." *College Literature* 25 (1998): 12–20.

Weiss, Piero, and Richard Taruskin. *Music in the Western World: A History in Documents*. Belmont, CA: Wadsworth, 1984.

Weller, Robert P. "Divided Market Culture in China." In *Market Culture: Society and Morality in the New Asian Capitalisms*, edited by Robert Hefner, 78–103. Boulder, CO: Westview Press, 1998.

———. *Resistance, Chaos and Control in China: Taiping Rebels, Taiwanese Ghosts and Tiananmen*. London: Macmillan, 1994.

Wilkinson, S., and G. Hough. "Lie as Narrative Truth in Abused Adopted Adolescents." *Psychoanalytic Study of the Child* 51 (1996): 580–96.

Winnicott, D. W. *Playing and Reality*. New York: Routledge, 1971.

Winslow, Elizabeth. *Meetinghouse Hill, 1630–1783*. New York: Norton, 1972.

Wolfson, Harry Austryn. *Philo: Foundations of Religious Philosophy in Judaism, Christianity, and Islam*. Cambridge, MA: Harvard University Press, 1962.

———. *The Philosophy of the Church Fathers*. Cambridge, MA: Harvard University Press, 1970.

Worringer, Wilhelm. *Abstraction and Empathy: A Contribution to the Psychology of Style*. Translated by Michael Bullock. Madison, CT: International Universities Press, 1953.

———. *Form in Gothic*. Translated by Michael Bullock. New York: Schocken, 1957.

Worsley, Peter. *The Trumpet Shall Sound: A Study of "Cargo" Cults in Melanesia*. New York: Schocken, 1968.

Wuhan Daxue Zhongguo Wenhua Yanjiuyuan, ed. *Guodian Chu Jian Guoji Xueshu Yantaohui Lunwen Ji*. Wuhan: Hubei Renmin Chuban She, 2000. [Chinese]

"Xing Zi Ming Chu." In *Guodian Chumu Zhujian*. Beijing: Wenwu, 1998. [Chinese]

"Xing'e." In *Xunzi*, edited by Ancient Chinese Text Concordance Series Institute of Chinese Studies. Hong Kong: Commercial Press, 1996. [Chinese]

Yaffe, Martin D. *Shylock and the Jewish Question*. Baltimore: Johns Hopkins University Press, 1997.

Zielyk, Ihor V. "On Ambiguity and Ambivalence." *Pacific Sociological Review* 9 (1966): 57–64.

Index

Note: Page numbers in italics indicate illustrations.